MARKETING MANAGEMENT FOR INDIAN BUSINESS ENVIRONMENT

MARKETING MANAGEMENT

FOR

INDIAN BUSINESS ENVIRONMENT

B. BALAJI SATHYA NARAYANAN

MBA, M.Phil

Asst. Professsor, Marketing

Karaikudi Institute of Management

KIT & KIM Technical Campus

Karaikudi, Tamil Nadu, India

UNIVERSITY SCIENCE PRESS

(An Imprint of Laxmi Publications Pvt. Ltd.)

An ISO 9001:2008 Company

BENGALURU • CHENNAI • COCHIN • GUWAHATI • HYDERABAD

JALANDHAR • KOLKATA • LUCKNOW • MUMBAI • RANCHI • NEW DELHI

BOSTON (USA) • ACCRA (GHANA) • NAIROBI (KENYA)

MARKETING MANAGEMENT FOR INDIAN BUSINESS ENVIRONMENT

Printed and bound in India
Typeset at ABRO Enterprises, Delhi
First Edition : 2015
ISBN 978-93-5138-252-2

Branches

Bengaluru	080-26 75 69 30	
Chennai	044-24 34 47 26,	24 35 95 07
Cochin	0484-237 70 04,	405 13 03
Guwahati	0361-254 36 69,	251 38 81
Hyderabad	040-27 55 53 83,	27 55 53 93
Jalandhar	0181-222 12 72	
Kolkata	033-22 27 43 84	
Lucknow	0522-220 99 16	
Mumbai	022-24 91 54 15,	24 92 78 69
Ranchi	0651-220 44 64	

PUBLISHED IN INDIA BY

UNIVERSITY SCIENCE PRESS
(An Imprint of Laxmi Publications Pvt. Ltd.)

An ISO 9001:2008 Company
113, GOLDEN HOUSE, DARYAGANJ,
NEW DELHI - 110002, INDIA
Telephone : 91-11-4353 2500, 4353 2501
Fax : 91-11-2325 2572, 4353 2528
www.laxmipublications.com info@laxmipublications.com

C—
Printed at:

DEDICATION

I Dedicate This Book to the Students of India
Pursuing Marketing as Their Area of Specialisation

CONTENTS

LIST OF EXHIBITS

Chapter 1: Overview of Marketing Management

Chapter 2: Market Analysis and Market Planning (STP) in Marketing

Chapter 3: Marketing Mix

Exhibits Related to 'Product' in Marketing Mix

Chapter-3 covers the role of marketing mix or 4Ps in marketing. A special focus is given to Packaging of Products with latest laws, real time information and trends in the field of packaging. In this chapter, a special discussion is provided on recent communication techniques like Punk marketing Campaigns, Surrogate Ads, Ambush Marketing Campaigns, Comparative Ads and of course Scam Ads.

Chapter-4 explains the importance of understanding buyer behaviour to be a successful marketer, how to conduct marketing research and a detailed discussion on marketing of industrial products and marketing of services.

Chapter-5 deals with famous time tested marketing strategies along with recent strategies like Blue Ocean Strategy, Bottom of the Pyramid and CRM Strategies. The last page of this chapter is being provided with the template of 'One-Page Marketing Plan' with a Sample Marketing Plan for the practical exposure in developing an effective marketing plan for any business.

Finally, *Chapter-6* contains detailed explanation on emerging trends in marketing which explains Rural Marketing, Social Marketing, Green Marketing, Viral or Buzz Marketing, Online Marketing, and Permission Marketing.

Comments on the book will be acknowledged with gratefully.

—Author

PREFACE

After 1990s, India's face in global business has changed tremendously. Thousands of new businesses have emerged. Business firms that have survived the last three decades of global economic mayhem are today leaner and meaner than ever before. Every company today realise that gaining and sustaining competitive advantage is harder than ever before. Just gaining a competitive advantage is not enough. It has to be utilised to the fullest extent. For that purpose marketing management comes handy.

Today consumers have become extremely price sensitive and have become reluctant purchasers of products and services. When they decide to purchase, they look for value for money. This purpose is also served by means of marketing. Marketing has evolved for several years since its inception. Social networking and e-commerce have altered marketing to its core since its humble beginning.

Any marketer who goes to the market place must remain updated with the latest marketing trends to survive in the field of marketing. Hence this book covers special topics under marketing promotion like Ambush Marketing, 360 Degree Promotion, Guerilla Marketing, Surrogate Advertising, and Scam Advertising. It also throws light on famous business and marketing strategies with simplified explanation for Rural Marketing, Social Marketing, Green Marketing, Viral or Buzz Marketing, E-Marketing and Permission Marketing.

This book includes one-page case studies, one-page marketing plan template, simple & straight forward explanation with real time examples from Indian companies and MNCs operating in India, along with marketing glossary to understand and update with latest marketing terms.

It will definitely serve the needs of students who pursue B.Com, BBA, M.Com, MBA, MCA, M.Phil in Management and the students of Doctoral Programme for their Marketing Management Course Work. The book attempts to explain each and every aspect of marketing management using Indian Companies and MNCs operating in the Indian Business Environment.

The text has been divided into six chapters. *Chapter-1* sets tone for understanding the fundamentals of marketing management where the reader will learn what Marketing Management. What its Core concepts are What marketing managers do in an organisation, How the Sales-Orientation has evolved into today's marketing, The role of Marketing Department with other functional areas, How marketing is different from sales, Do we really have to see them as a separate entity, What a Market is and how it is classified, and finally, the various categories of players in the market.

Chapter-2 discusses on the Role of Market Environment Analysis in Marketing Management and the role of Market Planning – (STP) Segmentation, Targeting and Positioning in Marketing Management.

Chapter 6: Emerging Trends in Marketing

ACKNOWLEDGEMENTS

I would like to thank Mr. T. Parvathinathan, Retired Principal and Head, Department of Business Administration, Alagappa Government Arts College, Karaikudi, Tamilnadu, India for helping me to kick start my career in teaching line by giving me an opportunity to serve the students from rural background. I would also like to thank the Management of J.J. College of Arts and Science, Pudukkottai, Tamil Nadu who gave me an opportunity to pursue the career of teaching in the Department of Management Studies in their esteemed institute.

I thank Dr. Parasuraman, Principal, J.J. College of Arts and Science, Pudukkottai, Tamil Nadu, India for his extended support in the institute. I am thankful to SASTRA University for offering a chance to work in their esteemed university. I thank the Management of the Karaikudi Institute of Technology and Karaikudi Institute of Management, Karaikudi, Tamilnadu for providing me an opportunity to serve in their esteemed institute. A Special Thanks to Rev. Fr. J. Pushparaj, Former Principal, Ananda College Devakottai for providing with the most important moral support when I was desperately in need of it. I thank colleagues Prof. Kasi Viswanathan and Prof. Gopu of Ananda College for being supportive in completion of this book.

I am grateful to Mr. Pari Raman Palani, Assistant Director, Directorate of Distance Education, Alagappa University, Karaikudi and to my M.Phil Guide Dr. V. Balasubramaniam, Associate Professor, Department of Commerce, Alagappa Government Arts College, Karaikudi, Tamil Nadu who guided me effectively to complete my M.Phil in Management Successfully. I also thank Mr. D. Napoleon, Assistant Professor, School of Computer Science Engineering, Bharathiar University, Coimbatore, Tamil Nadu, India, who motivated me effectively to clear my UGC-NET examination in the first attempt itself.

Fulfilling this dream would never have been possible for us without the support and constructive suggestions of the student fraternity who I believe form the backbone of any civilized society. I would be failing in my duty if I do not thank Mr. R.S. Ramasamy, a retired engineering faculty, for sharing his valuable time to motivate and guide me on the right direction in completion of this book. I thank the publisher from the bottom of my heart for accepting the book for publication.

I wholeheartedly thank my mother for tolerating me and helping me morally till this moment. I thank Mr. SLV Moorthy, an IIM-A Alumni and a famous business consultant in India for creating an urge in my mind to write this book as an inspiration. I am profoundly influenced by his writing and publications on business and marketing.

—Author

Chapter 1

OVERVIEW OF MARKETING MANAGEMENT

Chapter Objectives

After studying this chapter, you should be able to understand the following:

1.1. Marketing Management Process—Definition and Conceptual Framework
1.2. Core Concepts in Marketing Management
1.3. What do Marketing Managers do?
1.4. Evolution of Sales and Marketing Management
1.5. Role of Marketing Department with Other Functional Areas
1.6. How Marketing is Different from Sales
1.7. Market and its Classification
1.8. Categories of Players in the Market

UNIT 1.1: MARKETING MANAGEMENT

The Case of Tata-Nano

One day, Mr. Ratan Tata, the erstwhile Chairman of Tata Group of Companies, observed families arriving on a two-wheeler. The father driving in a Scooter, young kids standing in front of him, his wife sitting behind him, holding a baby. He asked himself whether one could conceive a Safe, Affordable, and All Weather form of transport for a set of family vehicle that could be affordable and low cost enough in everyone's reach. Now, Tata Motors identified the needs and wants of the specific target market which is a four-member family that requires a Safe, Affordable, and All

Weather-proof transport vehicles. This need is then converted into a small car and sold through dealers. The company makes reasonable profits with its ₹ 1 lakh price tag.

EXHIBIT 1.1.1 **Ratan Tata's Press Meet at the Launch of Nano-World's Cheapest and Smallest Car**

Source: www.youtube.com

EXHIBIT 1.1.2 **Mr. Ratan Tata on People's Car**

It started years ago when I observed families arriving on two wheelers, the father driving in Scooter, the young kids standing in front of him, his wife sitting behind him, holding a baby and

I asked myself whether one could conceive a Safe, Affordable, and All weather form of transport for a set of family that could be affordable and low cost enough in everyones' reach

A People's Car!

(a) What is Marketing?

Marketing is a process that involves:

1. Identifying the specific needs and wants of the target market or customers.
2. Converting those needs and wants into product and services.
3. Moving them to the final users.
4. Satisfying the specific needs and wants of the target market.
5. Making reasonable profits.

The above steps can be better understood by applying them on Tata-Nano Case. Tata Motors identified the needs and wants of the specific target market which is a four-member family that requires a vehicle that is Safe, Affordable, and All Weather-proof transport. These needs are then converted into a small car and sold through dealers. The company makes reasonable profits with its ₹ 1 lakh price tag.

(b) Defining Marketing Management

The following definition was approved by the American Marketing Association's Board of Directors in the year 2007: "Marketing is the activity, set of institutions, and processes for creating, communicating, delivering, and exchanging offerings that have value for customers, clients, partners, and society at large".

But, all time appropriate definition would be Malcolm Mc Nair's definition. According to him, Marketing is defined as, "Creating and Delivery of Standard of Living". It means marketing of a product leads to the upliftment of the living standard of the people. Say for instance, at one point of time, owning a car was a luxury but today Tata Motors has made it a necessity. Thus yesterday's luxury has become today's necessity by Tata Motors' Nano.

UNIT 1.2: CORE CONCEPTS IN MARKETING MANAGEMENT

Before one gets into the subject of marketing, it is essential to understand the meaning of the key terms in marketing. The important key terms are as follows:

1. Market
2. Market place
3. Market space
4. Meta market
5. Marketeer
6. Prospects
7. Needs, wants and demand
8. Product
9. Exchange
10. Transaction
11. Supply Chain
12. Market share

1. Market

A market is a collection of buyers and sellers who transact over a particular product or a service. In the world of marketing, often the term 'offering' is used which refers to product or a service.

2. Market Place

Market place refers to the physical store where goods are sold. The retail outlets are called as (POP) Point-of-Purchase or (POS) Point-of-Sale.

3. Market Space

A market space is a virtual or digital medium by which products are sold online. It is also called as web-based marketing or e-marketing (Electronic-Marketing). For instance, www.amazon.com, www.ebay.com, www.snapdeal.com, and www.paypal.com sells their offering only by online medium.

4. Meta Market

It was postulated by Mohan Sawhney. It refers to a group of complementary or dependent products and services that are closely related to a particular industry.

For instance,

Product : Two-wheeler

Meta-market : Automobile market viz. two-wheeler manufacturer, Auto-Finance Companies, Spare Parts Dealers, Mechanics, Auto Magazines, online auto related internet websites, and auto magazines.

5. Marketer

Marketer is a person who commercializes the company's offerings (products and services).

6. Prospects

Those people who could become the buyers of the company's offerings in the near future are called as prospects.

7. Needs, Wants and Demand

Needs are the basic requirements for human survival. One needs food, water and shelter to survive. Marketers understood this hence we have purified water brands, viz. Kinley from Coca-Cola, Aquafina from Pepsi and Bisleri from Parle. Strong needs become wants. An Indian needs food but wants Chappati and Dal. An American needs food but wants Burger and Coke. When needs backed by financial strength and propensity (willingness) to consume, it leads to demand.

8. Product

Anything that is offered into the market to satisfy human needs and wants are called as products. They are often referred as 'offerings'.

9. Exchange

Transfer of ownership of goods and services against money is known as exchange.

10. Transaction

Trade or business deal between two or more parties is called as transaction. A transaction can be monetary transaction or barter transaction. Exchange of goods against goods is known as barter trade and exchange of goods against money is called monetary transaction.

11. Supply Chain

Transportation (and storage) of goods from the place of production to the place of consumption with minimal or no wastage at the optimal cost is known as supply chain management.

12. Market Share

Market share of the companies show their competitive position in the market. The market share of the companies is always expressed in terms of percentage. For instance see the Exhibit 1.2.1.

EXHIBIT 1.2.1 **Market Share of Scheduled Domestic Airlines – Nov. 12**

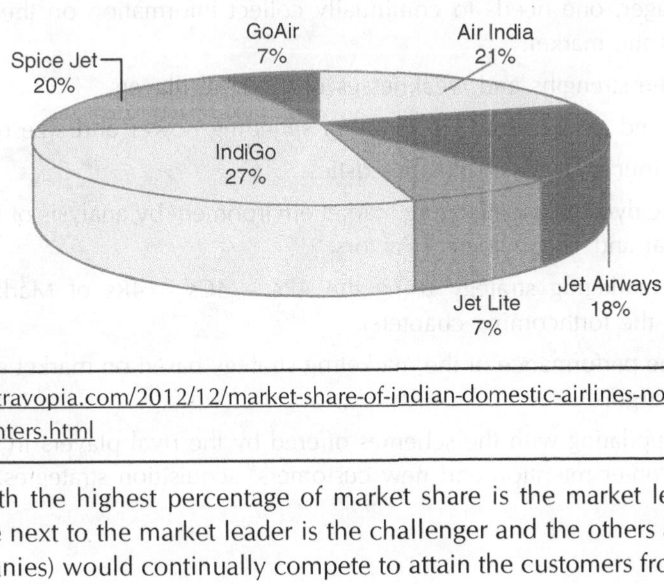

Source: http://www.travopia.com/2012/12/market-share-of-indian-domestic-airlines-nov12-indigo-still-leads-other-interesting-pointers.html

The player with the highest percentage of market share is the market leader and the player having market share next to the market leader is the challenger and the others are followers. All the rival players (companies) would continually compete to attain the customers from each other so that their market share shall increase and decrease along with the profitability. In simple words, the highest market share in India's Airlines Business is held by IndiGo 27%, which means, when 100 people travelled by air, out of these 100, 27% had travelled by IndiGo. It simply means, sales decide the market share and profitability of the company, which in turn determines the company's competitive position, viz. the market leader, challenger and the followers in the market.

UNIT 1.3: WHAT DO MARKETING MANAGERS DO?

Following are the steps involved in the marketing of a product or service offering of the company:

1. Conduct Market Analysis to know the opportunities and challenges available in the market.
2. Segment and target the market.
3. Identify the unsatisfied needs and wants of the customers using market and marketing research.
4. Analyze the competitive offerings, including the substitutes.
5. Convert the needs and wants of the customers into product or service offerings.
6. Give an attractive brand name.
7. Give an attractive packaging.
8. Distribute or channelize the products and services through dealers or intermediaries.
9. Promote the brand using (USP) Unique Selling Proposition and (ESP) Emotional Selling Proposition.
10. Build the brand image using brand personality and (CSR) Corporate Social Responsibility initiatives.

As a marketing manager, one needs to continually collect information on the following to make appropriate moves in the market:

1. Identifying the strengths and weaknesses of the rival players.
2. Market size and attractiveness in terms of spending power and size of population
3. Buyer behaviour and market characteristics.
4. Analyzing the dynamic or changing market environment by analysis of Political, Economic, Socio-Cultural and Technological Factors.
5. Developing marketing strategy using the 4Ps – 4Cs – 4Rs of Marketing mix (will be discussed in the forthcoming chapters).
6. Evaluating the performance of the marketing strategy based on market share, sales volume, and profit margins.
7. Continually updating with the schemes offered by the rival players in the market so as to develop customer retention and new customers' acquisition strategies.

UNIT 1.4: EVOLUTION OF SALES AND MARKETING MANAGEMENT

The Philosophy and Marketing Orientation Concepts

What is Marketing Orientation?

Marketing orientation explains how marketing in India evolved (changed and progressed) over the years, till date.

Marketing Philosophy?

Philosophy simply means what the company believes in and what it is intending to follow on a particular matter. To understand the orientation concept, it is important to put it in perspective by reviewing other philosophies (what a company believe and does) that once were predominant.

While these alternative concepts prevailed during different historical time frames, they are not restricted to those periods and may still be practiced by some firms even today.

EXHIBIT 1.4.1 **Marketing Orientation Concepts/Philosophies**

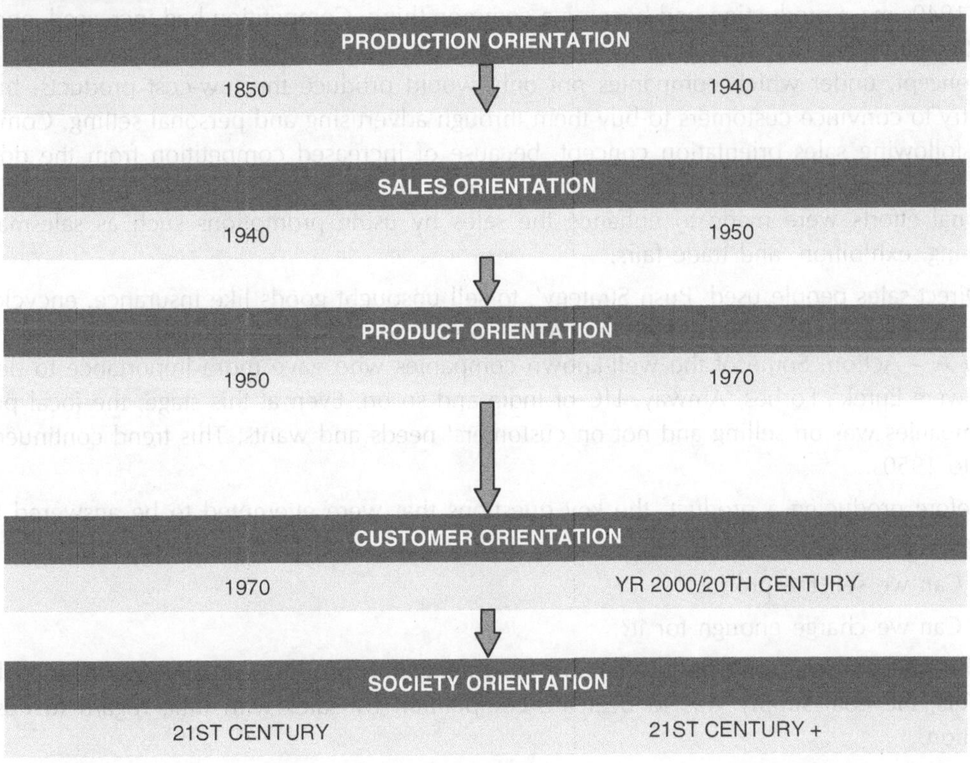

Note: Orientation means what a company believes in and what it follows or followed earlier.

STAGE-1: Production Orientation

At the first stage, marketing concept was based on production orientation. The focal point was on production of goods. The companies did not identify what the customers want, instead thought that producing a product most cost-efficiently and supplying it to the market at a low-cost would itself create the demand for the products.

In short, companies did not identify what the customers' want but focused on

- What they can produce?

  and

- How much they can produce?

This orientation was very successful till 1940s due to two key reasons:

1. Companies at that time operated only in a closed economy hence no competition from foreign players.
2. Less domestic competition as no privatization policy resulted in almost monopoly in business/ market.

STAGE-2: Sales Orientation

By the 1940s mass production had become a common thing. Competition had increased, and there was little unfulfilled demand. Around this time, market players (companies) began practicing the sales concept, under which companies not only would produce the low-cost products, but also would try to convince customers to buy them through advertising and personal selling. Companies started following sales orientation concept, because of increased competition from the domestic players and were eager to earn more profits through increased sales of their product offerings. Additional efforts were made to enhance the sales by using promotions such as salesmanship, advertising, exhibition, and trade fairs.

Direct sales people used 'Push Strategy', to sell unsought goods like insurance, encyclopedia and so on. They simply followed AIDA formula which denotes A – Attention / I – Interest / D – Desire / A – Action. Some of the well-known companies who gave more importance to personal selling were Eureka Forbes, Amway, LIC of India and so on. Even at this stage, the focal point of the companies was on selling and not on customers' needs and wants. This trend continued from 1940s to 1950s.

Before producing a product, the key questions that were attempted to be answered by the companies were:

- Can we sell the product?
- Can we charge enough for it?

The sales concept paid little attention to whether the product actually was needed by the customers; the goal simply was to beat the competition by sales with little regard to customer satisfaction.

STAGE-3: Product Orientation

At this stage, companies followed this concept to overcome the severe competition from other existing and new entrants. Marketers viewed this concept to develop new products which helped them overcome the boredom of customers and in turn enhance their market share.

According to Philip Kotler, "consumers will favour those products that offer the most quality, performance and features". Managers in product-oriented organizations focused on developing quality product offerings and continually added features (attributes) to the existing products thus improving them over time. Marketers viewed – product quality and performance as the two Critical Success Factors (CSF) where people were ready to shell extra money for the new product.

But sometimes it is alleged that focusing only on product development and upgradation led to ***Marketing Myopia***. It was a concept which was promulgated by Theodore Levitt in his paper "Marketing Myopia"[1]. It refers to development of new products or adding features to an already existing product without identifying the consumer needs. It is a coloured perception or short-sightedness about business.

When marketers without understanding the needs of the customers started developing new products or added new features to the existing products, it failed in the market. This concept can be easily understood with the example of Motorola's world's First Mobile Handset.

Brand Name	:	DynaTAC 800 x (AKA Brick)
Battery Life	:	30 Minutes
Price	:	US $ 3995
Outcome	:	Failed in the market as it was heavy, not compact and costlier.
Reasons	:	The product was nick named "Brick" due its size, which means not compact to hold it in hand comfortably. It took 10 hours to charge the battery for a battery backup of 30 minutes. Price was also seemed to be costly. Market acceptance was poor as it did not address the customer needs.

Hence, could not do well in the market. Motorola was the market leader in Pager service when it launched in 1995, in India. In 2004, Pager service was out of market and lost its pager business as text messaging got better with mobile, and telecommunication telecom became cheaper in India. It did not think beyond text messaging, which is indeed a classic example of marketing myopia where they lost their business against mobile handset which not only offered SMS service but also other value added services like MMS and so on. Net Books in India pushed off the shelves. Lightweight and sleek laptops, cheap tablets and high-end smartphones have lead to the death of the netbooks, that are now available at less than ₹ 20,000, half the price of laptops[2].

---

1 "Marketing Myopia", Published in *Harvard Business Review*, in July – August 1960 journal.

2 "Tablets, smartphones push netbooks off the shelves", by T.E. RAJA SIMHAN, The Hindu Business Line, dt. April 5, 2013, http://www.thehindubusinessline.com/industry-and-economy/info-tech/tablets-smartphones-push-netbooks-off-the-shelves/article4585340.ece.

EXHIBIT 1.4.2 Marketing Myopia

Motorola's Dynatac	Motorola's Pager	Asus Net Book
	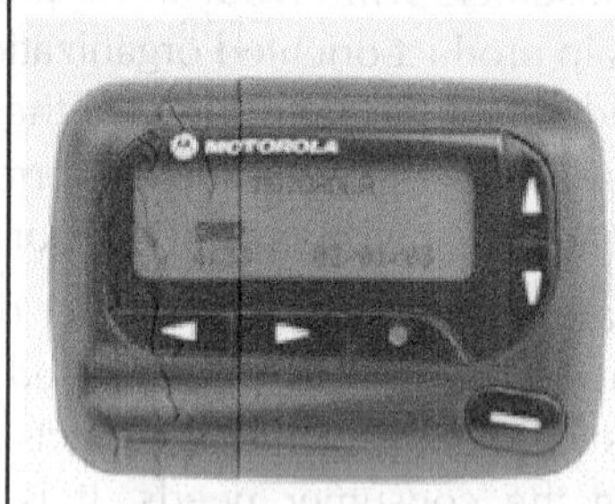	

Dynatac: http://www.retrobrick.com/moto8000.html
Motorola Pager: http://www.itexaminer.com/pagers-are-almost-history.aspx
ASUS Netbook:
http://upload.wikimedia.org/wikipedia/commons/thumb/e/e5/ASUS_Eee_White_Alt.jpg/220px-ASUS_Eee_White_Alt.jpg

STAGE-4: Customer Orientation

The modern marketing concept is based on the philosophy, 'Customer Orientation'. It says that all business activities revolve around customers, in fact, they start and end with customers. Without customers there is no need for production and so the marketing activities. Hence, there will be no business. Therefore customer is the king of any business. Peter F. Drucker used to say that, 'the purpose of any business is to create customers'. Consequently all business marketing activities revolve around customers.

Customer-oriented organizations followed the marketing as below:

- The market is segmented
- Target market is identified
- Common unfulfilled needs are identified
- Those needs are converted into products and services
- Branding and packing of products and services given due importance.
- Promoted by using Unique Selling Proposition (USP) and Integrated Marketing Communications (IMC).
- Profit and market standing through customer satisfaction and delight.

Modern marketers believe in pull strategy rather than push strategy. Modern Marketing concept is based on 'Freedom of Consumers', which means the consumers are free to choose and buy any product or service they want.

STAGE-5: Society Orientation

It is also called as management orientation concept or social marketing. Peter F. Drucker used to say that "Society's problems must be considered as an opportunity for organization." Healthy business cannot ignore issues like anti-tobacco smoking, safe drinking water, AIDS and so on. Commitment to social welfare activities will help out to acquire positive corporate image, brand awareness, loyalty and improved sales. According to Philip Kotler, "Management orientation aimed at generating consumer satisfaction and long-run consumer and public welfare as a key to satisfying organizational goals and objectives". Marketers today have recognized that the cause related marketing or societal or social marketing is a way for sustainable growth.

Conclusion

There is a popular saying that, "Nothing is permanent except change". Change is the essence of life and marketing is no exception to this. Hence the marketing concept may once again get remoulded, remodeled and redefined as per the changes that take place in the business environment and the society as a whole in future. The readers of the Marketing Orientation Concepts must realize that nothing is correct or wrong in the marketing world. The only thing is that it must help the organization to make money through sustainable or long-lasting growth.

UNIT 1.5: ROLE OF MARKETING DEPARTMENT WITH OTHER FUNCTIONAL AREAS

EXHIBIT 1.5.1 **Marketing with Other Functional Areas**

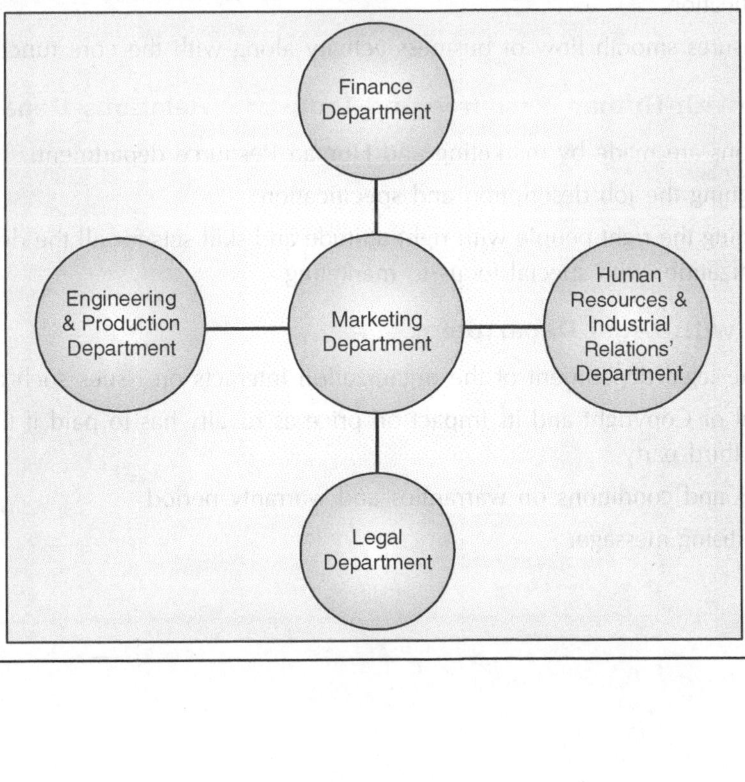

1. The relationship between the marketing department with other departments or functional areas of business is important as it facilitates the co-ordination of company's business.
2. Following are the relationships that is adopted in any organization:
   (a) Marketing with Finance Department
   (b) Marketing with Engineering and Production Department
   (c) Marketing with Human Resource and Industrial Relations' Department
   (d) Marketing with Legal Department

(a) Marketing with Finance Department

Following decisions are made collaboratively by marketing and finance department:

(i) Amount and time limit on credit sales to dealers
(ii) Norms on accounts receivables
(iii) Norms on account payables

All the above do have an effect on the smooth functioning of the marketing department.

(b) Marketing with Engineering and Production Department

Following decisions are made by marketing and production department:

(i) Selecting quality suppliers
(ii) Make or buy (outsource manufacturing process) decision of product
(iii) Quality Check and acquiring ISO (International Standards Organization) Quality Certification

All the above ensures smooth flow of business activity along with the core function, marketing.

(c) Marketing with Human Resource and Industrial Relations Department

Following decisions are made by marketing and Human Resource department:

(i) Designing the job description and specification
(ii) Selecting the right people with right attitude and skill sets for all the departments of the organization, with special focus to marketing

(d) Marketing with Legal Department

Marketing and the legal department of the organization interacts on issues such as:

(i) Patent or Copyright and its impact on price as royalty has to paid if they are acquired from third party
(ii) Terms and conditions on warranties and warranty period
(iii) Advertising message.

UNIT 1.6: HOW MARKETING IS DIFFERENT FROM SALES?

Following are the key differences between marketing and sales:

Sales	Marketing
• Focus is only on sales promotion	• Focus is on customer needs and sales promotion relevant to customer needs
• Importance given only to the products and their features or attributes	• Importance is given to customers where the offerings (products and services) are customised according to the customer requirements
• Focus is on converting the products and services into cash through hard core selling. Results in push strategy	• Converting customer needs into products. Results in pull strategy
• Profit through sales volume	• Profit through customer satisfaction
• Management follows a fragmented approach to sell its products	• Management follows an integrated approach to market its products
• Principle of Caveat Emptor is followed	• Priciple of Caveat Vendor is adopted
• Sales is a one-way communication from the company to consumers	• Marketing is a two-way communication process between the company and the customers
• It focuses on finding the prospects and sell them the product in hasty manner	• It focuses on brand building
• Sales programme is a short-term activity	• Marketing programme is a long-term process
• Sales are one of the activities under marketing	• Marketing includes sales

Conclusion

In totality, the learners are advised not to focus too much on finding the differences between marketing and sales, as all marketing activities must end up in sales in order to make money in the market. Thus, it is concluded that marketing without sales is incomplete and sales without marketing will not succeed in the market. That is why we have 'Marketing & Sales Department' and not just 'Marketing Department'.

UNIT 1.7: MARKET AND ITS CLASSIFICATION

Traditionally, market refers to a place where buyers and sellers gather to buy goods and services. But economists describe a market as a collection of buyers and sellers who transact over a particular product or a service.

Marketers define that

- Sellers constitute the industry
- Buyers constitute the market

Classification of Market

A market can be classified into four types:

(i) Consumer Market

(ii) Industrial or Business Market

(iii) Non-Profitable and Non-Governmental Markets

(iv) Global Market

In broader terms it can be classified as Domestic Markets and Global Markets.

EXHIBIT 1.7.1 Market Classification

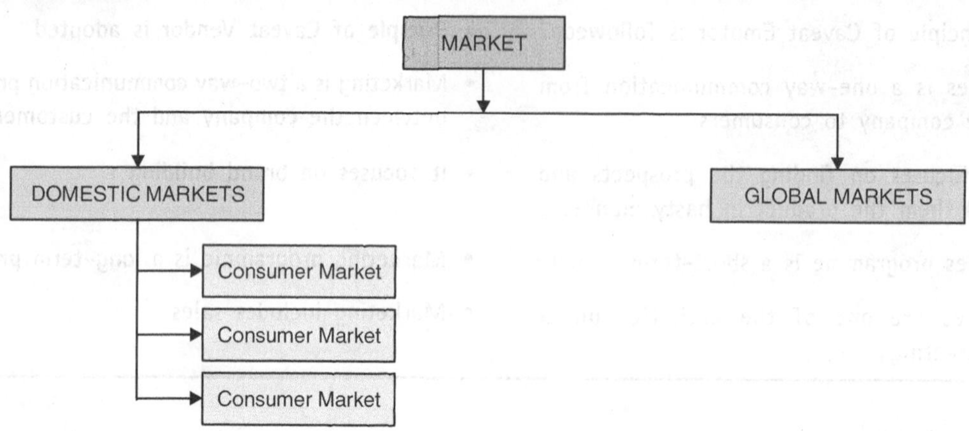

Consumer Market

It is a market where people buy goods and services for own use and not for resale. This market is called as B2C or Business-To-Consumer Market. These goods are called as consumer goods. For instance, Television Sets, Tooth Paste, Two-Wheeler and so on.

There is one more market called C2C or Consumer-To-Consumer Market. It is a market where second hand goods are sold. Well established companies are also in this market. Say for instance, Maruti's True-Value Cars sell Pre-Owned Cars, ebay.com an online C2C player (retail company) and so on.

Business or Industrial Market

It is a market where people buy goods and services for resale and not for own use. This market is called as B2B or Business-To-Business market. These goods are called as business or industrial goods. For instance, Nuts and bolts, Tyres, Engine for a Two-Wheeler or Four-Wheeler Manufacturing company and Industrial paints.

Non-profit Market

It refers to non-profit organizations such as churches, universities, non-governmental organizations and government procurements through open-tender. These organizations and the government call for the lowest bid from the sellers-cum-suppliers as they have a limited purchasing power.

Global Market

Global market refers to foreign markets. A global company sells its products and services (offerings) throughout the world. Such companies operate in two or more nations, hence called as MNCs or Multi-National Companies.

Example: Coca-Cola and Pepsi.

UNIT 1.8: CATEGORIES OF PLAYERS IN THE MARKET

Companies make competitive moves to outsmart their rivals in the competition. These moves would change with the role, the company plays in the target market. The roles played by the players in the market are as follows:

Market Leader

The company with the largest market share in an industry is the market leader. It usually leads other firms in price changes, new product introductions, distribution coverage and promotion spending, *e.g.,* HUL in skin care industry.

Market Challenger

A company which fights hard to enhance its market share plays the role of the challenger in an industry, *e.g.,* Godrej challenging HUL in skin care industry.

Market Follower

Those companies which attempt to hold or retain its market share in an industry are market followers. These companies focus on retention of their existing market share. Other players in the skin care market.

Market Niche

Those companies that serve small well-defined market segments which have been overlooked or ignored by mass marketers. Often tend to be a premium player in the industry, *e.g.,* HUL's Dove Soap in FMCG, Tupperware in Plastic Storage and AMWAY in FMCG products.

EXHIBIT 1.8.1 **Categories of Players in the Market**

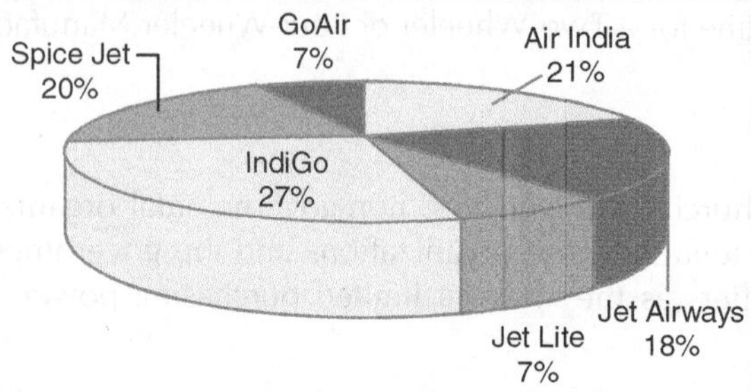

Market Leader:
IndiGo with 21% Market Share.

Market Challenger: Air India with 21% Market Share.

Followers: Other players viz. Spice Jet, Jet Airways, Jet Lite and GoAir.

Source: http://www.travopia.com/2012/market-share-of-indian-domestic-airlines-nov12-indigo-still-leads-other-interesting-pointers.html

LEARNING EXERCISES

1. Develop your own live example of Marketing Process (use any product or service offering of your choice)
2. Identify at least five players, each in at least five categories of market that are operating in your city or town. (Category of Businesses: Automobile, FMCG, Telecom, Diary Products, Cement etc.)

❑❑❑

Chapter 2

MARKET ANALYSIS AND MARKET PLANNING (STP) IN MARKETING

Chapter Objectives

After studying this chapter, you should be able to understand the following:

2.1. Role of Market Environment Analysis in Marketing Management.

2.2. Role of Market Planning—(STP) Segmentation, Targeting and Positioning in Marketing Management.

(a) How to Segment and Target a Market?

(b) How to Position a Brand in the Minds of the Target Market?

UNIT 2.1: MARKETING ENVIRONMENT

There are three important market environments in marketing for any business. Learning these environments before entering the business or expansion of business is very important as it becomes the deciding factor for the success of any business. A Marketing Director studies the environment of the business to know whether it is favourable or unfavourable to commence a business or continue to invest for the expansion of business in the given market condition, based on a feasibility study.

Whether it is India or any other country, following environmental conditions or environments exist:

1. Internal Environment
2. Micro Environment
3. Macro Environment

1. Internal Environment

Internal environment denotes all those factors that are internal to the organization and are controllable by the management of the company. The internal environmental factors that are analyzed by the business are 5 Ms viz. Men, Money, Materials, Machinery and Methods. In short, they are within the firm's control. This analysis is important as it helps the firm to know its strengths and weaknesses while competing with the competitors or the rival players.

2. Micro Environment

Micro environment is the one that influence the organization directly. It includes, the consumers, suppliers and the other stake holders. Stake holders are those people who are directly or indirectly associated with a business. They are banks, shareholders, debenture holders, employees, suppliers, customers and the government.

To understand stake holders, one needs to put himself or herself in the place of a business person. Assume that you are about to start your own business, your need to get the approval from the Government officials like license, VAT registration and so on. You are in need of seed money, which is nothing but capital. This capital can be mobilized from banks, shareholders and debenture holders. Then you need employees to work for the company. To manufacture the product you need suppliers of raw materials and last but not the least, all the products and services produced by you need to be sold in the market which consists of customers. Now read the meaning of stake holders again.

Thus, it is understood that a business revolves around stake holders. Hence, one cannot do business without taking them into account.

3. Macro Environment

This environment is the one which is external to the business and out of organizational control. Analyzing the factors involved, this environment helps the organization to understand the threats and opportunities of its business.

It is often analysed by the taking following environmental factors into account and is termed as PEST.

P – Political Environment
E – Economic Environment
S – Socio-Cultural Factors
T – Technological Factors

Let us see each of these factors and what are to be specifically analysed to measure the future prospects of the business:

P – Political Environment

Before a company enters into a specific industry, it needs to analyze what is the political environment in the market. To be more specific one needs to look for the answers for the following questions:

(a) *How Stable is the Political Environment in the State or States where the Business is to be Established and/or Expanded?*

Say for instance, Central Government of India has allowed **51%** (FDI) Foreign Direct Investment in Multi-Brand Retail Sector[1]. But implementing this policy decision is handed over to each state. Punjab, one of the states of India, is ready to implement it. But Tamil Nadu is not ready to implement it. Hence, the retail majors like Carre Four (French Retailer), Wal-Mart (US Retailer) are hesitating to commence their retail business in India. Ultimately, what does it mean? It means when the government changes, the policy also changes along with it. Hence, companies look for stability of the government before investing in businesses.

(b) *What is the Government's Policy on a Specific Industry?*

Government Policy is nothing but the Rules or Guiding Principles of the Government that are established for streamlining the smooth functioning of an industry. Let us again take the Retail Sector as an example to understand the government policy. According the Central Government of India's FDI policy on multi-brand retail trade, if a foreign retailer wants to setup its business in India it has to source at least 30% of manufactured or processed products from (SMEs) Small and Medium Enterprises operating in India[2].

(c) *What is the Government Policy on Marketing of the Company's Offerings?*

This area can be understood with a few examples

(i) *Infant Milk Substitutes:* Based on Infant Milk Substitute Act, any company is legally allowed to manufacture infant milk substitutes like Cerelac, Farex and so on but cannot promote in any form in India as Government of India found that it is indeed indirectly de-promoting breast feeding among mothers, which subsequently affects the health of the child.

(ii) *Cigarette:* Indian Companies like ITC are legally allowed to produce Cigarettes but are not legally permitted to promote them in any media. The excise duty (manufacturing tax) on cigarettes is being continually raised by the Government in order to discourage the sales. But do check the Exhibit-2.1.1 of ITC's performance where even today revenue from cigarettes are quite high as compared to its any other business.

(iii) *Chewing Tobacco:* Recently (from 2013), Government of Tamil Nadu banned the sales of chewing tobacco for 2 years.

(iv) *Liquor:* Liquor manufacturing and sales are legally accepted in India but promotion of any liquor in any media is not legally allowed. In Gujarat, permits are pre-requisites for

[1] "30% sourcing from SMEs not possible, Walmart tells Govt". by Bindu D. Menon, The Hindu Business Line, dt. 24-07-2013, pg-2.

[2] Ibid.

consumption of liquor. In the year 2013, Government of Gujarat raised the limit of monthly income level of consumers, for obtaining liquor permit on health grounds from ₹ 5,000 to ₹ 25,000.[1]

EXHIBIT 2.1.1 ITC's Performance

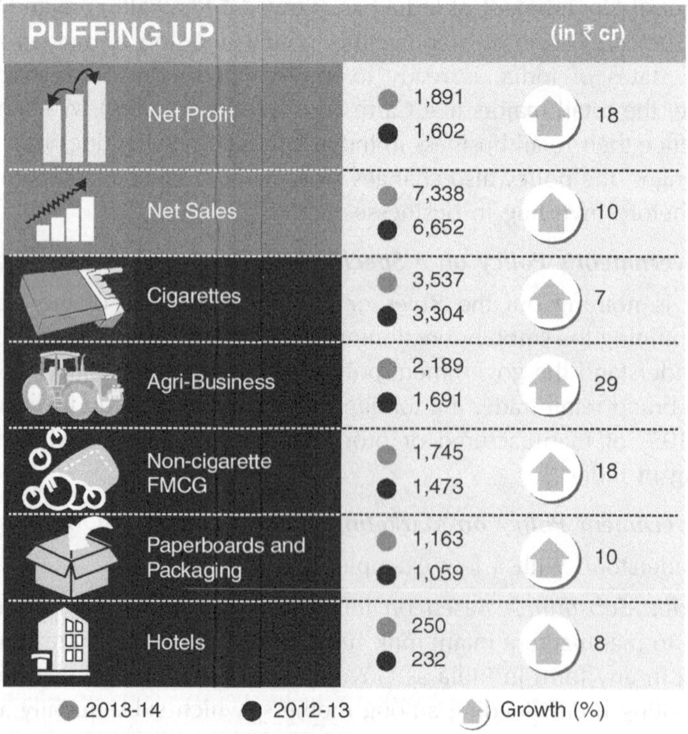

Source: http://www.thehindubusinessline.com/companies/itc-q1-net-up-at-rs-189133-cr-noncigarettes-fmcg-segment-back-in-red/article4952195.ece?ref=wl_economy

(v) *Lottery Tickets:* Sales of Lottery Tickets are banned in Tamil Nadu.

Above examples would help a business to decide whether to enter a particular state to do any of the above businesses in India.

(d) *Does the Government have a View on Culture and Religion?*

Our Indian banking system is based on the core functions, viz. deposit mobilization and lending. But Islamic banks do not operate in such a way. As per their Holy Book, Kuran, Interest is not to be charged on lending. Instead, they become partners of the borrowers' business where they take a share of profit from the business. Reserve Bank of India is yet to allow Islamic banks to operate

[1] http://articles.timesofindia.indiatimes.com/2013-07-02/ahmedabad/40328719_1_liquor-permit-fees-health

in India. This prevents any Islam or Muslim to start a commercial bank based on Islamic banking system in India.

(e) *Is the Government Involved in any Trading Agreement (Treaty) with Other Nations?*

This must also be checked as it helps us to know whether the marketers are about to face domestic competition alone or the global or international competition in the market.

E – Economic Environment

Economic environmental factors are analyzed by the business houses in order to forecast the future economic scenario based on the past and present trends in economic conditions. Several Economic Indicators are used by the companies to analyze the economy of the nation or the market. Following are the environmental factors that are analyzed:

(i) *Interest Rates on Borrowings*

RBI would come out with its Credit Policy on Quarterly basis. Businesses keenly watch on the (CRR) Cash Reserve Ratio, Repo Rate, Reverse Repo Rate, Bank Rate, Prime Lending Rates and so on. To know whether the interest on borrowing is going to be high (dear money) or low (cheap money). Moreover, companies today borrow at floating rate, rather than fixed rate, which would fluctuate based on international scenario. Obviously, to have favourable business scenario, the interest rate on borrowings need to be low.

(ii) *Level of Inflation*

Today India is facing a problem of growth-less and jobless inflation. Inflation refers to a continuous rise in price of a commodity over a period of time. Inflation leads to reduced purchasing power. Say for instance, if one kilo of sugar was priced at ₹ 50 last year, and this year due to demand-supply mismatch, the price of the same one kilo sugar has risen to ₹ 75, then a customer will not be able to buy the same quantity of sugar for ₹ 50 (will be able to buy less than a kilo only). This means drop in sales volume and profitability of the company. Check both Consumer Price Index and Whole Sale Price Index.

(iii) *Employment Level and Per-capita Income*

The business houses will also look at the level of employment and per-capita income of each state before deciding where to do their businesses. The simple logic behind this is that it helps the company to whether the market has the purchasing power to buy their offerings and also fix price for their offering based on their purchasing power.

(iv) *GDP*

GDP stands for Gross Domestic Product; it refers to overall production of a country during a year. Each state in India contributes towards the GDP of the nation. Companies choose those states that have a high rate of GDP growth rate (refer Exhibit-2.1.3) in order to make sure their business grow along with the economic growth.

EXHIBIT 2.1.2 **Per Capita Income: How the States Compare**

State	2005-06	2006-07
Delhi	58665	66728
Puducherry	48477	52669
Harayana	41988	49038
Maharashtra	36090	41331
Punjab	36759	40566
Gujarat	32991	37532
Himachal	33817	36656
Kerala	30668	33609
Tamil Nadu	29958	32733
Andhra Pradesh	26226	29582
Sikkim	26412	29521
Karnataka	26015	28830
West Bengal	25041	28753
Uttarakhand	24870	27800
Tripura	25700	27777
Arunachal Pradesh	22335	25836
Mizoram	23900	25679
Meghalaya	22847	24672
Manipur	20326	22495
Jharkhand	18803	20733
Orissa	17610	20240
Assam	18211	20166
Rajasthan	17306	19512
Madhya Pradesh	15304	16578
Uttar Pradesh	13316	14685
Bihar	7930	9702

Source: *The Hindu Business Line,* dt. 4-12-2013, pg-19.

EXHIBIT 2.1.3 **States and its Corresponding GDP Growth Rate**

SIZE OF STATE GDP

TODAY			2020		
1	Maharashtra	13.94	1	Maharashtra	13.43
2	Uttar Pradesh	9.08	2	Uttar Pradesh	8.86
3	Tamil Nadu	7.43	3	Tamil Nadu	8.49
4	West Bengal	7.17	4	West Bengal	8.27
5	Andhra Pradesh	7.07	5	Andhra Pradesh	7.22
6	Gujarat	6.40	6	Gujarat	6.85
7	Karnataka	5.84	7	Karnataka	6.69
8	Rajasthan	4.23	8	Rajasthan	4.89
9	Madhya Pradesh	3.95	9	Madhya Pradesh	4.58
10	Punjab	3.54	10	Punjab	3.01

Note: 'Today' denotes Indian States' GDP in 2000-1 and GDP forecast for 2020-21.

Source: http://indiatoday.intoday.in/story/projections-2020-how-some-major-indian-states-are-likely-to-perform-in-the-future/1/195629.html

(v) ***Labour Cost***

The cost of labour is another important external or macro environmental factor to be taken into account in-order to decide whether to establish the manufacturing base in a particular state in India. In general, companies prefer low cost labour to cut costs there by to earn sustained profits and to stay relevant in the hyper-competitive markets.

S – Socio-Cultural Factors

As far as the social factors are concerned, companies attempts to get the answers for the following questions:

(i) What is the dominant religion in the state where they intend to do their business?

(ii) What are the food habits of the people?

(iii) What are the attitudes of the people towards the company's offerings (product and services)?

(iv) How much time do the consumers have for their leisure?

(v) What are the roles of men and women in the family and in the society?

(vi) Is the older generation wealthy?

(vii) What is the trend on pocket money and spending attitudes of youngsters?

Based on the answers to above cited questions, companies decide and design their offerings.

T – Technological Factors

Companies today need to invest a lot in Research and Development (R&D), to develop new products and make them succeed in the market. Technology plays a very vital role not only in developing a new product but also decides the fate of any new product to see sustainable growth in the market.

Following questions are asked by the market players (companies) to analyze the technological environmental factors:

(i) Can the technology make the product and service affordable and quality to the customers?

(ii) Can it facilitate innovation? Example: Internet banking, mobile baking and so on.

(iii) Can the distribution process be made more convenient to customers using the new technology? (GIS – Geographical Information System, GPS – Global Positioning System and E-CRM modules) say for instance, LIC sells its Insurance plans using its online portal other than through its agents and bancassurance channels.

(iv) Can the new technology make offerings (product or service) obsolete? Say for instance, Due to the arrival of SMS facility in cellular phones, Text Messaging Service of Pager (RPG was a major service provider in Pager segment) got obsolete, not only that from the Month of July 2013, Telegram services were stopped by the India Post Office as there are only a very few takers for this service due to cell phone and e-mail invasion.

Conclusion

Thus, it is very important for every business entity to understand the various marketing or business environments to do business successfully, in India.

UNIT 2.2: ROLE OF MARKET PLANNING IN MARKETING MANAGEMENT

Market planning in planning in marketing management involves STP or Segmentation, Targeting and Positioning. This unit deals each of these activities in details.

Market Segmentation

(a) Market Segmentation – Meaning

(b) Need for market segmentation – Why should a marketer today need to segment the market?

(c) Benefits of Market Segmentation

(d) Types of Market Segmentation

(e) How do marketers segment in recent times?

(f) Assignment

(a) Market Segmentation – Meaning

Segmentation is a process of disaggregating (or) dividing the entire market into a number of sub-markets based on similar needs or characteristics of the people. It is the one where the heterogeneous (diverse) market is broken up into a number of relatively homogeneous (identical) units.

(b) Need for Market Segmentation – Why should a Marketer Today Need to Segment the Market?

No seller or a company can serve and satisfy all the customers in the market. Because, the customers are too numerous and each one of them have diversified or different needs and wants. Moreover, for any player (company or seller), the resources are limited. Say for instance, a company has a land, it can either use it for building a factory or use it for constructing a cinema theatre. It can not do both simultaneously as it has got a land space only for either of the business purpose. Initially, companies were following mass production and sales. In short it is nothing but mass marketing.

In mass marketing, a company or seller engages in mass production, distribution and mass promotion where it offered one product for all types of customers. It is based on the philosophy "One Size Fits All!" Henry Ford, Founder of Ford Motor Company, USA, did this at its initial stage. He followed this marketing strategy when he offered "Model T-Ford only in black colour" where he said "In any colour, as long as it's black". Once, Coca-Cola was sold only in a 6.5-ounce bottle and no other choice. One would definitely ask "Why these companies followed mass marketing?" The reason is that it leads to lower cost due to Economies of Scale, which in turn helps to price its offerings competitively. But it is not a sustainable strategy as the needs and want vary from customer to customer, where the single offering of the company would not be able to satisfy the need and wants of all the customers.

Assume a company has ignored a differing customer's need; a rival player would definitely enter the market with a product to satisfy the dissatisfied customers. Let see this with the example of Indian Telecom Industry. Before 1990s, India had only one national company offering telecom service. Later after adapting Liberalisation, Privatisation and Globalisation, through (FDI) Foreign Direct Investment, Both Indian Private telecom companies like Tata, Reliance and foreign players like Vodafone entered into the Indian Telecom Market. Before 1990s, customers literally had only one choice—BSNL, but now, there are more than 15 telecom companies competing in the market for their chunk of market share. It is a cut-throat competition. Hence, they address different customer groups with different offerings and schemes. Customers are today segmented as Corporate, Individual Customers, educational institutions and so on based on their similar needs and characteristics so as to garner the profitable market segment and achieve a sustainable growth.

(c) Benefits of Market Segmentation

Following are the key benefits of market segmentation:

(i) It helps the marketer to know people who have common characteristics which influence them (tend) to act in a similar way.

(ii) It helps to identify various customer groups within the market.

(iii) It helps to target the specific customer group.

(iv) It facilitates for an in-depth study of buyer behaviour.

(v) It helps to formulate marketing programmes on reliable and predictable base for an effective result.

(vi) It also helps to identify the less satisfied customer groups or market segments and make successful business by satisfying such segments.

(d) Types of Market Segmentation

(i) ***Geographic segmentation:*** Dividing the market or customers based on area is called as geographic segmentation. Customers may be segmentation based on any one or more following area such as Continent, Region, Country, State, District, Urban, Rural, Climate of the area and so on.

(ii) ***Demographic segmentation:*** Dividing the market or customers based on people's population size is called as geographic segmentation. Customers may be segmentation based on any one or more following areas:

EXHIBIT 2.2.1 Demographic Market Segmentation and Offerings of the Companies

Demographic Variables	Offering / Brand	Target Market Segment
Age	Pepsi, Close-up	Teenagers
Gender	Axe Deodrant, Brylcream Fair and Lovely, Ponds, Lux	Male Customers Female Customers
Family size	Tata Nano	Small Family
Language	The Hindu, The New Indian Express	English Daily Readers
Social level	Dove	High Class Ladies
Occupational level	Raymonds	Corporate People
Income level	Ginger Hotel	Budget Travellers

Some of the famous terms used for describing demographic market segments are presented below for the readers' convenience. DINKY – Double Income No Kids Yet, GLAM – Greying, Leisured, Affluent, Middle-aged, NILKIE – No Income, Lots of Kids, OINK – One income, no kids, OPAL – Older People with Active Lifestyles, PANSES – Politically Active and Not Seeking Employment, RAPPIES – Retired Affluent Professionals, SINBAD – Single Income, No Boyfriend and Absolutely Desperate, SINDI – Single Independent and Divorced, SITCOM – Single Income, Two Kids Outrageous Mortgage, SUPPIES – Senior Urban Professionals, TINKIE – Two Incomes, Nanny and Kids, WOOF – Well Off

Older Folk – a demographic grouping, WOOPIES – Well – Off Older People, YAPPIES – Young Affluent Parents, YUPPIE – Young Urban Professional. Say for instance, following demographic markets may be taken as the relevant markets for Tata Nano, World's Smallest and Cheapest Car: DINKY – Double Income No Kids Yet, OINK – One income, no kids, SINBAD – Single Income, No Boyfriend and Absolutely Desperate, YAPPIES – Young Affluent Parents, YUPPIE – Young Urban Professional and YOUTH MARKET which denotes to young customers, typically those aged between 16 to 24.

(iii) ***Psychographic segmentation:*** It refers to market segmentation based on individual's activities, personality, interest, opinion, Lifestyle and Values. *Example:* Page3Gen or Party Crazy Generation. Today youth have got lots of earning capacity. A few are there who really don't care about the society. They say they have the capacity to earn and so they will spend and party as they wish. This has indeed become a good income generating market in India.

(iv) ***Usage or user based segmentation:*** Dividing the customers based on their usage or the users themselves is called as User or Usage based segmentation. This can be easily understood by using smoking or smokers as example. Smoking (usage) or Smokers (users) can be classified into four categories, viz. heavy users/smokers, medium smokers, occasional smokers and non-smokers.

(v) ***Volume segmentation:*** Segmenting or dividing the customers based on potential quantity of bulk purchase is the basis for Volume based segmentation. Industrial Buyers and Government Institutions are seen as bulk purchasers upon tenders.

(vi) ***Loyalty based segmentation:*** When a customer purchases a specific brand for a long period of time, he is a loyal customer. Dividing the customers based on their loyalty is called as loyalty based segmentation. They can be of three types:

Hard-Core Loyalists : These customers buy only one specific brand

Soft-Core Loyalists : These customers buy two to three brands

Switchers : These customers are unloyal to any brand. Hence, buy any brand that is available

(e) How do Marketers Segment the Market in Recent Times?

Let us understand how marketers today segment their customers using Telecom.

As the mobile-services industry starts to mature, executives must find new ways to sustain growth – especially by generating value from existing customers. Customer life-cycle management, though a likely and proven strategy, presents a vexing challenge to prepaid mobile operators: the nature of their transactions does not permit the exchange of vital marketing details, such as age, gender, and address. Operators therefore resort to blanket promotions that risk destroying value by needlessly cutting prices or offering free services. But companies can find alternate ways to overcome the data shortfall, as our experience shows. One solution is for marketers to look more closely at their billing systems, which conceal a wealth of information; to create segments, often as small as 100,000 subscribers; and to plan tailored promotions for each group.

EXHIBIT 2.2.2 **Segmenting Mobile Operator's Prepaid Customers**

Illustrative example of mobile operator with prepaid subscribers

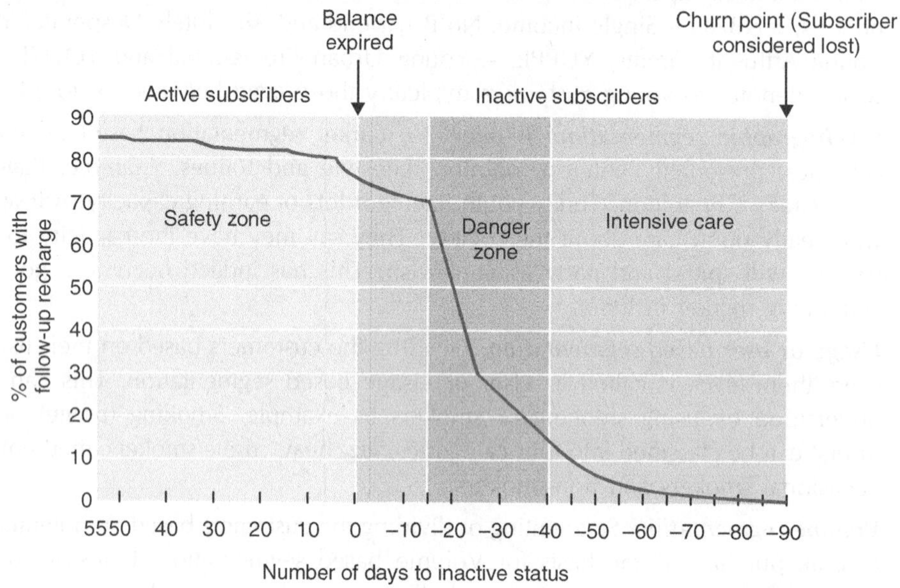

Safety zone

- No indication that higher churn is probable

Effective offers

- Target offers to recent customers to decrease early churn
- Sell bundles and other low-cost offers
- Increase stickiness through loyalty and point programs

Danger zone

- Goal is immediate recharge

Effective offers

- Vary recharge offers by value of customers; offer extra top-up amount bonus airtime, Short Message Service (SMS)
- Roll out more aggressive offers to subscribers who remain inactive over time

Intensive care

- Low likelihood of recovery; recharge offers will have low acceptance rates

Effective offers

- Offer free credit accessible only when customer tops up

Source: *The McKinsey Quarterly News Letter,*"New ideas for customer segmentation", "Getting more from prepaid mobile services" (February 2008).

The above exhibit – 2.1.5 illustrates one prepaid mobile operator's strategy to reduce churn rates by segmenting subscribers through their usage patterns. Tracking the number of days before a customer is "lost" helped the company to introduce promotions most likely to increase usage and retention while minimizing revenue lost to scattershot offers and unnecessary discounts.

Additional Information for Market Segmentation: Socio-economic Classification

In addition to income classification and consumer classification, Indian households can also be segmented according to the occupation and education levels of the chief earner of the household (the person who contributes most to the household expenses). This is called as Socio-Economic Classification (SEC), which is mainly used by market planners to target market before launching their new products. SEC is made to understand the purchase behavior and the consumption pattern of the households. The urban area is segregated into: A1, A2, B1, B2, C, D, E1, E2.

EXHIBIT 2.2.3 Socio-Economic Classification

Occupation	Education						
	Illiterate	Less than 4 yrs in school	5–9 yrs of school	School certificate	Some college	Graduate	Post-graduate
Skilled	E2	E1	D	C	C	B2	B2
Unskilled	E2	E2	E1	D	D	D	D
Shop owner	D	D	C	B2	B2	A2	A2
Petty trader	E2	D	D	C	C	B2	B2
Employer of-							
Above 10 persons	B1	B1	A2	A2	A1	A1	A1
Below 10 persons	C	B2	B2	B1	A2	A1	A1
None	D	C	B2	B1	A2	A1	A1
Clerk	D	D	D	C	B2	B1	B1
Supervisor	D	D	C	C	B2	B1	A2
Professional	D	D	D	B2	B1	A2	A1
Senior executive	B1	B1	B1	B1	A2	A1	A1
Junior executive	C	C	C	B2	B1	A2	A2

Source: Indian readership survey (IRS).

What is Socio Economic Classification (SEC)?

A common classification that is used by marketers to describe the Indian population is the Socio Economic Classification (SEC). SEC is the classification of Indian consumers on the basis of two parameters: Occupation and Education of the chief wage earner (Head) of the households. The SEC classification, created in 1988, was ratified by Market Research Society of India (MRSI) is used by most media researchers and brand managers to understand the Indian consuming class.

According to SEC, the Urban Indian households are classified on the basis of the two parameters Education and Occupation into SEC A1, A2, B1, B2, C, D, E1, and E2. Sections A & B refer to High-class- constitutes over a quarter of urban population. Sec C refers to Middle-class—constitutes 21% of the urban population. Sections D & E refer to low-class—constitutes over half the urban population. In urban households, SEC A1 include those with graduation/post graduate holding senior positions like CEO's and Middle level managers and also those entrepreneurs having some college education and employs more than 10 staffs. The chart is self-explanatory. The 'Rural Indian Households' are classified into SEC R1, R2, R3, R4. In the rural classification, the parameters are Education of the chief wage earner and the type of the house is presented in the following table:

EXHIBIT 2.2.4 **Rural Classification, Based on Education of the Chief Wage Earner and the House Type**

Education of chief wage earner	Type of House		
	Pucca	Semi-pucca	Kuchcha
Professional degree	R1	R2	R3
Graduation/ PG	R1	R2	R3
College	R1	R2	R3
SSC/HSC	R2	R3	R3
Class 4-Class 9	R3	R3	R4
Up to class 4	R3	R3	R4
Self-learning	R3	R4	R4
Illiterate	R4	R4	R4

The SEC classification helps the marketers to identify segments that have high consuming potential. The high potential types: A1, A2, the medium ones and the bottom of pyramid ones. The SEC classification is used by Media planners to decide the media which gives the client maximum effectiveness. The research team at the media houses uses the (NRS) National Readership Survey and (IRS) Indian Readership surveys' raw data to identify the reach of the media in these SEC segments and uses this input for pitching their campaign to large advertisers[1].

Target Market and Targeting Strategies

(a) Selecting the target markets

(b) Targeting Strategies

[1] cks.in,readbetweenps.blogspot.com,agencyfaqs

(a) Selecting the Target Markets

Once the marketers segment (divide) the market they identify and choose the markets they would like to serve. Most marketers would select or target only those markets that are potentially profitable and sustainable. Marketers usually use the market size in terms of population and income which is directly correlated with the spending power. Of course, it is quite dangerous to generalize that all those with high income would spend on the company offerings. Hence, marketers consider 'Response Sensitivity', which means the likelihood of the given market segment (group of prospects) to react positively towards the company's marketing programmes, which in turn leads to purchase action.

Say for instance; assume that a company has decided to sell its organic fertilizers in villages. Hence collects data on rural population of India and it is given below for the scrutiny of the readers. After reading it, select or target the market which has the highest population.

EXHIBIT 2.2.5 Rural Population Classified by Village Size

Village Size (No. of Persons)	% of Villages	% of rural population	Average Village Population
Less than 200	15	01	100
200 to 499	21	06	345
500 to 999	24	14	724
1000 to 1999	22	25	1410
2000 to 4999	14	32	2974
5000 to 9999	02	13	6630
10000 +	02	09	16026
Total	100	100	–

Source: *The Hindu Business Line*, "Truly Rural", by Sudhanshu Ranade, dt. 6-3-2009, pg-5.

When marketers target their specific markets, they would get ready to face challenges. Some of them are as follows: when the marketers target the largest market in terms of population size, they would face the challenge in the form of heavy and cut-throat competition. Assume, they attempt to target the bottom of the pyramid, the economically backward people, niche players cannot offer them products and services as they do not have economies of scale to reduce costs and thereby reduce price of the offerings.

(b) Targeting Strategies

Once the marketers have evaluated the potential of every available market segment, their next task is to decide the following:

(i) How many target markets to be chosen?

(ii) Which segment of the target market will become the targets of the organisation's marketing programme?

To know answers for the above two important questions, the marketers have three strategies to choose from. They are as follows:

(1) Concentration

(2) Differentiation

(3) Atomisation

(1) Concentration Strategy

When marketers decide to serve a single market segment, they are pursuing concentration strategy. This helps the marketers to direct all their efforts towards satisfying the single target market segment. This makes the marketing programme more relevant, effective and cost effective, as there would not be any spillover effect. But they do have the risk of putting all their eggs in one basket. If customers move away from the company's offerings due to technological development or change in tastes and preferences, then the company would stand to lose their market share and revenue altogether. Example: Export Credit Guarantee Corporation of India offering policy coverage against FOREX transactions targets only the Indian Exporters and Importers. When global economy slows down, its revenue would also slow down.

(2) Differentiation Strategy

This strategy is also known as multi-segment strategy. It is the one where marketers direct all their efforts toward satisfying more than one market segment, *i.e.,* satisfying several market segments simultaneously. It is done by following varying marketing mix such as adopting different pricing, different brand names, different distribution channels, different media of communication in different target market segments. Example, Hindustan Unilever, Tata Group of Companies.

Say for instance, Spectacles retailer Lawrence and Mayo launched "stylish and colourful" pens targeting working women, women executives and professionals. The 135 year old eyewear retailer opened its first retail outlet in 1877 in India. Big pen brands like Cross and Mont Blanc targets men. But Lawrence and Mayo is targeting professionals like CEOs, Doctors etc[1].

(3) Atomisation

Each consumer is treated as an unique market segment. Customization plays a vital role in this kind of market targeting strategy. Hence it is also called as micro level marketing or one-to-one marketing. For example, Homes are constructed by the engineers as per the tastes and preference of the clients (customized), Tailors stitch blazers, suits as per the style, preferences and size of the customers, and five star hotels offer customized suites to their VIP customers.

---

[1] *The Hindu Business Line,* "Eyewear retailer makes the pen special for women", by Purvita Chatterjee, dt. 12-5-12, pg-1.

Positioning of Products and Services

(a) **Positioning**

(b) **Positioning Strategies**

(c) **7–Strategic Ways to Position a Product or a Service.**

(a) Positioning

Every product or service has its own unique features. These unique features in marketing are called as attributes. These unique features that would facilitate to market the products and service offerings are called as USP or Unique Selling Proposition. Using these USP imaginatively and effectively to occupy the mind space of the target market is called as positioning. Positioning is done in the minds of the people. It is done by using both USP and ESP. ESP refers to Emotional Selling Proposition. It is used for developing a long-term emotional bond between the target market and the service brand.

(b) Positioning Strategies

A marketer has 3 strategic options for positioning a service. They are as follows:

1. ***Create:*** Grab an unoccupied position in the minds of the target market
2. ***Reinforce:*** Strengthen the existing position in the minds of the customers
3. ***Change:*** Reposition an existing brand in the minds of the customers.

1. Create: Grab an Unoccupied Position in the Minds of the Target Market

When companies were focusing on their sachet milk, dairy business, AMUL (Anand Mill Union Limited) offered Milk Powder. It positioned its brand as an Instant Milk Maker using its tagline "A dairy in your home". It also offered Amulya which was positioned as "Dairy Whitner".

2. Reinforce: Strengthen the Existing Position in the Minds of the Customers

Heinz's Complan reinforced its existence in the Health Food Drink by communicating that it contains 23 vital nutrients for the proper physical and mental growth of a child. It communicates this message to its target market quite frequently with the tagline "A Complete Planned Food".

3. Change: Reposition an Existing Brand in the Minds of the Customers

Historically, Xerox, a US based company positioned itself as "Photocopier Company", now it has repositioned itself as "Complete Documentation Company". So when you think of office documentation, you are made to think of Xerox.

(c) 7–Strategic Ways to Position a Product or a Service Offering

1. **Attribute based positioning**
2. **Benefits based positioning**
3. **Use or application based positioning**
4. **User based positioning**
5. **Competitors based positioning**
6. **Category based positioning**
7. **Value based positioning**

1. Attribute Based Positioning

When a company uses the unique features of the brand or its product offering in the minds of the customers, is known as Attribute based positioning. For instance, Kinetic Honda scooter was the first scooter in India to have button start along with Kick Start facility. This indeed became the ultimate (USP) Unique Selling Proposition of the brand to differentiate itself from other rival brands and occupy the minds of the market using this feature or attribute. Thus if a person wanted to buy a scooter with button start facility or feature, he would immediately think of Kinetic Honda and that is where the success of positioning lies.

2. Benefits Based Positioning

When a company uses the benefits of using its brand to occupy the mind space of the target market or the customers, it is known as benefits based positioning. For instance ICICI bank's ad on extended branch working hours from 8 am to 8 pm. A.C. Nivea, a body lotion targeted towards women offers it benefits clearly which are whitening, cell repair and UV protect.

3. Use or Application Based Positioning

When a company positions its offerings (products and services) as the best one for a specific application in the market, it called as Use or Application based positioning. For example, Microsoft positioning its MS Office Application as the Best for Office Documentation. Google search engine website for searching information on the web. Heinz's Complan is positioned towards kids' growth which offers "A Complete Planned Food".

4. User Based Positioning

When a company positions its offerings as the best for a specific user groups or people, it is called as User based positioning. For example, Old Spice, an after shave lotion position its brand for Man by using its taglines, 'Mantastic' and "Smells like a man, man" in its advertisement., Gokul Sandiva, talcum powder, fairness cream and face wash are positioned towards women as "Pure Sandalwood. Beautiful Skin......", Horlick, a malt based health food drink is positioned as "A Great Family Nourisher". India has got many Diabetic patients who cannot take sugar in their food. This need is clearly addressed by Sugar Free Gold.

5. Competitors Based Positioning

When a company positions its offerings better than its competitors' offerings in order to occupy the minds of the target market, it is called as Competitors based positioning. For instance, it happened in the case of Heinz's Complan Vs. GSK's Horlicks, HUL Surf Vs. P&G's and among major airline of India. Companies do this by Comparative Advertisements in order to show their rivals that they are always better than the rival brands available in the market. This is done so as to bring in brand preference among the customers.

6. Category Based Positioning

When a company positions its offerings as No.1, in a particular business category, it is known as Category Based Positioning. Example LIC of India in Insurance, Airtel etc.

7. Value Based Positioning

The service provider uses values (benefits) such as price, quality to position its service. For example, when Reliance Infocom was Launched, it positioned its service based on low call charges just 40 paise/min.

LEARNING EXERCISES

1. Prepare a market analysis report for Mushroom marketing in your city or town.
2. Develop a Market plan on how to segment, target and position your brand of mushrooms in your city or town.

❑❑❑

Chapter **3**

MARKETING MIX

Chapter Objectives

After studying this chapter, you should be able to understand the following:

1. Role of Marketing Mix in Marketing a Product Offering of a Company.
2. Understand Various Aspects That Are to be Learnt Regarding 4Ps of Marketing Mix.
   - **3.1.** Role of 'Product' in the Marketing Mix.
   - **3.2.** Role of 'Place' in the Marketing Mix.
   - **3.3.** Role of 'Price' in the Marketing Mix.
   - **3.4.** Role of 'Promotion' in the Marketing Mix.

1. ROLE OF MARKETING MIX IN MARKETING OF A PRODUCT

The readers now would have segmented and targeted (selected) the market (customer groups) with similar needs and characteristics. The next stage would be to design a suitable marketing mix in order to see increased sales and sustained growth of the company. To facilitate this, the marketers use the Marketing Mix. It is otherwise called Marketing Tactics. Any marketer will have to do the following to market their offerings in the select target market:

(1) Product design

(2) Fixation of price for their product offering

(3) Promotion

(4) Sales

(5) Distribution

The term 'marketing mix' became popular by Prof. Neil H. Borden who published his article, "The Concept of the Marketing Mix" in 1964. Borden used the term in his teaching in the late 1940's when James Culliton described the marketing manager as a 'mixer of ingredients'. The ingredients in Borden's marketing mix included product planning, pricing, branding, distribution channels, personal selling, advertising, promotions, packaging, display, servicing, physical handling, and fact finding and analysis.

American Prof. Edmund Jerome McCarthy later grouped these ingredients into the four categories which are famously known as the 4Ps of marketing, and they are – Product, Place, Price and Promotions. These four Ps are the parameters that the marketing manager can control, subject to the internal and external constraints of the marketing environment. The goal is to make decisions that center the four Ps on the customers, the target market, in order to create perceived value and generate a positive response.

For the sake of the reader's convenience, please refer the first case — 'The Case of Nano' once again inorder to understand the application of 4Ps — the marketing mix in detail through Tata Motor's Nano – The People's Car. (Refer Chapter 1)

Marketing Mix of Tata Motors' People's Car – Nano

P – Product

Product Design

Built to meet all safety standards designed to meet or exceed emission norms and low in pollution and high in fuel efficiency that offers 20kms per liter. A Value for Money.

Emmission Standards

It conforms to Bharat-III but the engine conforms to 'EURO-4' International Pollution Standards.

Safety Standards

It has passed full frontal crash test that is required in India also designed to pass the side crash test that is required internationally

Brand Name

'Nano' – Denotes Hi-technology and Small Size.

P – Promotion

The brand launch event itself was utilized as a promotional tool. Media people from all over the world visited the Tata Nano's Launch Event and reported live, on the event. The car was promoted by positioning the brand as ***"People's Car"*** and ***"The Most Fuel Efficient Car in the Country"*** targeting a four-member family. Now it is repositioned as ***"Celebrating Awesomeness"***. It is promoted aggressively in print media, Audio-Visual media and electronic media by the company.

Brand Positioning and Re-Positioning of Tata Nano

Source: http://2.bp.blogspot.com/_YMPU4XCOUb0/TUjwFG6ny9I/AAAAAAAAAQI/fUc7wwC1Ku0/s400/Tatanano1.2.jpghttp://burnyourfuel.com/gallery/2013/08/Tata-Nano-TV-Ad-Celebrate-Awesomeness.jpg

P – Place

It is distributed through the authorised dealers of Tata Motors.

P – Price

The standard car will have a dealer price of ₹ 1 lakh only where VAT and transport being extra. At the time of launch of the brand, Tata Motors successfully positioned it as One Lakh Car by using it its Launch Event.

2. VARIOUS ASPECTS THAT ARE TO BE LEARNT REGARDING 4PS OF MARKETING MIX

Following are the aspects you are going to learn in each Ps of the Marketing Mix in the forthcoming units:

Unit-3.1: P – Product	: Under 'Product', you will learn the meaning of Product, Classification and Types of product, Various levels of a product, Product mix, New Product Development, Branding, Packaging and labeling.
Unit-3.2: P – Place	: Under 'Place', you will learn the meaning of Distribution, Various Distribution Channels and how to select them.
Unit-3.3: P – Price	: Under 'Price', you will learn the meaning of Price, Various Pricing Strategies, and the factors influencing pricing.
Unit-3.4: P – Promotion	: Under 'Promotion', you will learn the Communication Process, meaning of Promotion, Various Communication or Promotion Mix options and of course the role of IMC or the Integrated Marketing Communication.

Learning Outcome

Once you have learnt the above aspects in the marketing mix, you will be able to develop marketing plans for enhancing the sales of the company product and service offerings using these 4Ps.

UNIT 3.1: ROLE OF 'PRODUCT' IN THE MARKETING MIX

1. Product

Now let us learn what is a product? A product is basically a tangible offering of a company which is developed based on the feedback of the needs, wants, tastes, preferences of the target market and latest trends in technology prevailing in the market by the corporate body. But I would say that a product is a combination of both tangibles and intangibles. Say for instance, we buy USB Memory Stick. Though it is tangible, it does the service of storage where it becomes intangible. Thus a product can be defined as a disguised form of service.

Just to understand how tangible characteristics of a data storage device evolved and how the very purpose of these devices remained the same can be viewed in the following Exhibit-3.1.1:

EXHIBIT 3.1.1 **Evolving Tangible Product – Unchanged Intangible Service**

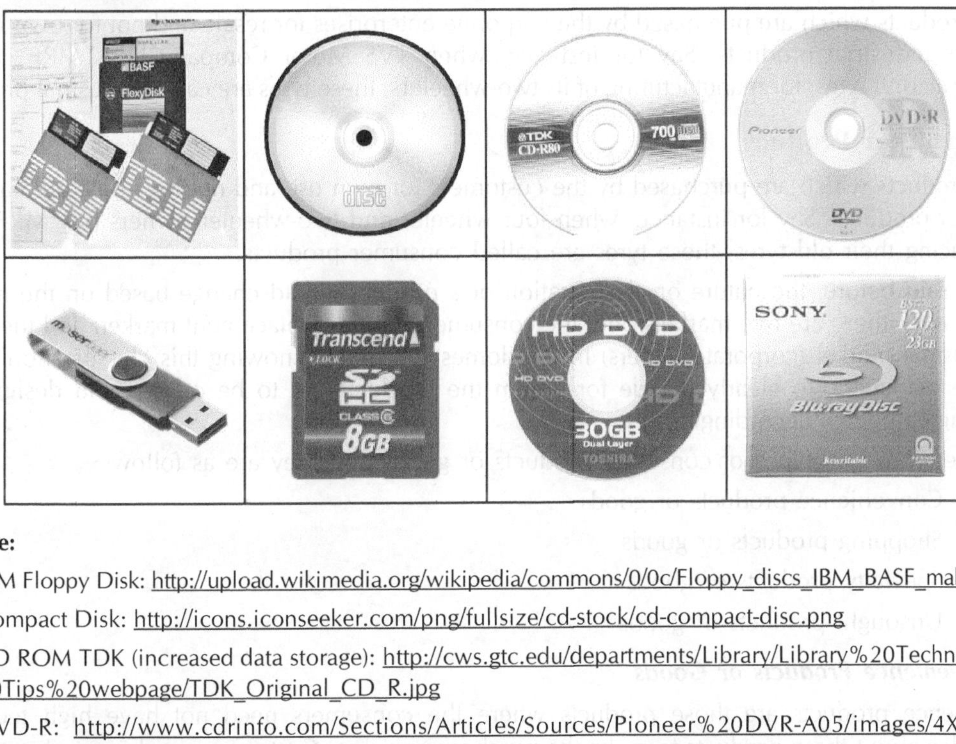

Source:

1. IBM Floppy Disk: http://upload.wikimedia.org/wikipedia/commons/0/0c/Floppy_discs_IBM_BASF_makffm.jpg
2. Compact Disk: http://icons.iconseeker.com/png/fullsize/cd-stock/cd-compact-disc.png
3. CD ROM TDK (increased data storage): http://cws.gtc.edu/departments/Library/Library%20Technology%20Tips%20webpage/TDK_Original_CD_R.jpg
4. DVD-R: http://www.cdrinfo.com/Sections/Articles/Sources/Pioneer%20DVR-A05/images/4X_DVD-R_Media_BIG_1.jpg
5. USB Memory Stick: http://logicterminal.com/shopping/images/moser-baer-pen-drive.gif
6. USB Memory Card: http://upload.wikimedia.org/wikipedia/commons/7/75/SDHC_memory_card_8GB.png
7. Toshiba's HD-DVD: http://media.teamxbox.com/dailyposts/hd-dvd/hd-dvd_disc_30gb.jpg
8. Sony's Blu-Ray Disc: http://www.blogcdn.com/www.engadget.com/media/2006/02/sony-blue-ray-disks.jpg

Definition

According to Prof. Philip Kotler, "anything that can be offered to a market for attention, acquisition, use or consumption that might satisfy a want or need" is a product.

2. Classification and Types of Product

A product can be classified into two. They are as follows:

(i) Industrial Product

(ii) Consumer Product

One must understand that the nature of a product would change according to the purpose for which a customer buys it. Let us take chairs for an instance. If these chairs are purchased for office purpose and not for personal use, they become industrial product. If the same chairs are purchased for personal use they become consumer products.

(i) Industrial Product

Those products which are purchased by the corporate enterprises for resale and not for own use are called as industrial products. Say for instance, when TVS Motor Company buys MRF (Madras Rubber Factory) tyres, for manufacturing of its two-wheelers, these tyres are called industrial products.

(ii) Consumer Product

Those products which are purchased by the customers for own use and not for resale are called as consumer products. Say for instance, when four wheeler and two-wheeler owners buy MRF tyres, for replacing their old tyres, these tyres are called consumer products.

As said before, the nature or classification of a product would change based on the market. Thus for MRF there are two markets one, the consumer market (replacement market) and the other, the industrial market (corporate buyers) in the domestic market. Knowing this classification would help the marketers, to clearly decide for whom the products are to be offered and design their marketing campaign accordingly.

There are four types of consumer products or goods and they are as follows:

(1) Convenience products or goods

(2) Shopping products or goods

(3) Specialty products or goods

(4) Unsought products or goods

(1) Convenience Products or Goods

Convenience products are those products where the consumers need not have high technical knowledge about these products to make the purchase decision. Customers need not go hunting for these products as they are extensively distributed. They are often purchased and consumed in regular intervals. The buyers may tend to substitute one product with another, if their most preferred brand is not available at a retail outlet (POS – Point-of-Sale). Example: Cola Products such as Coca-Cola, Pepsi and Thumps Up.

What must marketers do?

Marketers must understand that products like soft drinks are bought out of impulse (sudden urge). Hence aggressive promotion using ESP or Emotional Selling Proposition has to be used, to create an emotional bond between the customers and the brand. Say for instance, MILO, health drink used to offer free drinks to the Cricketers at League level Cricket Matches at Chennai, Tamil Nadu, India to promote its brand. Extensive distribution network is to be established. A life saving drug or medicine may not be available in every state of India. But Coke's Kinley, Parle's Bisleri and Pepsi's Aquafina are available at every nook and corner of India.

(2) Shopping Products or Goods

Shopping products are those products where the consumers consider factors like price, quality, style, colour and other such technical and non-technical factors before making a purchase decision. Consumers tend to visit several outlets before buying a product. This trend was prevailing before the internet was introduced in India. But today, all these data are collected by the prospective buyers by searching and comparing the features of the product using the official website and several online retailers in a few hours' time, at an arm's length.

What must marketers do?

Customers look for extensive information on the product. Hence, they establish an official website and give detail specifications of the products. Enroll with www.google.com's search engine optimization. These products are not purchased in regular intervals. Hence they are to be always priced more than convenience goods or products. Promotion of these products plays a vital role as consumers seek extensive information regarding the product. The promotional campaign must focus on the brand's USP or Unique Selling Proposition (Unique Features). Often price and features tend to influence the prospects' purchase action. Hence the marketers may resort to comparative advertisement. Because, the buyers may tend to substitute a higher priced product with the lower priced one, provided other things (features or attributes of the product) remain equal. Examples: white goods like refrigerators, washing machines, clothes, furniture, and other household appliances and electronic gadgets.

(3) Speciality Products or Goods

These speciality products have no substitutes. They have unique characteristics and strong brand identification among consumers. Hence, consumers pay high price for these products. Say for instance, General Motor's Rolls Royce, which is built with Aero Engine that reflects its uniqueness which is its (USP) Unique Selling Proposition.

What must marketers do?

Extensive distribution network is not required. Availability can be restricted to a few select dealership outlets. Aggressive promotions are required, where promotional budget is shared by the manufacturer and the retail dealers.

(4) Unsought Products or Goods

Those goods which are not voluntarily searched by the customers with purchase intention are called as unsought goods. Example, insurance policy, encyclopedia. Some of the players that are successfully marketing unsought goods are Eureka Forbes, Life Insurance Corporation of India and so on.

What must marketers do?

Develop an ad campaign to create awareness on the benefits of owning or the disadvantages of not owning it. This campaign must be supported with field sales persons to increase sales. Participating and demonstrating products in exhibitions and trade fairs would result in fruitful outcome. Example: Eureka Forbes' water purifiers and vacuum cleaners.

3. Various Levels of a Product

In order to explore the nature (classification) of product further, marketers must consider learning the five different levels of product, viz. the CORE product, the BASIC, the EXPECTED, the AUGMENTED and finally the POTENTIAL product. These are also known as the Five Levels of a Product.

EXHIBIT 3.1.2 **Various Levels of a Product**

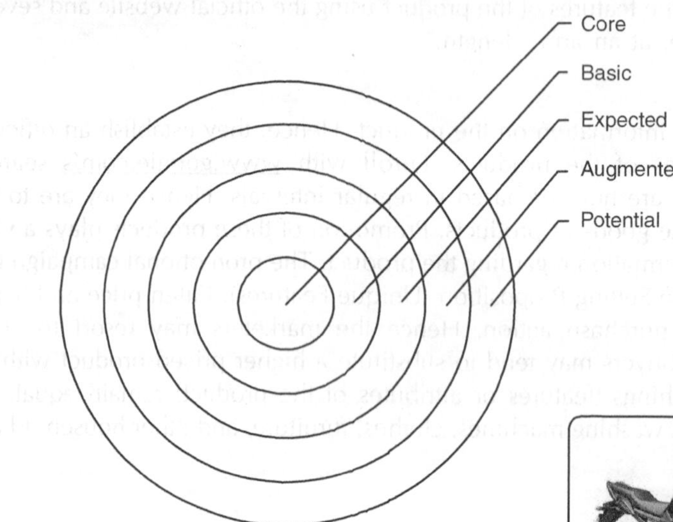

Well, now let us learn on what is the difference between these five products or the levels by using motorbike as an example:

(1) Core Level of a Product

It refers to the fundamental service offered by a product, the bike. The core benefit of owning a bike is convenience of travelling to any place at any point of time. In short, Travelling.

(2) Basic Level of a Product

It refers to the transformation of the intangible service of a product to a tangible product. It is like designing the physical characteristics of the bike like seat, light, horn, hand-bars, wheels, breaks and the body as a whole.

(3) Expected Level of a Product

It refers to the attributes or features that are expected by the prospective buyers from the product. Example: speed, mileage and stylish design in a bike. Sometimes, companies introduce the feature which could then become a trend. Say for example, 'electric start button', along with a 'kick-starter', in a bike. Kinetic Honda Scooter was the first to introduce this attribute in their scooters way back in 1990s in India. Today all bikes have this feature, as it is expected by the prospective buyers.

(4) Augmented Level of a Product

It refers to adding something new to an existing product. It may be an intangible part of the product. Say for instance, the warranty, the customer service support offered by the manufacture, and any after-sales service.

(5) Potential Level of a Product

It is the final stage of a product where the product cannot be upgraded further. Say for instance, electric bike or solar powered bike or hybrid fuel bike.

4. Product Mix

Following aspects are to be learnt in product mix:

- Product mix
- Product line

(i) Product Mix

Product mix is a combination of Width, Length, Depth and Consistency.

W – Width: It refers to a number of products produced by a company.

L – Length: It refers to a number of brands offered under each product category by a company.

D – Depth: It refers to a number of varieties in each product category by a company. It is done by offering the product with different colour, weight or grammage, size, taste or flavour, fragrance etc.

C – Consistency: All products produced by the company used for a similar purpose.

To understand all the above four components of product mix, let us see the example of Hindustan Unilever Ltd. (HUL):

EXHIBIT 3.1.3 **Understanding Product Mix with Hindustan Unilever Limited**

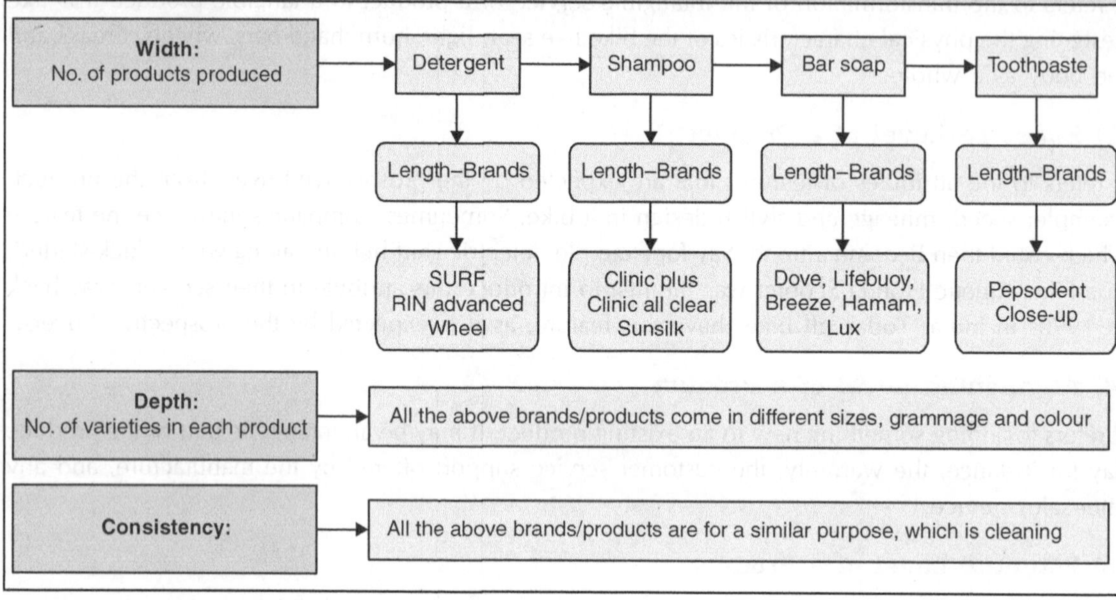

(ii) Product Line

Product line refers to a group of products produced by a company that shares a common set of characteristics. Say for instance, in the above HUL's example, shampoo, bar soap and toothpaste all the three products in the product line or width, share a common characteristic, and that is cleaning.

5. New Product Development

> *"If you have a creative idea and it doesn't create value, it is not technology. It is art."*
>
> *— Mr. Mathew Ganz,*
> *General Manager-R&D*
> *Boeing*

(1) Need for New Product Development in a company
(2) Classification of New Products
(3) Stages in New Product Development

(1) Need for New Product Development in a Company

In the age of scientific and technological advancement, change is quintessential. The change takes place in the market due to changes in customers' tastes and preferences. The firms respond to these changing customer requirements by using its new products and services.

There are three main bases for New Product Development (NPD):

- *Basis one:* People always seek better products, greater convenience, newer fashion, and more value (benefits) for money. The above said dynamic requirements of the people are then converted into new products and services.
- *Basis two:* It is always essential for a firm to bring in new products to replace its old, declining and losing products so as to make new profits.
- *Basis three:* New products for combating the environmental threats. Say for instance, bio-degradable plastics like paper cups, paper bags.

Thus companies develop new products to meet the changes in consumer demands and to earn more profits by replacing the existing old ones and declining product offerings with the new innovative products in the market for sustained market share and profits.

(2) Classification of New Products

New products can be classified based on technological innovations and marketing-oriented modifications.

Technological Innovation

Any new product arising out of technological innovation will have new functionality. Say for instance, India's (Bangalore based) Electric Car brand 'Reva' acquired by Mahindra & Mahindra.

Marketing-oriented Modifications

Any new version of an existing product with modifications such as additional features (attributes) and new packaging.

(3) Stages in New Product Development

Following are the seven stages involved in New Product Development (NPD) in any organization:

(i) Idea Generation
(ii) Idea Screening
(iii) Concept Testing
(iv) Business and Market Analysis
(v) Actual Development of New Product
(vi) Test Marketing
(vii) Commercialization

(i) Idea Generation

Companies generate new ideas for developing its new offerings (products and services) through its workforce, research staff and sales people or client relationship executives. They use tools or NPD techniques like Market Research, Brain Storming and Focus Group Sessions.

(ii) Idea Screening

In the second stage, a series of questions are to be answered regarding the new idea generated and they are as follows:

- Is there a need for new product?
- Is it an improvement over an existing product or is it going to be a completely new product?
- Is it with the current line of business of the company or is it totally a new line of business?

Usually, companies may commit two mistakes in this stage and they are as follows:

- *Drop Error:* It happens when a good idea has been dropped and not carried forward to the next stage of the NPD.
- *Go Error:* It happens when a bad idea has been selected and carried forward to the next stage of the NPD.

(iii) Concept Testing

This stage of NPD involves answering two key questions by the organization:

- Whether the market is actually in need of this New Product?
- Whether the market will try the new product?

If the answers for the both the above questions are "Yes", then the company would move to the next stage of the NPD, the business and market analysis.

(iv) Business and Market Analysis

In this stage, a feasibility study is conducted and it covers the following:

- ROI or Return on Investment.
- Cost and Availability of Technology.
- Cost and Availability of Materials.
- Cost and Availability of Skilled Work Force.

(v) Actual Development of New Product

At this stage, the company develops a model design of the new product, which is called as Prototype, by involving Research and Development, Production, Finance and the Marketing Departments of the company.

(vi) Test Marketing

At this stage, the product is marketed and sold only in a few selected market segments. Feasibility of full fledged marketing of the new product is tested with minimum costs and risks. Based on the results, the company will decide to pull back or commercialize the product.

(vii) Commercialization

Once the test marketing is successful, the company will go for a large-scale manufacturing and marketing of the new products where the product is launched nationwide.

6. Branding for Product Differentiation

1. Brand – Meaning and Definition
2. Characteristics of Branding
3. Need and Importance of Branding
4. Types of Branding
5. Brand Building Process

1. Brand — Meaning and Definition

Companies do product differentiation by using branding. In simple words, a brand is a name given to a product or a service. Branding is a process by which the true characteristics and the purpose of the company are communicated. A brand represents value, culture and personality. In general, all Indians have an American Dream. This is smartly utilized by Coca-Cola and Pepsi where they inculcated a thinking pattern in the minds of the Indians that consuming Coke or Pepsi will make them feel like Americans, and this is where personality and culture comes into picture.

Brand can be defined as "a name, term, symbol, or combination of them, which is intended to identify the goods and services of one seller or group of sellers and to differentiate from those of the competitors."

Say for instance, let's say a customer visits a retail store and asks for cola product. There are three cola products available in Indian market, viz. Coca-Cola, Pepsi and Thumps Up.

If branding is not done and no brand preference is created using the promotions, the companies selling these brands cannot ensure sale of their own brands in the market. Hence, branding becomes important to stay relevant in today's hyper-competitive market.

2. Characteristics of Branding

Following are the characteristics of a good and effective branding:

(1) A good brand name should be distinctive.

(2) It must be easy to pronounce.

(3) Easy to remember and recognize.

(4) It must be attractive and appealing.

(5) It must denote or symbolize the nature of the product.

All these can be found in Indian brand Fevicol.

EXHIBIT 3.1.4 **Clear Brand Positioning**

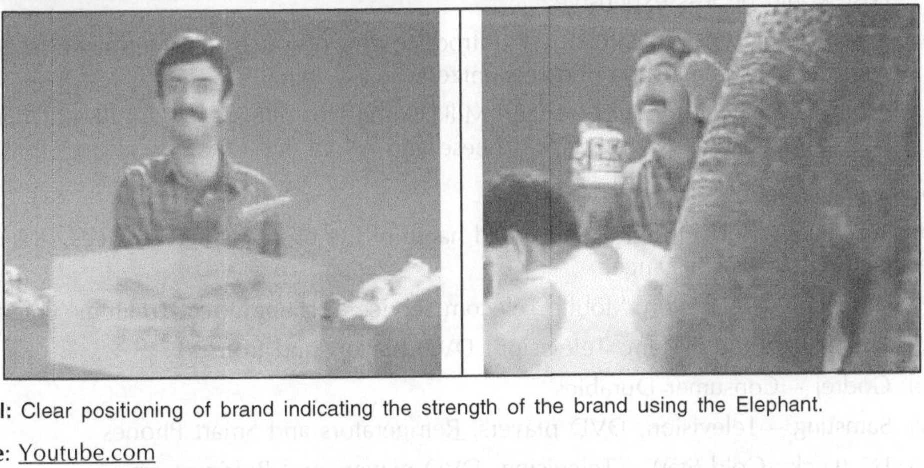

Fevicol: Clear positioning of brand indicating the strength of the brand using the Elephant.

Source: Youtube.com

3. Need and Importance of Branding

(a) It helps to identify the products and services of a seller.

(b) It helps to differentiate one company's brand from the rival brands or competitors' brands

(c) It helps to increase the price of the product over the time using the brand loyalty.

(d) It helps to introduce or launch new brands easily into the market when the parent brand is well-established.

(e) Since, branding is done after market planning, i.e. market segmenting and targeting, the spill-over effect will be minimal and this will help the companies to optimize its marketing costs.

(f) It helps the manufacturers to push their product offerings to the dealers, since the brand is already well-recognized and accepted by the market.

4. Types of Branding

Following are various types of branding strategies followed by leading business houses in India:

1. Family Branding
2. Corporate Branding
3. Individual Branding
4. Multiple Branding
5. Middle-man's Branding
6. Brand extension
7. Brand rejuvenation

1. Family Branding

When different products of a company are marketed under one same brand name, it is called as family branding. The benefits of Family branding are as follows:

(i) Since all products are marketed under one brand name, the marketing and advertising cost would be less expensive.

(ii) It will be easy for the company to introduce new products into the market as the brand name is well established and recognized.

Example: AMUL India Ltd. (Anand Milk Union Ltd) offers AMUL milk powder, AMUL Milk Chocolates, AMUL Butter, Cheese and AMUL Ice Cream.

2. Corporate Branding

When company name itself is used as the brand name of the products and services, it is called as corporate branding. Say for instance,

(i) Videocon – Television, Mobile Telecom Service, DTH or Direct-To-Home Entertainment

(ii) Philips – Audio System, Television, DVD players and Iron Box

(iii) Godrej – Consumer Durables

(iv) Samsung – Television, DVD players, Refrigerators and Smart Phones

(v) LG (Lucky Gold Star) – Television, DVD players and Refrigerators

In this branding strategy, once the corporate brand name is well established, it facilitates easy establishment of it new product offerings in the market. Since the brands are marketed and promoted under the corporate banner, the cost of marketing and promotions tend to be low compared to individual branding.

3. Individual Branding

When a company assigns an independent brand name for each of Its offerings, it called as individual brand name. Example: Hindustan Unilever's.

Tooth pastes : Pepsodent, Close-Up

Bathing Soaps : Dove, Lifebuoy, Lux , Hamam, Breeze, Pears, Liril, Rexona

Tea : Red label, Three Roses, Lipton, Taaza, Lipton Yellow Label, Taj Mahal

Shampoo : Sunsilk, Sunsilk Plus, Clinic All Clear, Dove

Detergent : Sunlite, Wheel, Rin Advanced, Surf Excel

Since each of these brands are promoted separately, the promotional expenditure tends to be high.

4. Multiple Branding

When the product of a company is marketed under different brand names in different markets, it is called as multiple branding. Say for instance, Hyundai's ATOS Prime in European Union markets is Santro in India, Mahindra & Mahindra's Scorpio is Mahindra Goa in EU markets, Tata Motors' Indigo is City Rover in the European Union (EU) markets.

One of the key reasons for having multiple branding is that the original brand name might be already registered by some rival player in that foreign market. Say for instance, in the above example we see, Mahindra & Mahindra's Scorpio is branded as Mahindra Goa in the EU markets. Because, the brand 'Scorpio' is registered by FORD in the EU markets.

5. Middle-man's Branding

When small companies do not have the required financial strength to market (promote and distribute) their offerings, they resort to middle man's branding. Example: Spenser Soda.

6. Brand Extension

When a company extends its existing brand name across a range of products, it is called as Brand Extension. For example, Marico Industries' Parachute Hair oil brand extended to its shampoo, body lotion and hair cream. One simple requirement for brand extension is that there should be some kind of relations for the extension of brand name. In the case of Parachute, it is Hair Care (remember '*Consistency*' in Product Mix). GSK's Horlicks did it very well with its series of products. Its consistency is healthy food.

7. Brand Rejuvenation

Brand rejuvenation is the process of adding value (benefit) to the existing brand by improving the product. Since, people may feel bored to see the same kind of product for years, the sale may get affected. Therefore, in order to sustain sales, the product is re-launched in the market.

HUL re-launched Fair & Lovely as "Ayurvedic Fair & Lovely", GSK re-launched Horlicks as "New Horlicks", with additional (values/benefits) nutrients, calcium, and proteins in an attractive jar. It also re-launched it with new flavours like Honey and Chocolate. It still continues to do so with Junior Horlicks, Horlicks Lite, Horlicks Women and so on. RIN Supreme Bar was rebranded and re-launched as Surf Excel Bar.

EXHIBIT 3.1.5 **Types of Branding**

Source: Family Branding: AMUL-http://www.cpdubai.com/images/cpd_product_images/Amul-all-products.jpg

Individual Branding: HUL Soaps: http://3.bp.blogspot.com/__TH9FtDBYmM/TKiJ_Bq2v4I/AAAAAAAAAAM/VakYGFxRHUw/s320/soaps-250x250.jpg

Multiple Branding – Hyundai Atos Prims is Santro: http://images.caradisiac.com/photo/8/2/9/9/38299/S0-ATOS-PRIME-3-4-ARRIERE-photo40934-38299.jpg

Brand Extension: Parachute – http://she.sulekha.com/content/blogphotos/hair-care/parachute-hair-oil-review_2012_5.jpg; http://www.prlog.org/11826947-parachute-advansed-body-lotion-summer-fresh.jpg; http://www.thehindubusinessline.in/bline/catalyst/2004/08/05/images/2004080500060303.jpg

Brand Rejuvenation: http://www.hul.co.in/Images/fal-ayurvedic-care-450x450_tcm114-296606.jpg http://www.hul.co.in/Images/fal-forever-glow-450x450_tcm114-296613.jpg

Re-Branding: Rin to Surf Excel bar: http://3.bp.blogspot.com/_BeJ_SGTxpLs/SCkX1_jInFI/AAAAAAAAALk/oNi9r94J0Aw/s200/surfrin.gif

6. Brand Building Process

Before we enter into the brand building process the marketers must understand that not all steps that are about to be discussed here be followed systematically and in sequential order for brand building. It is an art and will evolve according to the changing market conditions and consumers' preferences. Following are the initiatives towards brand building.

(i) Create a strong brand image and symbol (MRF muscle man).

(ii) Appoint a strong spokesperson to represent the company or brand. Often company resort to Appointing a brand ambassador for this purpose. (Kapil Dev, Sachin, Shewag brand ambassadors for Boost, Health Drink).

(iii) Developing ad campaigns using USP and ESP.

(iv) Create a club in the name of the brand and invite customers to join as members. (Maagi club).

(v) Establish own and Exclusive Retail Outlets (Wills Lifestyle outlet of ITC).

(vi) Promote public welfare services, donate for social welfare and sponsor well regarded events.

(vii) Invite public to factory to promote transparency (Pepsi & Coke did that to overcome the Pesticide Residue row) to ensure quality.

(i) Create a Strong Brand Image and Symbol (MRF Muscle Man)

As a marketer of your brand, it is essential to design a logo along with a tagline to capture the minds of the target market. This has to be done, because customers cannot remember the brand easily all the time. In general people try to remember things by relating to something they like. Using tagline is essential to communicate, for what the brand stands for in a short and crisp manner. Say for instance, let's take Nestle's Maggi, its logo is red coloured Heart symbol and its tagline is "2Minutes Noodles" i.e. it can be prepared in just 2 minutes and as a good, evening-snack for the children, which contains proteins and calcium. The most relevant brand logo would be MRF's muscle man which stands for tyre's strength.

(ii) Appoint a Strong Brand Ambassador

Appoint a strong spokesperson to represent the company or brand. Often companies resort to appointing a brand ambassador for this purpose. Boost did that very efficiently by appointing famous cricketers, quite consistently such as Kapil Dev, Sachin Tendulkar, Veerendra Shewag brand ambassadors for Boost, Heath Food Drink.

(iii) Developing Ad Campaigns using USP and ESP

The promotional campaign designed by the marketer must clearly specify the Just Noticeable Difference (JND) *i.e.,* the unique feature of the brand which helps to differentiate it from its rival brands. The brand must clearly say "How it is different from others" and "what value would it offer on purchasing it" to the consumer market. See how HUL' Knorr positioned its noodles "Soupy Noodles". Good

USP to differentiate its brand from Maggi. This JND is also called as Unique Selling Proposition (USP). On the other hand ESP is also seemed to be important for positioning the brand successfully in the minds of the target market. This is fantastically, done by HUL's SURF using 'Lalitaji' in 1980s. She created a lifetime bond between the brand 'Surf' and the Housewives in India.

(iv) Club Membership

Create a club in the name of the brand and invite customers to join as members. It is well handled by Nestle's Maggi as Maagi club. To become the member of this club in 1980s, the children have to cut the 'Heart' Shaped Maggi Logo and send them to the company office. Contests are conducted quite frequently to keep them engaged. Thus brands must know how to keep its customers engaged to have life time emotional bond.

(v) Establish Own and Exclusive Retail Outlets

The companies today establish their own retail outlets to promote their brands. Say for instance, Wills Lifestyle outlet of ITC.

(vi) Promote Public Welfare Services

Companies now are moving towards social marketing where CSR or Corporate Social Responsibility comes into picture to build brand by creating a positive image about the brands in the minds of the target market. Companies organize Blood Donation Camps and Sponsor well regarded events, for this purpose.

(vii) Inviting Public to the Factory to Promote Transparency

Companies today understand the importance of having PRs or Public Relation Officers to handle crisis situation. Say for instance, Coke and Pepsi overcame the Pesticides row in 2006 when Centre for Science and Environment came in public and revealed that these Carbonated Softdrinks contained high level of pesticide traces. Rajiv Bakshi, Chairperson of Pepsi himself acted as a PR, came in a media campaign saying "Your Pepsi is Absolutely Safe" to ensure quality. Both the brands invited the public to visit their manufacturing plants, promoting transparency and trust among them.

7. Brand Personality

As discussed earlier, brand denotes values, culture and personality. Companies use brand personality to position (occupy the mind space of the target market) their offerings in a way where the customers associate themselves with the brands which is similar to their personality. Here brands become persons. It is done to create an emotional bondage between the brand and the consumers. For instance, refer 3.1.7.

EXHIBIT 3.1.6 **Brand Building Process**

Sources:

Maggi Noodles: http://www.redeneeds.com/index.php?main_page = products_all&disp_order = 6&page = 106
http://d-tux.blogspot.com/2011/09/maggi-25-years-of-being-different.html

Boost Brand Ambassadors: https://sphotos-b-ord.xx.fbcdn.net/hphotos-prn2/p480x480/10188_175397002614546_254694696_n.jpg
http://3.bp.blogspot.com/-hsmz-pele1A/TiGT8_nFecI/AAAAAAAAAY4/-IVu_dQALhw/s1600/70-109-large.jpg

Knorr Soupy Noodles: http://www.afaqs.com/news/story.html?sid = 29546

Maggi Club: http://simplycreativeideas.com/wp-content/uploads/portfolio-images/enlarge/online-advertising/maggiMailer_1.2_30July07.gif

Wills Lifestyle: http://pune.mallsmarket.com/sites/default/files/photos/news/WillsLifestyle_Amanora_Pune_NewStore_March2012.jpg

EXHIBIT 3.1.7 **Brand Personality**

S.No	Brand	Personality
1.	Old Spice	Masculine
2.	Sunsilk	Feminine
3.	Pepsi	Young Teenagers
4.	Raymonds	Complete Man
5.	Titan	Ritualistic

It is concluded that to create brand personality, it takes a long time with consistent and enduring promotional mix efforts.

8. PACKAGING AND LABELING

1. What is packaging?
2. Reasons and functions of packaging a product
3. The recent trends in packaging.

> **Fact File**
>
> ***Flexible Packaging India Pvt Ltd***, a subsidiary of ***Essel Propack***, supplies packaging material to FMCG majors like **P&G, Hindustan Unilever Ltd, Emami and Britannia.**

1. Packaging

Packaging of a product is like providing a beautiful and suitable dress to a new born baby. So that the baby looks attractive, protected from the insects and scratches and so on. Similarly, the core role played by packaging of product in marketing is protecting the quality of the product from the time of production till the time of consumption. Thus, well packaged brand of product is placed on the (Point-of-Purchase) store shelves waiting for consumers to purchase it.

Apart from this core functions, other ancillary functions of the packaging are increasing the visibility of the brand in a cluttered market and distinguish one's brand apart from its rival brands. Ultimately, in today's cluttered market somehow, the package must attract the eye-balls of the target market in order to create an urge in the, minds the customers.

2. The Functions of Packaging

The marketing managers must understand the need for packaging in order to become better marketers. To be more specific, we are about to learn the reasons why packaging developed and is in use today.

(a) Containment

The kind of packaging needed to contain a product depends on the physical form of the product and the nature of the product itself. Today Coca-Cola comes in PET bottles in family size pack, one liter plastic bottles, aluminum tins and of course in glass bottles. Initially, it was available only in glass bottles and these bottles's shapes were patented. Similarly, this can be observed with GSK's Horlicks, too, in India. Marketers must learn how to design a container that is relevant to the market tastes and preferences. Check how Parle's Frooti Pacakaging evolution.

EXHIBIT 3.1.8 **Packing Containment**

Source:

Coca-Cola Bottles:
http://www.coca-cola.co.uk/content/en_GB/img/125/AM_706x264_Bottle_Chronology.jpg

GSK's Horlicks Bottles: http://www.digitalimpulse.in/insights/wp-content/uploads/2013/02/horlicks.jpg

Parle's Frooti: http://www.exchange4media.com/image2010/Frooti220711.jpg

(b) Preservation and Convenience Pack

The preservation function plays the role of stopping chemical reactions and changes to the product by or due to its packaging. The most common example would be Ready to Eat packaged food products like Nestle India, which has taken the lead by extending its Maggi soups brand to Maggi Hot Cup in single-serve sachets, priced at an aggressive ₹ 3 per sachet in a couple of variants.

Along with the single serve sachets, Nestle's Maggi soup is now available in three sizes viz. four-serve packs in six variants priced at ₹ 20 each, and two-serve packs priced at ₹ 10 per pack in two variants. Its rival Hindustan Lever's Knorr-packaged soups are priced in the same range[1]. This would definitely help to increase the shelf life of a food product beyond its natural life. It plays a very vital role in maintaining sterility in food or medical products. Preserving a product requires understanding of the conditions beyond which unacceptable deterioration may occur, say for instance, India has a very hot climate where chocolate melt easily if not stored in proper temperature. For this purpose, Cadbury's, Carbonated Soft drinks major Coca-Cola India provides refrigerators to preserve its quality for a longer period which also serves as an attractive (PoP) Point-of-Purchase Display. Another example is milk product like AMUL's which needs cold-storage system in the retail outlets.

EXHIBIT 3.1.9 Preservation and Convenience Pack

Knorr Soup

Coca-Cola Cold Storage

Cadbury's Cold Storage

Source:

Knorr: http://www.hul.co.in/Images/Packshot-CUP-SOUP-450x450_tcm114-302835.jpg

Coca-Cola: http://images.jdmagicbox.com/jaipur/d1/0141px141.x141.120223121115.m7d1/catalogue/37fa3d222c245fd6cb9c41f6e6d675c6.jpg

Cadbury's: http://www.thehindubusinessline.com/multimedia/dynamic/00861/kirana_861761f.jpg

[1] "Branded soups packing it hot" by Ratna Bhushan, http://www.thehindubusinessline.in/2002/12/09/stories/20021209 01830100.htm.

EXHIBIT 3.1.10 Convenience of Handling

Source:

C.K. Ranganathan: http://www.exchange4media.com/StoryImages/fs_53093.jpg

Chik Shampoo: http://www.cavinkare.com/images/chik_product_image.png

Parachute: http://www.ishopindian.com/images/D/d_989-01.gif, http://parachutehaircare.com/image/cache/data/Parachute-Coconut-oil-500x500.jpg, http://4.bp.blogspot.com/-t8CzUPDD45o/TvnL8EQVktI/AAAAAAAAAl8/x0fJB0iq2EU/s400/Parachute+advanced+ayurvedic+hair+oil+cap.jpg, http://3.bp.blogspot.com/_RoZOCtRoIGc/RoNy3kfPZmI/AAAAAAAAALc/Mn5Etv6SdIc/s320/para_small.jpg

(c) Protection

The protection function helps in guarding against physical damage. This could arise through shock, vibration or compression damage while transporting the products from the place of production to the place of consumption. Mostly, the corrugated cardboard boxes are used protection against these hazards while transportation.

Another important aspect, one must focus, is the package shape. A regular size-package can be stacked between each package so that too much space is not being wasted. This means that more packages can be transported in a container or a lorry. But, unusually and abnormally-sized packages lead to the wastage of space which would be uneconomical in case of distribution costs.

(d) Convenience of Handling

It means the marketer must focus on all aspects of the movement and usage of the product from the time of packaging till final use and disposal. The most apt example is the brand's availability in sachets. The entire credit goes to Kavin Care's Chic Shampoo which was offered in sachets targeting the rural Tamil Nadu customers with a price point of 50 paise per sachet. This directly addresses Prof. C.K. Prahalad's Bottom of the Pyramid strategy. Today one cannot see any small kirana store without these sachets. HUL did this by introducing a pack like carry bag for Surf. This created the convenience of carrying the pack without a carry bag. One can understand the importance of packaging in marketing by looking at the Marico's Parachute hair oil's packaging evolving as per the changing taste and user convenience. It offered flip-top cap for greater convenience to customers.

(e) Providing Information on a Product's Packaging

It means communicating information on a pack to a consumer that is legally required. As well as helping to identify and market the product, there may also be legal requirements as to the information a pack must contain. These vary from industry to industry, depending on the nature of the product being packaged. This includes, ingredients, sell by dates, expiry date, price, special offers, manufacturers address, contact information, product title, barcode and more. Infact, companies use Quick Response (QR) Codes to disseminate information regarding their brands to the consumers. QR Code is a modern day update of the bar code, which carries information such as web links that can be read by smart phones. Now medical cards of the patients would carry a QR code which would carry their genetic information, which in turn can help the doctors for better medication of the patients[1].

Since 2001, packaged food products sold in India ought to be labeled with a mandatory mark in order to distinguish them from vegetarian and non-vegetarian. The symbol is to be followed as per the Food Safety and Standards (Packaging and Labeling) Act. According to this law, vegetarian food should be identified by affixing a green dot symbol and non-vegetarian food with a brown dot symbol on the brand's package.

Recently, the government has made it mandatory for FMCG companies to pack and sell specific products like biscuits and milk powder in standard sizes only with effect from November 2012.

The government brought this law by amending the Legal Metrology (Packaged Commodities) Rules 2011[2]. Even before this law came into force, ITC company's Divisional Chief Executive, ITC's foods division, Chitranjan Dar said that the Rising inflation, coupled with a new packaging legislation, will make price hikes of packaged foods inevitable in India.

---

1 "Biometric QR Codes", *The Hindu Business Line, dt.* 7-8-2012, pg-18

2 "New standard packaging norms for FMCG cos from Nov: Govt", dt. August 21, 2012, http://www.thehindubusinessline.com/marketing/new-standard-packaging-norms-for-fmcg-cos-from-nov-govt/article3803431.ece

EXHIBIT 3.1.11 **Product Information on Packaging**

Vegetarian mark and non-vegetarian mark

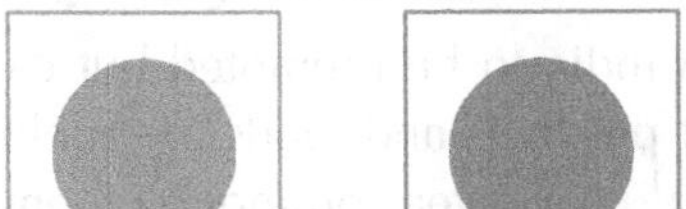

The green dot symbol identifies vegetarian food, and the brown dot symbol identifies non-vegetarian food.

How Quick Response (QR) Code Works?

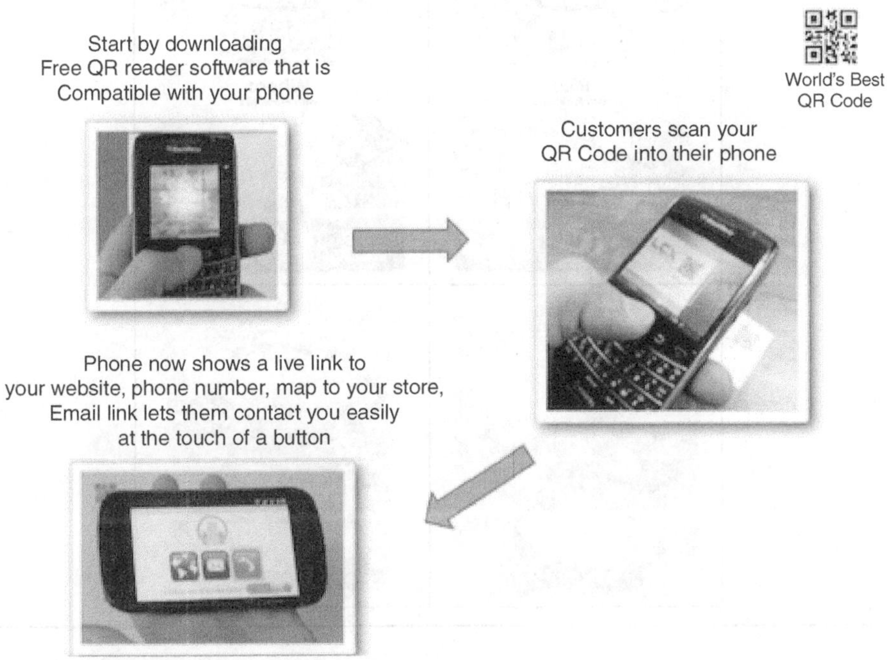

Source

Veg and Non-Veg Dots:

Aachi Veg masals: http://www.in.all.biz/img/in/catalog/52929.jpeg

Mc Donald's Chicken Food Non-Veg:

http://static2.demotix.com/sites/default/files/imagecache/a_scale_large/800-0/photos/1315307420-the-indian-chicken-maharaja-mac-from-mcdonalds-_819090.jpg

How QR Code works?: http://herbstmarketing.com/wp-content/uploads/2011/11/how-qr-codes-work.png

(f) Sales

A well designed packaging can play a pivotal role in promotion of the brand. It can be done by displaying the product, using illustrations, branding the product using its brand name or the company that manufactures it, as well as using tantalizing pack shapes, colours and designs.

Think of a products or brands which are prohibited in India to be promoted but can legally be sold. I am talking about infant foods. Marketing of Infant products and foods are prohibited by the Government of India by using 'Infant Milk Substitute Act[1], to prevent promoting them in India as it discourages breast feeding among mothers. This is a big challenge for brands like Cerelac and Farex but still they succeed in the market by attractive packaging. Check the window display of any Medical Shop and you will see attractively coloured infant food brands.

EXHIBIT 3.1.12 Packing Assists Sales

Source:

Nestle's Serelac:

http://www.baronepharmacy.com.au/baby-care/nestle-cerelac-rice-200g-p-22364.html

http://www.baronepharmacy.com.au/baby-care/nestle-cerelac-wheat-200g-p-22365.html

Heinz Farex

http://www.baronepharmacy.com.au/baby-care-c-93.html?v=all

http://www.baronepharmacy.com.au/baby-care-c-93.html?v=all

---

[1] http://www.bpni.org/cgi/update7.pdf

(g) Stacking and Storage

The most important thing malls would look for is "Space Must Not Be Wasted". Because, Lost space on shelves leads to a lost opportunity to sell a customer. Hence, super markets and malls look for possibilities to stack (load) packages where the space is not wasted on the shelves. The company must also remember that the package must be designed in such a way that all the important information, especially like the brand name and the special offer, can be seen by the prospects. Often packages are stacked or loaded on top and alongside each other so as to reduce space wastage. The shape and form of the package determines how efficiently they can be stacked or stored. See the following exhibit to understand how major brands do this in major malls and kirana or retail stores in India.

EXHIBIT 3.1.13 **Product Stacking and Storage**

Source:

http://www.thinkdesign.in/images/news/news27.jpg

http://www.popon.net/Files/Admin/ARTICLES%202011/ARTICLE-246-PIC-2.jpg

http://3.bp.blogspot.com/-fiPyY-qVZGc/UHGTMeKch5I/AAAAAAAAAHw/ULcEe88rM6k/s1600/Picture3.png

http://www.thehindubusinessline.com/multimedia/dynamic/00861/kirana_861761f.jpg

Conclusion

Thus, product packaging plays an important role as a medium in the marketing mix, in promotion campaigns, as a pricing criterion, in defining the character of new products, as a trend setter (an innovative pack to make 'new products' out of familiar ones, like coffee byte offered in 'Combo Pack' instead of loosely sold toffee[1]), as an instrument to create brand identity and shelf impact in all product groups.

In totality today's packaging must have Eye-catching appearance, attractive Design, shape, colour, creative printing and finishing to allure the consumer. Aroma protection, hygiene, environmental responsibility and practical handling (in both use and storage) are important to improve comfort of the users.

3. Recent Trends in Packaging and Labeling

Fact File-2: Krishna Printernational for Cost-effective Labeling Solutions

Krishna Printernational, headed by Divya Keshav, suplies self-adhesive labels for pharma, airlines and consumer durables industries. Her clients are LG, Samsung, Usha, Eicher, Naturelle Safari, Indigo, Spicejet, DHL, Cadbury and Havells. The company would prepare self-adhesive labels based on client's requirements such as label design, size and finish. Strict quality checks are in place to deliver defect-free lables. The estimated revenue of the company is ₹ 2 Crore..

Source: "Bringing Cost-effective labeling solutions", by Richa Mishra, *The Hindu Business Line*, dt. 14-5-2012, pg-4.

EXHIBIT 3.1.14 Branding Potential In Packaged Foods

Branding potential in packaged foods

Food item	Market size (in $ million)		Percentage growth per annum (2010-30)		Branded product as a percentage of total category
	2010	2030	2010	2030	
Milk	7,767	32,900	8	31	73
Cheese	144	1,958	14	NA	NA
Butter	254	1,340	9	6	19
Vegetable and edible oils	3,931	10,331	4	32	59
Sweet and savoury snaks	1,286	16,399	13	42	66
Atta	574	8,158	13	4	44
Processed poultry	398	8,340	17	6	49
Fruit and Beverages	720	12,204	15	NA	NA
Biscuits	2,753	13,145	8	NA	NA

[1] http://www.interpack.com/cipp/md interpack/custom/pub/content,lang,2/oid,7773/ticket,g u e s t/~/Product packaging plays an important role in the marketing mix.html

Just to understand the scope of packaging and labeling in India, an article from *The Hindu-Business Line* is reproduced here. The budding managers are urged to read this article carefully to understand the scope.

The packaged food segment is likely to grow 9 per cent annually to become a ₹ 6 lakh crore industry by 2030, dominated by milk, sweet and savoury snacks and processed poultry, among other products, says a new report. The CII-McKinsey report on "India as an agriculture and high value food powerhouse by 2030" says the emphasis on branding could further enhance realisations of packaged foods by up to 30 per cent, besides driving the growth of the country's processed food sector.

Packaged milk, as a category, is projected to grow from $7.76 billion to $32.9 billion by 2030, registering an annual growth of 8 per cent. About 73 per cent of the milk sold by 2030 would be branded, against 31 per cent at present. Sweets and savoury snacks will be second largest category at an estimated $16.39 billion by 2030 from $1.28 billion in 2010, clocking a 13 per cent growth annually.

Processed poultry products will clock the fastest growth of 17 per cent per a year to $8.34 billion by 2030, against $398 million in 2010. Similarly, biscuits will see an 8 per cent growth to touch $13.14 billion in 2030, followed by fruit beverages at $12.20 billion and vegetable and edible oils at $10.33 billion. Packaged atta (wheat flour) is expected to grow 13 per cent to $8.15 billion from $574 million in 2010[1].

CASE-1: Cadbury's Worm Infestation Controversy

Cadbury Ropes in Big B as Brand Envoy

Will Amitabh Bachchan as brand ambassador help Cadbury India Ltd overcome the worm infestation controversy? The top brass at Cadbury is confident that a turnaround would come about through a series of initiatives the company has taken including, new improved packaging, appointment of Bachchan as the brand ambassador and several new launches to follow.

"There is going to be renewed effort in re-establishing the category", Bharat Puri, Managing Director, Cadbury India Ltd, said at a news conference to announce these initiatives. Cadbury India Ltd will suffer a 3 – 5% decline in sales value on account of the controversy. However, sales have shown signs of improvement in, December 2003.

In a bid to prevent any incidence of infestation, Cadbury has introduced a double packaging for its 13 gm ₹ 5 Cadbury Dairy Milk chocolate, its flagship brand. The chocolate is wrapped in aluminium foil and enclosed in a polyflow pack, which is sealed on all sides. The larger Cadbury Dairy Milk packs will come in poly-coated aluminium foil, which will be heat-sealed and

[1] 'Milk, snacks, poultry to drive packaged food industry growth to 9% a year in 15 years'- Thrust on branding could further push growth to 30%: CII-McKinsey report, BY Vishwanath kulkarni, DT. April 12, 2013; http://www.thehindubusinessline.com/industry-and-economy/agri-biz/milk-snacks-poultry-to-drive-packaged-food-industry-growth-to-9-a-year-in-15-years/article4610841.ece

then wrapped in the branded outer package. Both these are first ever in chocolate packaging in India.

The new packaging is going to add to the company's cost of production to the extent of 12 – 15%. But at the current juncture, Cadbury does not plan to raise the price of its products. "Our margins could be under pressure, but we are hoping to ramp up volumes, thereby neutralising the cost increase," Puri said. The new ₹ 5 pack of Cadbury Dairy Milk chocolate bar has been rolled out in Maharashtra and will be rolled out nationally in three weeks, officials said. The new packaging is being introduced for its moulded chocolates.

The capital expenditure of setting up new machinery is to the tune of ₹ 12 – 15 crore. Bachchan has been signed on as the brand ambassador for a period of two years, during which period he will endorse and promote Cadbury chocolates. On queries about Bachchan endorsing far too many products, Puri said that he has a universal appeal cutting across ages.

Cadbury has a 70% market share in chocolates. Cadbury Dairy Milk chocolate has a market share of 30%. "Daily 2.7 million chocolate bars are sold, of these 1 million bars are Cadbury Dairy Milk," Sanjay Purohit, General Manager – Marketing, said.

Following the controversy, the company carried out quality checks at its facilities as well as its C&F warehouses and distributor warehouses and found products free of infestation. "Our quality control goes beyond the factory gates to the distributors, but our control over the retail chain does diminish," he said adding that Cadbury products are sold across 650,000 outlets.

"Improper storage and its consequences is not unique to Cadbury. Every food items is affected. Unfortunately, though there is adequate legislation, ensuring compliance at the retail level is impossible," he said.

In the aftermath of the controversy, the company launched Project Vishwas, a retail education programme under which 190,000 retailers in key states were covered. The program entailed generating awareness and providing assistance in improving storage quality. Cadbury suffered a major impact in sales in Maharashtra and Kerala. These states account for 20–23% of the total sales[1].

Case Discussion

1. Why do you think Cadbury's was faced with the worm controversy issue? Who is to be blamed for this mess?
2. What was the impact of this controversy on the brand image of Cadbury's?
3. What are the measures taken by Cadbury's to recover its brand image in the market place? Do you agree with the solutions of the company to overcome the worm infection controversy?
4. What would have you done, if you where the marketing manager of the company to recover the brand image?

---

[1] http://www.thehindubusinessline.in/2004/01/08/stories/2004010800690600.htm

UNIT 3.2: ROLE OF 'PLACE' IN THE MARKETING MIX

1. Physical Distribution or Place—Meaning

'Place' in Marketing Management also refers to the 'Physical Distribution' or 'Channels of Distribution'. It means movement or transportation of goods from the place of production to the place of consumption. In simple words, Distribution means – making the products available to customers when and where they need them, by what modes or ways are the marketers going to make their products reach the target consumers is called as Channels of Distribution.

2. Types of Channels of Distribution

For any marketer, there are two important channels of distribution available to take the company's offerings to the customers, and they are as follows:

(a) Direct marketing distribution channel

(b) Indirect (marketing) distribution channel

(a) Direct Marketing Distribution Channel

Direct marketing channels of distribution is the one where the company sells its offerings directly to the customers without any intermediaries and through internet. It is also called as e-marketing or electronic marketing. Say for instance, www.olx.com, www.snapdeal.com etc.

(b) Indirect (Marketing) Channels of Distribution

It is the one where a company sells its products to the customers through middlemen or intermediaries such as:

(i) C&F or Clearing and Forwarding Agents

(ii) Wholesalers

(iii) Retailers

(i) C&F or Clearing and Forwarding Agents

C&F agents secure an order for the producer and take commission for it. The C&F agent will not provide storage facility. The title of ownership of goods will remain with the producer.

(ii) Wholesalers

Wholesalers buy products in bulk quantity and distribute them in small packages to the retailers for resale. Hence, they got the name, 'distributors'. The 'distributors' take ownership of goods, provide storage facility and earns their share of profit margin on sale.

(iii) Retailers

Retailers have direct contact with the customers. The retailers' selling price is the final selling price which is also called as MRP or Maximum Retail Price. Retailers hold several brands in each product category, which facilitates consumers' freedom of choice. They provide credit purchase facility to the customers and earn their share of profit margin on sale.

EXHIBIT 3.2.1 Types of Channel of Distribution and Intermediaries

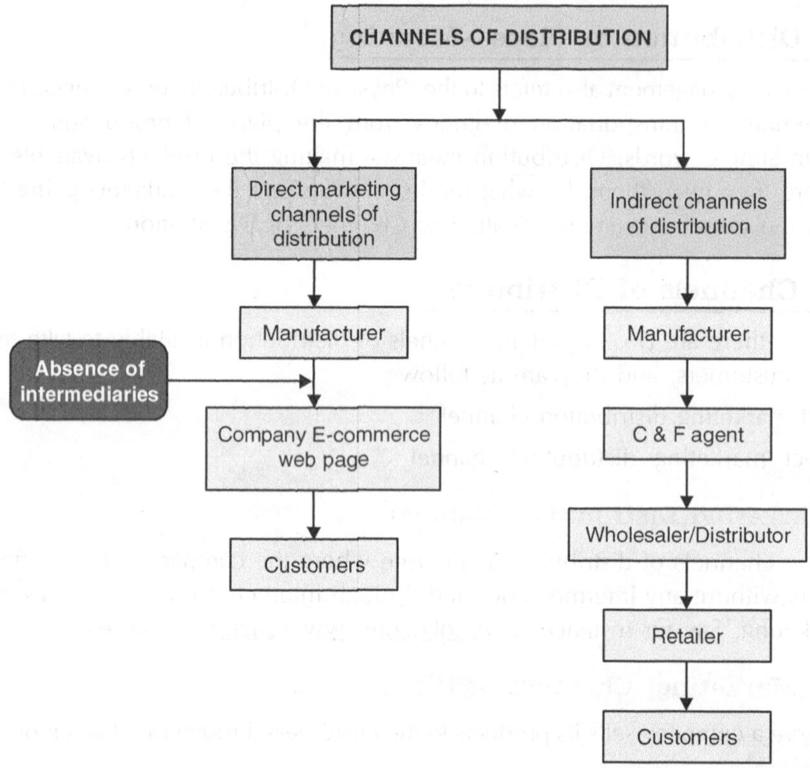

3. Factors Influencing Determination of Channel of Distribution

Before selecting a suitable distribution channel, the marketing managers must make channel decisions based on various aspects, which are converted into questions for the sake of convenience of the marketers:

(1) Are we going to use direct or indirect distribution channels?

(2) Are we going to use single or multiple channels of distribution?

(3) What type of intermediaries or middlemen are we going to use?

(4) How many intermediaries or middlemen are we going to use?

(5) How to select the intermediaries carefully, to avoid intra-channel conflict?

(6) Is the distributor familiar with the company's target market segment?

(7) Is there the synergy or match in the policies and image of the company and the distributors?

(8) Is the intermediary having required qualification, experience track record, and sound financial background to become our channel partner?

(9) How much training and support is required to equip the distributors?

Conclusion

Deciding on the above issues clearly during the Channel Decision will enhance the products' (offerings') availability in the market place for the right customers, at the right time. This will in turn lead to increase in turnover of the company.

CASE-2: The Magic of Mumbai Dabbawallas!

– Road for an efficient distribution channel.

> **"A model of managerial and organizational simplicity."**
>
> –Prof. C.K. Prahalad
>
> University of Michigan Business School
>
> [Commenting on the Mumbai Dabbawalas' operations]

(a) Introduction

Day after day, confronting the traffic and crowds of Mumbai city, the Mumbai Dabbawalas, consistently deliver thousands of tiffins to the hungry people their home-cooked meals from clients' home and later returns the empty tiffin boxes to where they came from.

All over the world, Logistics has always been a mantra for building competitive advantage. Mumbai's dabbawalas developed their own homegrown version of efficient transportation system. Their approach of ***competitive collaboration*** has lead to an excellence in their operation process. The Dabbawalas were invited to speak at Confederation of Indian Industries (CII) meets and at leading Indian business schools such as IIM, Bangalore and Lucknow. Corporation Bank, Mumbai, has banked the Supply Chain efficiency of the Mumbai Dabbawallas. Now these dabbawallas will not only deliver the hot meals but also the banking services as a facilitator. These dabbawallas will deliver important mails and collect the filled in applications for opening deposit accounts. In return, they will get ₹ 2 per form for distribution and ₹ 5 for collecting the filled in application form.[1] Understanding this case helps the marketers to analyze, what has made them so special and what could the business fraternity learn from them?

Origin of Dabba Wallahs

The **M**umbai **T**iffin **B**ox **S**uppliers **A**ssociation **(MTBSA)** is a 120-year-old organization with over 4,500 illiterate and semi-literate members providing a quality door-to-door service to a large and loyal customer base. Descendants of soldiers of the legendary Maharashtrian warrior-king Shivaji, dabbawalas belong to the Malva caste, and arrive in Mumbai from places like Rajgurunagar, Akola, Ambegaon, Junnar and Maashi.

The service is believed to have started in the 1880s but officially registered itself only in 1968. The proud owner of a BA (Hons) degree, Raghunath Meghe, President of MTBSA, is a rare graduate.

---

[1] "Corporation Bank ties up with dabbawallas", *The Hindu Business Line,* dt.5-5-2007.

(b) The Dynamic Organization

1. Organizational Structure

MTBSA is a remarkably ***Flat Organization*** with just three tiers: the Governing Council (President, Vice President, General Secretary, Treasurer and Nine Directors), the Mukadams and the Dabbawalas. Its first office was established at Grant Road. Today it has offices near most railway stations which prove to be an extensive distribution network.

This decentralized organization assumed its current form in 1970. Dabbawalas are divided into sub-groups of fifteen to 25, each supervised by four mukadams. The mukadams are the experienced old-timers, who are familiar with the colours and codings used in the complex logistics process.

EXHIBIT 3.2.2 Dabbawala's Organisational Structure

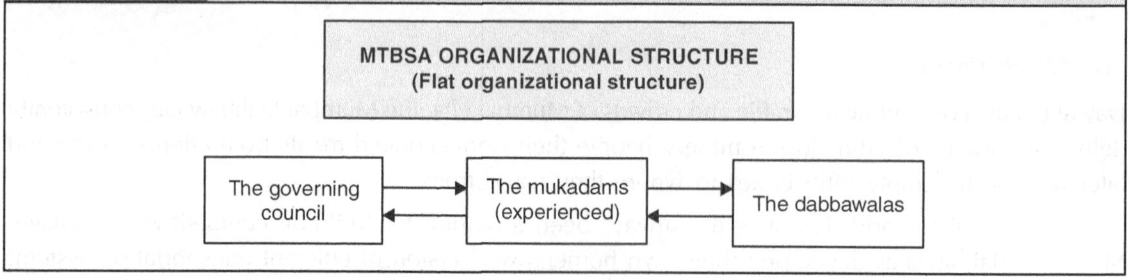

2. Human Resource Practices

Here nobody is employer and none are employees. The service provider follows the HR principle of—"Treat Employees as partners". Each dabbawala considers himself a shareholder and an entrepreneur.

Job Description

Their key responsibility of dabbawala is sorting tiffins. Apart from that they also play a critical role in resolving disputes; maintaining records of receipts and payments; acquiring new customers; and training junior dabbawalas on handling new customers on their first day. Each group is not only financially independent but also coordinates with others for deliveries. Each group is also responsible for day-to-day functioning which is the fundamental of TQM (Total Quality Management) where all the partners of the system are accountable for the jobs assigned to them.

Job Specification

Education till standard seven is a minimum prerequisite to join the club of the **M**umbai **T**iffin **B**ox **S**uppliers **A**ssociation **(MTBSA)**

Entrepreneurial Spirit

Apart from commitment and dedication, each dabbawala, like a businessman, has to bring capital with him. The minimum investment is two bicycles approximately ₹ 4,000, a wooden crate for the tiffins ₹ 500, at least one white cotton kurta-pyjama ₹ 600, and ₹ 20 for the trademark Mahatma topi.

Dabbawala's investment	
2 Cycles	= 4000
1 Wodden crate	= 5000
1 Cotton pyjama kurta	= 600
Total investment ₹ 5,120	

Source of Manpower

The **M**umbai **T**iffin **B**ox **S**uppliers **A**ssociation (**MTBSA**) believes in employing people from their own community. So whenever there is a vacancy, elders recommend a relative from their village. Typically, a twenty-member group has 675 customers and earns ₹ 1,00,000 per month, which is divided equally irrespective of size of the customers possessed by each group. The moral is groups compete with each others but not members within.

Welfare Measures

One dabbawala could collect 40 tiffins in the same time that it takes another to collect 30. From his earnings of between ₹ 5,000 to ₹ 6,000, every dabbawala contributes ₹ 15 per month to the association. The amount is utilized for the community's upliftment, loans and marriage halls at concessional rates.

3. Marketing

The Customer Profile

The range of customers includes students of both colleges and schools, small business entrepreneurs, managers, bank staff, and mill workers. They have a client base of around 1.25 lakh office goers and 50,000 students.

They generally tend to be middle-class people who, for reasons of economy, hygiene, and dietary restrictions, rely on the dabbawala to receive their home cooked mid-day meal.

4. Client Relationship Management

Creating Customers

New customers are generally acquired through referrals. Some are solicited by dabbawalas on railway platforms. Addresses are passed on to the dabbawala operating in the specific area, who then visits the customer to finalize arrangements. Today customers can also log onto the website www.webrishi.com to access the service.

Handling Customer Complaints

Meetings are held in their office on the 15th of every month for Performance Review. During these meetings, emphasis is paid to customer service. If tiffin is lost or stolen, an investigation is promptly instituted. Customers are allowed to deduct costs from any dabbawala if found guilty of such charge.

If a customer complaints of poor service, the association can shift the customer's account to another dabbawala. Before looking into internal disputes, the association charges a token amount of ₹ 100 to ensure that only genuinely grieved members come to it with their problems, and the officials' time is not wasted on paltry squabbling. Ruling of association is binding.

Pricing and Corporate Norms

Service charges vary from ₹ 150 to ₹ 300 per tiffin per month, depending on the location and collection time. Money is collected in the first week of every month and remitted to the mukadam (Senior Worker) on the first Sunday. He then divides the money equally among members of that group. It is assumed that one dabbawala can handle not more than 30–35 customers assuming every tiffin weighs around 2 kg. And this is the benchmark that every group tries to achieve.

5. Operations Management—The Blue Print

How do the Dabbawallas do it? The answer lies in a process that unites competitive collaboration between team members and high level of technical efficiency in logistics management. It works like this.

The Critical Success Factors (CSF)

The two Critical Success Factors of Mumbai Dabbawalas are time management and teamwork. The entire system depends on the teamwork and meticulous timing.

EXHIBIT 3.2.3 Teamwork and Time Management: Two CSF of Dabbawalas

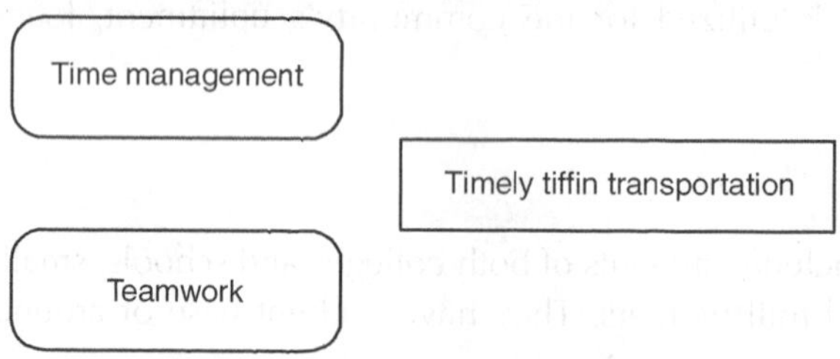

Teamwork and Time Management

Tiffins are collected from the clients' homes between 7.00 am and 9.00 am, and taken to the nearest railway station. At various intermediary stations, they are pulled onto platforms and sorted out for area-wise distribution, so that single tiffin could change hands three to four times in the course of its daily journey.

EXHIBIT 3.2.4 The Blueprint of Mumbai Dabbawalas

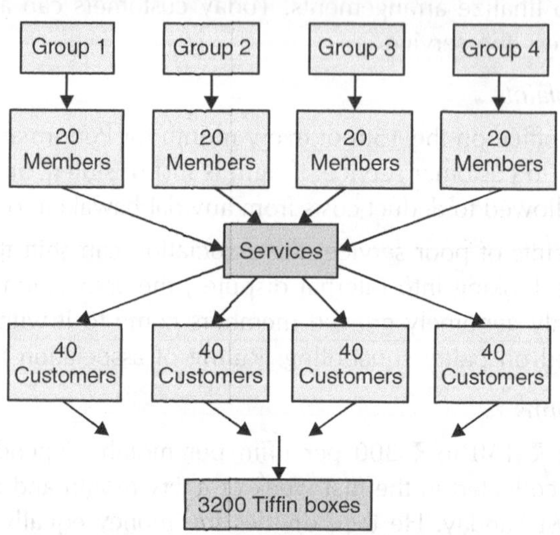

Calculation for your convenience:

20 members × 40 customers × 4 batches = 3200 Tiffin Boxes

To better understand the complex sorting process; let's take an example. At Mumbai's Vile Parle Station, there are four groups of dabbawalas, each has twenty members and each member services 40 customers. That makes 3,200 tiffins in totality.

These 3,200 tiffins have to be collected by 9.00 am, reach the station and sorted according to their destinations by 10.00 am, it is the when the Dabbawala's train arrives.

EXHIBIT 3.2.5 How Do Dabbawalas Do It?

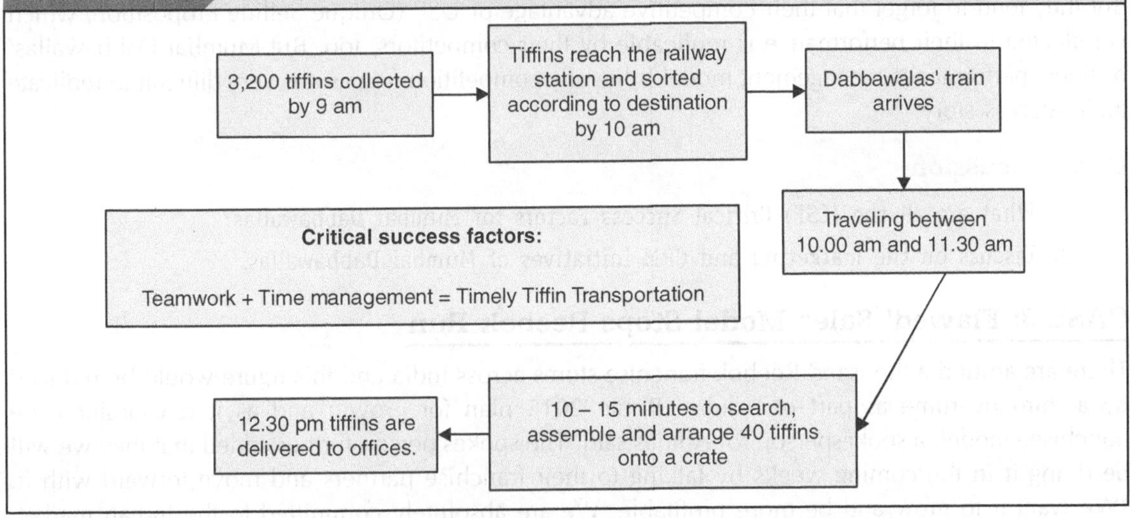

The railways provide sorting areas on platforms as well as a compartments on trains traveling between 10.00 am and 11.30 am. During the sorting process, each dabbawala will be concentrating on locating only those 40 tiffins which is their quality standards that would come under his charge, this makes the entire system efficient and error-free irrespective of the place they come from. During the journey, these 80 dabbawalas regroup according to the number of tiffins to be delivered in a particular area. If 150 tiffins are to be delivered in a station area, then four people are assigned to that station, keeping in mind one person can carry no more than 35-40 tiffins. Typically, it takes about ten to fifteen minutes to search, assemble and arrange 40 tiffins onto a crate, and by 12.30 pm they are delivered to offices.

(c) *Elegant Logistics – The Supply Chain Management*

The Mumbai dabbawalas' elegant logistics system uses 25 kms of public transport, 10 km of footwork involving multiple transfer points. But mistakes rarely happen. According to a Forbes 1998 article, one mistake for every eight million delivery is the norm. Now this could baffle all of us on 'How do they achieve virtual six-sigma quality with zero documentation'?

Error free–6 Sigma Quality

In 1998, Forbes Global magazine conducted a quality assurance study on the Dabbawalas' operations and gave it a ***Six Sigma*** efficiency rating of 99.999999; the Dabbawalas made one error in six million transactions. This has put them on the elite list of Six Sigma rated Multinational National Corporations (MNCs) along with Motorola and GE. The system limits the routing (***Seiso – Orderliness***) and sorting (***Serrie – Proper Arrangement***) to a few central points. Secondly, a simple color code (***Kanban-Visual Display***) determines not only package routing but also package prioritizing as lunches get transferred from train to bicycle to foot[1].

(d) Conclusion

The major players talk about their competitive advantage on many aspects including their efficient system of Supply Chain Management to compare (***Benchmark***) their performance with other players. But they tend to forget that their competitive advantage or USP (Unique Selling Proposition) which is reflected in their performance is replicable by their competitors, too. But Mumbai Dabbawallas' business performance management model is literally competition-free as it is very difficult to replicate their success story.

Case Discussion

1. What are all the (CSF) Critical Success Factors for Mumbai Dabbawallas?
2. Discuss on the marketing and CRM initiatives of Mumbai Dabbawallas.

CASE-3: Flawed' Sales Model Stops Reebok Run

There are around a thousand Reebok franchise stores across India and this figure would be reduced by a third overtime as part of Adidas' Route 2015 plan for growth and as it re-examined the franchisee model, a spokesperson for Adidas said. The spokes person further added that they we will be doing it in the coming weeks by talking to their franchise partners and move forward with it. "We want it to grow and be more profitable. We are absolutely committed to the Indian market, and we are only restructuring the Reebok part of it, the brand Adidas will not be touched," he added.

What could have really gone wrong with the way Reebok was run in India? According to a top North India-based distributor, the 'franchisee model' run by the company for the past few years was flawed. According to him some stores were picked on very high rental, where the sales were lower than the cost of running the outlet," says an anonymous distributor.

It is observed that the Reebok's contract with the franchisees was working based on a minimum guarantee (MG) basis, which is used for encouraging speedy network expansion, and a certain income was guaranteed to each outlet, regardless of sales. However, this model had its own negative effect, where the franchisees got lazy as they knew that a certain amount of revenue was guaranteed, sources in the distribution chain say. This compelled the more profitable stores to cross-subsidise the larger number of loss-making retail outlets. As a result of the minimum guarantee deal, the company was in a strange position to compensate these loss making franchisees, which Reebok was not able to pay immediately due to its under performance.

Thus, the management decided to change this business model by taking back the MG deal from loss-making outlets, or asking them to close for inability to meet targets. The Group had said that a third of the 1,000 Reebok outlets in India could be shut in the near future.

[1] Based on "How the dabbawallas do it?", Pradip Thakker; dt. 25-7-06, Moneycontrol.com

What Could Have Went Wrong?

Devangshu Dutta, CEO, Third Eyesight, a retail consultant firm, says most global brands, including Reebok and Adidas, went on an expansion spree during 2004-08. The company was quite optimistic of the Indian growth story and went on to open stores at places they shouldn't have, he adds. A franchisee owner of Reebok would invest anywhere between ₹ 40 lakh and ₹ 1 crore, depending on the value of the real estate. Say for instance, if a franchisee opens the retail outlet in Noida, it itself has five Reebok outlets, apart from stores in two malls. In comparison, a shopping area such as New Delhi's Connaught Place has three outlets within a distance of half a kilometre from each other.

Things changed from 2009 onwards where several stores had started either resizing, closing down or halting expansion. The Indian market for sports footwear is still largely dominated by unorganised players. Franchisees in India are new retailers and know little about retail strategies; they want immediate return on investments and when they don't get it, they try to cut costs, inventory, working capital and also failed to invest in manpower. This impacted the brand image. However, it is also learnt that the stores operating as 'factory outlets' and offering year-long discounts are expected to be closed first. These stores, which generally sell older unsold stocks of previous seasons, are believed to be the key reason for the 'brand dilution' of Reebok. It is noteworthy to remind here that Reebok is positioned as a premium brand, and these stores are affecting the business of the bigger stores which pay high rentals for operating in top shopping malls[1].

Case Discussion

1. What are the lessons you have learnt from Reebok's Distribution Model?
2. Is shutting down of 'Factory Outlets' stores offering long-term discount, a right decision? - Discuss.
3. Do you fully agree with the revamp of Reebok's new sales distribution model? If 'Yes' Justify. Don't you think shutting of stores immediately could impact its brand presence in key markets? - Discuss.

UNIT 3.3: ROLE OF 'PRICE' IN THE MARKETING MIX

1. What is a Price? Why Fix a Price for a Product Offering?

Price refers to the exchange value of the product and service offering, produced by a company. It is always expressed in terms of money. Price of any product or service revolves around two elements viz. Utility and Value.

---

[1] Source: "'Flawed' sales model stops Reebok run", by Roudra Bhattacharya Priyanka Pani, The Hindu Business Line http://www.thehindubusinessline.com/industry-and-economy/marketing/article3401274.ece

"Adidas Route 2015 plan ", *The Hindu Business Line*, *http://www.thehindubusinessline.com/companies/article3381077.ece*

Utility – it refers to the want satisfying power of the product or brand.

Value – it refers to the quantitative worth of the product.

In fact, it is the competition and market forces, *i.e.,* demand – supply mismatch that makes pricing of a brand dynamic (fast changing). Companies view pricing as an important strategic route for managing their brands of portfolio.

Why adopt Money as a medium of Exchange? In the early days of civilization, cavemen attempted to fulfill their requirements among themselves. In the passage of time, the cavemen realised that it is quite impossible to satisfy all their needs by themselves. This influenced the cavemen to exchange their produce with each other. This system of exchange of goods against goods is called as Barter System. The most important limitation of this system is inconsistency in quantity and preciousness of commodities exchanged. This had lead to consideration of gold as the common medium of exchange. Since, gold is scarce in supply; it paved way for gradual adoption of money as a medium of exchange. In simple words pricing is done in terms of money. Tomorrow we will trade using virtual currencies like bit-coins.

2. Objectives of Pricing

Following are the objectives of pricing a product or service offering by a company:

1. To penetrate deep into the market. Example: Chick shampoo offered at 50 paise per sachet.
2. To enter new market segments. Example: Mahindra and Mahindra entering into electric car market segment by acquiring REVA, India's first Electric-Car.
3. To outsmart the rival players or competitors in three ways
   - (i) For early cash recovery through premium pricing.
   - (ii) To keep competition out using discount pricing.
   - (iii) To keep parity with competition
4. To earn maximum possible returns on investment.
5. To recover investment quickly and break-even quickly.
6. To provide products and services to the weaker section of the society at an affordable price. Example: Godrej Mini Refrigerators sold for ₹ 5000 through Indian Post Office. (Prof. C.K. Prahalad's Bottom of the Pyramid)
7. To stabilize price levels in the market.
8. To enhance sales volume of products.
9. To enhance market share of a brand.
10. To increase profit and market share on the entire product line. Example: HUL's Power brands.

3. Pricing Strategies

Following are the different pricing strategies that are widely practiced by the corporate – India:

1. What the traffic can bear – pricing strategy.
2. Economy Based Pricing or Cost based pricing strategy.
3. Innovation oriented pricing strategy.
4. Competition oriented pricing strategy.
5. Differential pricing strategy.
6. Psychological pricing strategy.

1. What the Traffic can Bear – Pricing Strategy?

When a seller fix the maximum price based on what the customers are willing to pay at any circumstances, it is called as 'what the traffic can bear pricing'. The positive side of this strategy is that the player or the company can earn maximum profit in the short-run but on the other hand this pricing strategy cannot be continued on the long-run. Example: South Indian Super Star Actor Rajnikanth's Movie Tickets are sold for ₹ 1000 per ticket for the first show in Tamil Nadu. The same price cannot be possible in the second week of the screening of the same movie.

2. Economy Pricing or Cost based Pricing Strategy

When a seller fix the price based on the cost of producing per unit of product, it is called as cost based pricing. Usually, cost of production is classified into two, viz. fixed costs and variable costs. If one needs to see profit, then the price per unit must not be less than variable costs per unit. Often this pricing strategy is adopted by Supermarkets to market their generic brands.

EXHIBIT 3.3.1 **Penetrating Price of Tide—Just ₹ 20 per Kg**

Source: http://www.toptomato.in/static/images/00/18/001872.jpg

3. Innovation Oriented Pricing Strategy

This pricing strategy is followed when a new product is launched or introduced in the market. There are two innovation oriented pricing strategies:

(a) *Skimming Price:* When a player fixes the maximum possible price to maximize the profits, it is called as skimming price.

(b) *Penetrating Price:* When a player fixes the lowest possible price to maximize the profits by penetrating deep into the market, where the price is so low which makes it affordable to the mass market to consume the product, it is called as skimming price.

4. Competition-Oriented Pricing Strategy

This pricing strategy is followed to outsmart the rival players in the market. It can be done in three ways:

(a) *Premium Pricing:* When a company, price its offering (products and services) more than the competitors' offerings, it is called as premium pricing.

(b) *Discount Pricing:* When a company, price its offering (products and services) less than the competitors' offerings, it is called as discount pricing.

(c) *Parity or Parallel Pricing:* When a company, price its offering (products and services) equivalent to the competitors' offerings, it is called as parallel or parity pricing.

EXHIBIT 3.3.2 Competition Oriented Pricing – Tide Vs. Rin

Source: http://3.bp.blogspot.com/-JaFoPIZa8P4/T2Akx-szq0I/AAAAAAAAATo/fEDLaV57aKE/s1600/getimage.dll.png

5. Geographical or Differential Pricing Strategy

If a company charges different prices for the same product in different markets, it is called as differential pricing. Petrol prices differ from state to state in India (See Exhibit-3.3.3 how 'Petrol Price' differs in each state in India due to different state levies).

6. Psychological Pricing Strategy

This pricing strategy is followed by the companies to make the customers feel that the product price is affordable, which is actually not. Say for instance, this strategy was pioneered by Bata Shoe Company for its shoes and slippers. Recently, in 2013, Air Asia's Air Ticket to Singapore priced ₹ 7777, one of its offers also includes flying from Kochi to Seoul via Kuala Lumpur for just ₹10,409, and Airtel Broad Band Internet was priced at ₹ 999, Aakash Tablet PC priced at ₹ 2,499 per piece, Check McDonald's Burger and McCurry Pricing, all in the Exhibit 3.3.4.

EXHIBIT 3.3.3 **Petrol Prices are based on 'Geographical Pricing' in India**

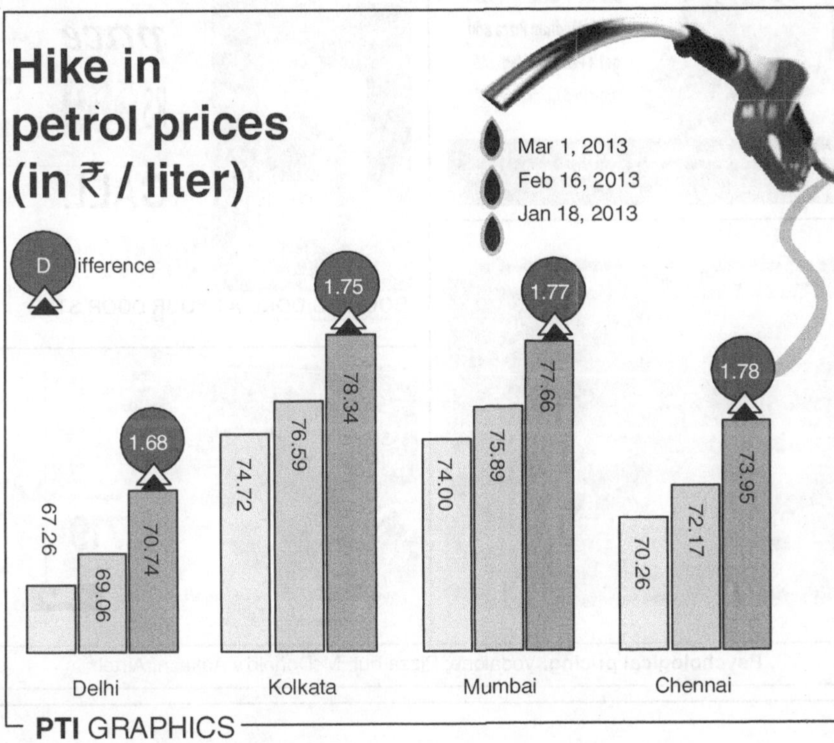

Source: www.thehindu.com/multimedia/dynamic/01381/Petrolhike_1381598f.jpg

EXHIBIT 3.3.4 Psychological Pricing Strategy

Psychological pricing: Vodafone, Pizza hut, McDonald's Aakash, Airtel.

Source:

Pizza hut: http://discountcouponsindia.in/wp-content/themes/couponpress/thumbs/ecoupon811.jpg?9d7bd4Mc Donald's: http://farm4.staticflickr.com/3139/2950181700_639b22b79b_z.jpg

Airtel broadband: http://media-s3.viva-images.com/vivastreet_in/clad/35/8/63784602/large/1.jpg?dt=537d3f47374ad038f38acd50a10e3277

AirAsia: http://www.airasia.com/iwov-resources/in/en/images/mb/2014-fly-aax-low-fares-473-inen.png

7. Product Line Pricing

Where there is a range of product or services the pricing reflect the benefits of parts of the range. Say for instance, it is obvious that any bathing bar soap's price will be less than the liquid soap.

EXHIBIT 3.3.5 Palmolive Product Line Pricing

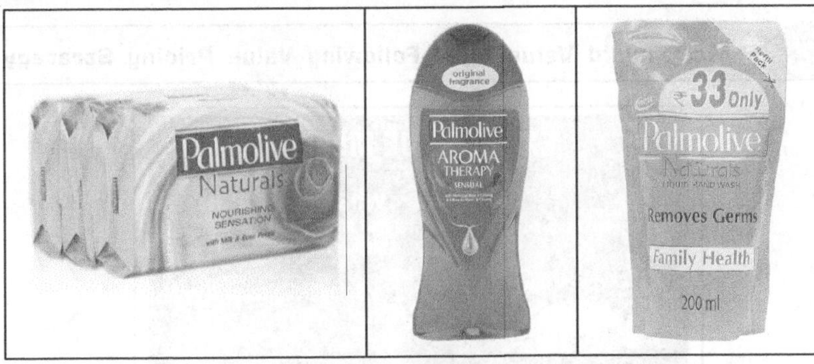

Source: http://images1.mysupermarket.co.uk/Products_1000/51/034251.jpg?v=4

8. Product Bundle Pricing

Sellers combine several products in the same package instead of selling them individually. Example, Diwali Crackers. They are now-a-days offered in package for an attractive price. Lotte's Coffy Bite (previously owned by Parry's Confectionery later acquired by South Korean Major Lotte) is offered in Combo pack priced at ₹ 5, individually, priced at ₹ 1, Vodafone offered a recharge voucher coupon at ₹ 1.

EXHIBIT 3.3.6 Product Bundle Pricing—Coffy Bite

Source: http://www.medplusbeauty.com/beautyproducts/lotte-coffy-bite-stick-packhttp://img.tradeindia.com/fp/1/419/779.jpg

9. Value Pricing

When Companies face external factors like recession, cut-throat competition and so on, they offer 'value' products and services at an attractive price to retain sales. Say for example, 'Value-Meals' at McDonalds, Surf Excel price in October 2013 slashed (from ₹ 98) to ₹ 70 due to economic slowdown in the country.

EXHIBIT 3.3.7 **McDonald'd Value Meal Following Value Pricing Strategy**

Source: http://collegers.net/pics/?di = UKUV & http://collegers.net/pics/?di = FLLR

4. Factors Influencing Pricing

Following are the two critical factors that affects or influence the pricing decision of the marketing managers:

1. Internal factors
2. External factors

1. Internal Factors

The internal factors are those factors that are controllable by the company's management and can be altered as per their requirements. A marketer must take following internal factors into consideration when setting price of a product:

(a) Company's marketing objectives

(b) Marketing strategy

(c) Costs

(a) Company's Marketing Objectives

Marketing objectives are guided by the overall objectives of the company. Following are the four main marketing objectives that affect the company's pricing decision:

(1) *ROI or Return on Investment:* The marketing manager has to determine an appropriate price that is needed to fulfill the Return on Investment objective of the company.

(2) *Cash Flow:* The marketing manager has to determine appropriate price that covers production costs, marketing costs and profitability (profit margin) through sales revenue.

EXHIBIT 3.3.8 Market Share of Smart Phone Players in India by 2013

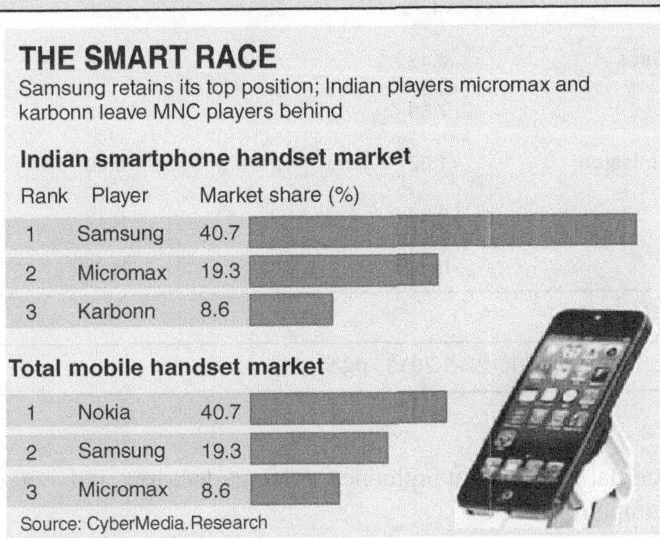

Source: http://bsmedia.business-standard.com/_media/bs/img/article/2013-07/09/full/1373312501-422.jpg

(3) *Market Share:* The marketing manager has to fix an appropriate price so as to capture a sizable portion of the market. Example, Micromax capturing the market share of Nokia using Discount Pricing Strategy in Smart Phone market. Or to retain the existing market share in the hyper-competitive market, where the competition is based on price. Example, P&G Ariel vs. HUL's Surf.

(4) *Maximization of Profit:* Here the marketing manager would determine a price that helps to maximize profits.

(b) Marketing Strategy

Marketing strategy helps the marketers to satisfy the target market and make profit out of it. Price, in fact, is one of the key marketing mix decision that influence the success of the product in the market.

(c) Costs

Companies fix price for their offering by adding up the cost of production, cost of distribution, dealers margin, taxes and duties. Price has to exceed the cost of production and cost of delivery to make profits. One must understand that the cost of production here refers to the variable cost per unit and not the fixed cost. For instance, take the example of price of petrol and Diesel in 2008 in India as shown in the following Exhibit 3.3.9:

EXHIBIT 3.3.9 How It Adds Up from Refinery to Petrol Pump

Components	Petrol (₹/ Ltr)	%	Diesel (₹/ Ltr)	%
Basic Price	21.93	48	22.46	71
Excise Duty	14.35	32	4.60	14
Education Cess	0.43	1	0.14	0
Sales Tax	7.59	17	3.78	12
Dealer Commission	1.02	2	0.60	2
Others	0.20	0	0.18	1
Total	45.52	100	31.76	100

Note: Prices as in Delhi

Source: *The Hindu Business Line,* dt. 27-5-2013, pg-9

2. External Factors

Following are the external factors that influence pricing decision and not controllable by the management of the company:

(a) Elasticity of Demand

(b) Consumer Expectations and the Channel Partners Expectations

(c) Market Competition

(d) Government Policy and Regulations

(a) Elasticity of Demand

Elasticity of demand refers to the capacity of demand to decrease or increase in response to change in price. In general, when price of Onion Increases, Demand for it Decreases. But if consumer expect future rise in price, they would buy more in order to avoid spending more on the same quantity of Onion in future. This leads to increase in demand of the Onion which in turn increases the price again. This helps to onion sellers to make sound profit.

(b) Consumer Expectations and the Channel Partners Expectations

Companies want to make profits, Consumers expects values (benefits) for the price they pay for a product or service and Channel partners expects financial returns in the form of commission and incentives from the sales they generate. Hence the final pricing should take care of all the parties simultaneously.

(c) Market Competition

Marketers will look into competitors' prices before fixing their product's price. Here the market should not only focus on the direct competitors' prices but also the indirect competitors pricing too. For instance, Pepsi was focusing only Coke' pricing but later on realized that its indirect competition is not just Coke but Parle's Bisleri – Mineral Water.

(d) Government Policy and Regulations

Marketers must clearly understand the government regulations and policy on products and services in each market they serve. Earlier in India Petrol and Diesel prices were controlled by the government. But since 25th June 2010, oil prices are deregulated[1] and are fixed by the oil refineries based on market forces like demand – supply mismatch and exchange rate fluctuations. But, prices of drugs and medicines are regulated by the Government of India.

5. Pricing Procedure

Following are the steps involved in fixing the price for the product:

1. Identify the target market or customer group.
2. Decide the desired market position and price image of the brand.
3. Determine the extent of price elasticity of demand. *i.e.,* how sensitive is the market or customers towards rise or fall of price of the brand.
4. Estimate various costs. Thumb rule, price per unit will always have to be more than the variable cost per unit.
5. Consider Patent or Copy Right Royalty to be paid for the using the product or services. Say for instance, royalty has to be paid for running a food chain.
6. Analyse the competitors' prices.

[1] http://www.moneycontrol.com/news/market-edge/who-really-gainedpetrol-deregulation_985689.html

7. Analyse the environmental factors.
8. Determine the company and dealers' margins and fix the final price of the product.
9. Review the pricing policy of the company periodically and take corrective action as per the changing market environment.
10. Government role in regulating prices of essential commodities and against cartelization.

The readers are provided with four mini-cases to understand the role of Government in regulating the prices of essential commodities.

CASE-4: Competing in India – The Cement Cartelisation

In June 2012, CCI slapped ₹ 6300 crore (50% of net profit) fine on 11 cement manufacturers for cartelization. Cartel is an agreement amongst the industry players to control production, distribution and pricing of goods, which is basically an anti-competitive agreement.

A complaint was filed by Builders Association of India on cartel and CCI was probing it under 'Director General of Investigation' and found that cement companies were controlling supplies and determined prices which is not only detrimental to the general public but also to the economy as a whole, where infrastructure development is dependent on cement[1].

Cement companies have said that they are disappointed at the order of CCI and would appeal against the penalty in the Competition Appellate Tribunal against the verdict and this is the beauty of true democracy[2].

CASE DISCUSSION

1. Where do you think the Cement Companies have gone wrong when pricing their offerings?
2. What would you do if your company is one of the players in the cement industry? who is slapped with a fine by CCI for Price based cartelization?
3. Do you think the CCI is interfering in the Cement Companies' parity pricing strategy by blaming the players to have formed cartel?

CASE-5: FDI in Pharma Industry

In June 2012, there was a public outcry that allowing FDI in pharma sector would be detrimental to the country's public health. It happened because of MNC pharma companies took over a few major India based pharma companies over the past few years:

Matrix by Mylan in 2006, Ranbaxy by Dai-ichi Sankyo in 2008, Shanta Biotechnics by Sanofi Aventis in 2009, Orchid Chemicals by Hospira in 2009, and Piramal Health Care by Abbott Laboratories in 2010 are to name a few. Those who are pressing the red button, says these acquisitions have become an easy entry for MNC pharmaceutical companies to enter India's generic drug market

---

[1] "Competition Panel slaps ₹ 6300 cr fine on 11 cement makers", The Hindu Business Line, dt.22-6-12, pg-1

[2] "Cement Companies disappointed with Competition Commission order", The Hindu Business Line, Dt. 22-6-12, pg-3.

which is its major rival for them in the international markets. They also add that at one point of time it will lead to almost monopoly like situation where Indians would be made dependent on theses foreign MNC Pharma companies when price and availability of drugs or medicines will be determined by them.

It is also alleged that it could result in aggressive price increase and diversion of the drugs to the more remunerative market across the borders which could in turn lead to artificial scarcity in the local market *i.e.,* in our country. But, Mr. P.Bhaskara Narayana, CFO of Natco Pharma, has defended this acquisition spree saying that CCI is there actively watching for unfair and anti-competitive trade practices, where a company is required to get the approval of CCI for merger deals beyond a threshold limit. Hence nothing would happen as alleged above[1].

CASE DISCUSSION

1. Is allowing FDI in Pharma Industry good or bad for the Pharmaceutical Industry of India? Discuss the pros and cons in detail.
2. Is the drug patent law favourable for Corporate India?
3. Does manufacturing of a generic drug at a much lower price compared to a MNC Pharma invites patent violation. If lawsuit is filed against your company, how will you handle it? Please answer from the Marketing Director's perspective.

CASE-6: Petrol Pricing in India

Government of India deregulated the pricing of petrol which means the oil companies can fix the prices of the petrol in response to the market forces *i.e.,* according to the demand-supply situation in international markets.

Once it is deregulated, the prices of petrol are fixed by the oil companies and not by government of India. Then how come the prices of petrol are the same across the nation (excluding VAT and other taxes)? Moreover, if one could watch closely, the price raise would also be the same by all the companies across India. If the oil price is said to have been deregulated and free market competition exist, why all the players are increasing the price to the same level simultaneously across India.

CASE DISCUSSION

1. If the oil prices are really de-regulated, why cannot every company can have its own different price levels?
2. Can the LPG cylinder price be fixed as per the company's market forces *i.e.,* demand and supply?
3. If the oil prices are de-regulated, why oil companies seek the permnissin of Indian Government every time it want to raise its oil price?
4. Assume Government of India has approved to increase the price of petrol by ₹ 2 only. As a marketing manager, can you increase the price of the petrol by ₹ 3 instead of ₹ 2? Discuss.

---

[1] "Why fear FDI in Pharma?" by Mr. P.Bhaskara Narayana, The Hindu Business Line, Dt. 6-6-12, pg-9.

CASE 7: Case on Pricing Strategy—The Story of GSM Mobile Telecom Market in India

India is proved to be the most exciting market for mobile telephony. When the Indian cellular sector was opened up for private sector in 1994-1995, the teledensity of the country was only 0.8 per hundred. Since then, the telecom landscape in the country has undergone a sea change. Today, the total teledensity has grown manifold to reach 906.93 Million as on September 2011[1]. Some of the prominent players in the Indian Telecom market are (ADAG) Anil Dhirubai Ambani Group's Reliance Communications, Bharti Airtel, Vodafone (previously Hutchison Essar), Idea Cellular, Aircel Ltd, MTNL, and BSNL.

EXHIBIT 3.3.10 Top Ten GSM Mobile Operators in India by 2011

Service Provider	Jun-11		Sep-11		Net Additions (in millions)
	No. of Subscribers (in millions)	Market Share	No. of Subscribers (in millions)	Market Share	
Bharti	169.19	22.95%	172.79	22.70%	3.60
Vodafone	141.52	19.19%	144.99	19.05%	3.47
Idea/Spice	95.11	12.90%	100.18	13.16%	5.07
Reliance	88.23	11.97%	91.94%	12.08%	3.71
BSNL	88.43	11.99%	90.91	11.94%	2.48
Aircel /Dishnet	57.98	7.86%	59.79	7.86%	1.81
Tata	49.06	6.65%	49.98	6.57%	0.91
Unitech	26.33	3.57%	29.65	3.90%	3.32
Videocon	7.13	0.97%	6.27	0.82%	–0.86
MTNL	5.23	0.71%	5.32	0.70%	0.09
S Tel	3.32	0.45%	3.50	0.46%	0.18
Loop	3.15	0.43%	3.20	0.42%	0.05
Etisalat	1.36	0.18%	1.52	0.20%	0.16
Quadrant (HFCL)	1.30	0.18%	1.16	0.15%	–0.13
Total	**737.33**	**100%**	**761.20**	**100%**	**23.86**

Source: The Indian Telecom Services Performance Indicators, July - September 2011, TRAI, www.trai.gov.in, DT. 9th January 2012, Table 1.12: Group-wise Market Share (in terms of subscription) within GSM Service, page-19.

[1] The Indian Telecom Services Performance Indicators, July - September 2011, TRAI, www.trai.gov.in, DT. 9th January 2012.

There are more than 15 GSM players and 6 CDMA players viz., Reliance, Tata, Sistema, BSNL, MTNL and Quadrant (HFCL) are in the market as on September 2011. Before allowing the private players to invest in telecom business, the only telecom service provider was the Government owned BSNL. Today in 2011, there are 14 to 15 players in the industry providing mobile telecom services (Please refer Exhibit-3.3.10). Just to show how fair competition benefits the consumers, have a glance at the 'Effective Charges per Minute' which was ₹ 16 per minute in 1998 steadily declined to 1-paise per second during 2010-2011 (Please refer Exhibit-3.3.11).

EXHIBIT 3.3.11 **How Competition in Circles Heats Up?**

Year	Effective Charges per Min (in ₹)	Average Revenue per minute	Subscribe Base (in million)	Average No. of Operators per Circle
1998	16.00	15.5	0.88	2
1999	15.70	15.5	1.20	2
2000	6.50	7.3	1.88	2
2001	4.10	4.3	3.58	3
2002	3.75	3.8	6.50	4
2003	3.00	3.5	13.00	6
2004	2.00	2	33.60	6
2005	1.20	1.2	52.20	6
2006	1.00	1.1	90.14	6
2007	0.90	1	165.11	6
2008	0.80	0.8	261.07	8
2009	0.50	0.6	450.00	10
2010	**1 paise per second**	**0.5**		**10-12**

Source:

1. "How many telecom companies should India have?", *The Hindu Business Line,* DT. 29-09-2009.
2. PwC-COAI-White-Paper-Indian-Mobile-Services-Sector "Indian Mobile Services Sector-Struggling to maintain sustainable growth" August 2011, "Decrease in ARPU", pg-16.

CASE DISCUSSION

1. Do you think that all GSM players did the right thing to reduce prices continually to capture the market share?
2. If every GSM player is going to follow the competition oriented pricing or discount pricing, how is sustainable in the long-run?
3. Why no GSM player has attempted to create a blue ocean market and every one competed in the red ocean market?
4. As a marketing manager of a GSM service provider, what kind of a pricing strategy would you follow? Please provide justification.

UNIT 3.4: ROLE OF 'PROMOTION' IN THE MARKETING MIX

1. The Basic Model of Communication

(a) Communication – Meaning.

(b) Basic Model of Communication – The Communication Process

(c) Conclusion

(a) Communication – Meaning

Communication is simply, passing of information, exchange of ideas, opinions and views between two or more persons. It is a process of establishing a commonness of thought between a sender and a receiver. Thus, communication is a process of having common thinking between two parties, where, information is passed from one person to another.

EXHIBIT 3.4.1 **The Communication Process**

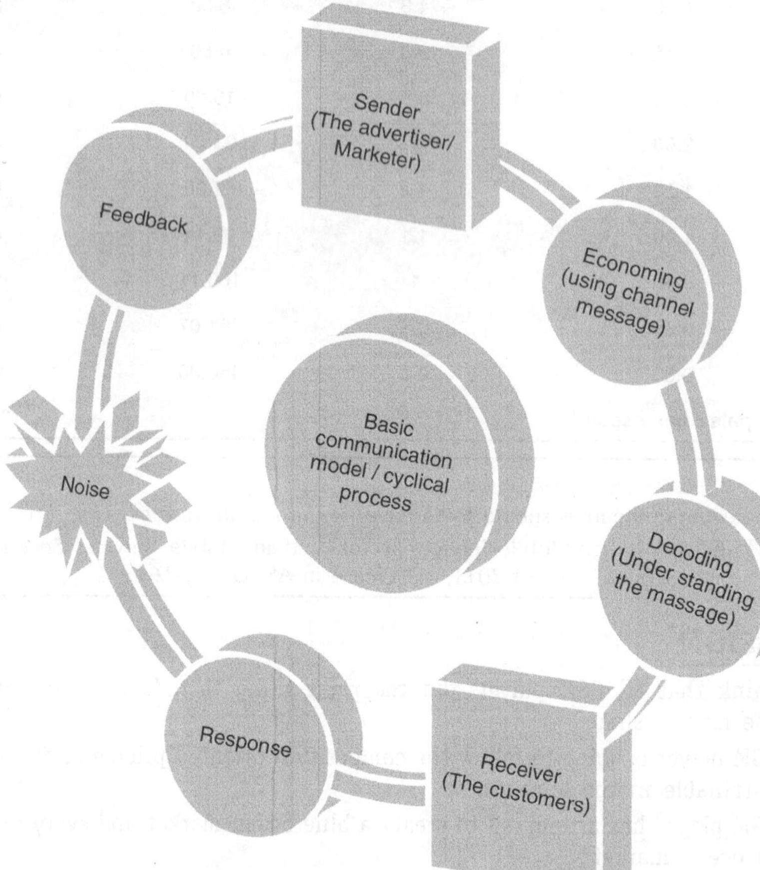

(b) Basic Model of Communication – The Communication Process

The communication process explains how advertisers (the companies), communicate and promote their brand benefits and how the message of the advertisement is understood and would end-up in purchase action.

The components of communication process are:

(i) *Participants* : The sender and the receiver

(ii) *Tools* : Message and Channel

(iii) *Functions* : Encoding, Decoding, Response and Feedback

(iv) *Noise* : An External Factor that affects effective communication.

(i) Participants: The Sender and the Receiver

The sender is the source of communication. It can be a person or an organization that has information to share with another person or a group of people. In our case the companies promoting their brands are senders and the target market or customer groups are the receivers.

(ii) Functions: Encoding, Decoding, Response and Feedback

Encoding – Sender encodes the message in a way, which will be understood by the receiver, the target market or the customer groups. Encoding involves putting selective words, thoughts, ideas etc. into a symbolic (symbols and pictures) form. Thus, sender uses words, signs or symbols that are familiar to the target audience to communicate the message. Say for instance. General symbols like the following communicate specific message of No Smoking, No Entry and No Parking:

EXHIBIT 3.4.2 Symbols Communicating Messages

No smoking	No parking	No Entry

Just like above, companies use symbols or logos to communicate their businesses.

EXHIBIT 3.4.3 Company Symbols or Logos Communicating Messages

India's first orange soda brand – Gold spot

Bharti Airtel's logo

Thums Up - communicating the message of challenging personality

Madras rubber factory's muscle man's logo- symbolizing strength as its cor quality

Decoding: Generally, the receivers are the target consumers who decode the marketer's message. Decoding is a process of interpreting and understanding the sender's message correctly on what the sender is trying to communicate. Understanding a message is influenced by the receiver's or customer's perception, attitude, values etc.

Response and Feedback: The reactions of the receiver after seeing, reading, or hearing the message in an advertisement is known as a response. *E.g.,* a person after reading or viewing an advertisement (hereafter please read 'ad') dialing a toll-free number to order a product advertised on a daily news paper or a television. Marketers are very interested in feedback/response as it let them (the senders) to know how the message is (decoded) interpreted and received by the customers (the receivers). Today, TV advertisers use tele-media campaign and stimulate the target audience to place order or make enquiry through mobile phone for getting immediate feedback on their ads.

(iii) Tools: Message and Channel

Message: Encoding leads to development of message that contains Information (or) Meaning. Such message may be Verbal, Non-verbal, Written or symbolic.

Verbal: Freebies or discounts with every purchase.

Non-Verbal / Written / Symbolic: Silk Sarees in India carry Silk Mark Logo which ensures quality of pure silk, Agricultural products carry AGMARK (written on the package) which ensures its quality and similarly, electrical and electronic products like pressure cookers, Gas Stoves and Electric Heaters carry BIS's ISI Mark which stands for Indian Standards Institution, which also ensures safety and quality.

EXHIBIT 3.4.4 **Non-Verbal Communication**

Silk mark	Agmark	BIS's ISI mark

Silkmark: http://www.discountsvu.com/saree/2005103113.jpg
AGMARK: http://2.imimg.com/data2/RQ/BN/MY-1939804/ag-250x250.jpg
ISI: http://m.silcharchronicle.com/wp-content/uploads/2011/08/isi-mark2.79105715_std.jpg

Channel: Channel is the medium by which the communicated message travels from the sender to the receiver. In general, the channels of communication are two types:

(i) Personal channel of communication

(ii) Non-personal channel of communication

(i) *Personal channel of communication:* Personal Channel of Communication is direct face-to-face contact between the Sales Person communicating the product's benefits to the prospects or the prospective buyer. Example: An Insurance Advisor of Bajaj Allianz Life Insurance Company, explaining the key benefits of insurance plan to the prospect.

(ii) *Non-personal channel of communication:* Non-personal channel of communication can be thro' broadcast media such as a TV Commercials, Radio Commercials or print media Newspapers, Magazines, Bill Boards and direct mail.

(iv) Noise

Noise refers to all external factors that disrupt the communication process *i.e.,* the message carried by an advertisement. Sudden disruption in receiving TV Signal in (DTH) Direct-To-Home Set-Top Box due to clouds while watching a commercial on TV could lessen its impact. This communication process can be understood with a simple example of Surf Excel brand of Hindustan Unilever in India:

(i) *Participants:* The sender and the receiver

- o *Sender*: Hindustan Unilever – the advertiser
- o *Receiver*: The Housewives

(ii) *Tools:* Message and Channel

- o *Message*: Save Two Buckets of Water during every wash using SURF EXCEL.
- o *Channel*: Television Media/Audio – Visual Media.

(iii) *Functions:*

- o *Encoding*:Symbolising of saving two buckets of water with comparing lots of foam and with less foam (using SURF EXCEL).
- o *Decoding*: Save two-buckets of water during rinsing the cloth when it is washed by SURF EXCEL.
- o *Response and Feedback*: Increase in Sales of the Brand.

(iv) *Noise:* An External Factor that affects effective communication.

A power-cut during the telecast of the commercial would affect its impact.

EXHIBIT 3.4.5 Communication Process

HUL's SURF EXCEL Campaign for North and South Indian Markets.

Source: www.youtube.com

(c) Conclusion

Thus, the students who are going to be tomorrow's marketers, must learn the process of communication clearly to understand how to communicate effectively with their customers by understanding who are their target audience, what do they feel about their company's offerings, how to communicate with the audience to influence their purchase action.

2. Marketing Communication Mix—Role of IMC or Integrated Marketing Communications Mix in Promoting a Brand

(a) What is Marketing Communication?

(b) Components of (IMC) Integrated Marketing Communication.

(c) IMC Process.

(d) Above the Line Marketing Vs Below the Line Marketing.

(a) What is Marketing Communication?

Marketing communication is all about "Telling and Selling". It helps to communicate the customers about the availability of a brand, its price, its USP or Unique Selling Proposition. Companies persuade the prospective customers to buy their brands using their communication mix or (IMC) Integrated Marketing Communications Mix.

(b) Integrated Marketing Communication

The components of IMC are as follows:

(1) Direct Sales Promotion

(2) Indirect Sales Promotion or Advertisement

(3) Direct Marketing

(4) Personal Selling

(5) PR or Public Relations

(1) Direct Sales Promotion

It refers to short-term incentives or inducements that create immediate demand for a product or a service. For instance, companies limit their freebies for a limited period of time as "This Offer is Limited only Upto Diwali – So Hurry!"

(2) Indirect Sales Promotion or Advertisements

Any paid form of non-personal stimulation of demand for a product or a service is called indirect sales promotion or advertisement.

(3) Direct Marketing

Use of non-personal communication mediums such as internet, e-mail, telephone, website banner ads to communicate and promote the offerings directly to the customers is called direct marketing. Example: Commercial Banks in India promote Credit Cards, Debit Cards, Loans through its tele-callers using cold-calls. Mostly used web-based promotions are banners, pop-ups and rich media like video, audio, animations etc.

(4) Personal Selling

When promotion and sales of products are carried out by the sales persons, it is called as personal selling. Mostly unsought goods like Insurance, Dictionary, encyclopedia etc are promoted through this channel of promotion. Examples: Eureka Forbes Vacuum Cleaners, AMWAY, LIC policy are sold through sales people in India.

(5) PR or Public Relations

It is unpaid form of publicity to build the corporate image among people or in a society is called as Public Relations. Example: Vijay TV, South Indian General Entertainment Channel's Campaign against Smoking.

(c) Integrated Marketing Communication Process

IMC process explains how to design a Integrated Marketing Communication using the components of the IMC. The steps involved in designing an IMC process are as follows:

1. Review of Marketing Plan
2. Analysis of Promotional Programme Situation
3. Analysis of Communications Process
4. Budget Determination
5. Develop Integrated Marketing Communications Programme
6. Integrate and Implement Marketing Communications Strategies
7. Monitor, Evaluate, and Control Integrated Marketing Communications Program

1. Review of Marketing Plan

In the first stage, the marketers do the following:

- Examine overall marketing objectives
- Competitive analysis
- Assess environmental influences

2. Analysis of Promotional Programme Situation

Analysis of promotional programme situation involves internal and external environmental analysis.

Internal Analysis: it involves analysis of

- Firm's ability to implement promotional program
- Agency evaluation and selection
- Review of previous program results

External Analysis: it involves analysis of

- Consumer behaviour analysis
- Market segmentation and target marketing
- Market positioning

3. Analysis of Communications Process

In this stage, marketers analyse the following:

- Analyse receiver's response processes
- Analyse message, channel factors
- Establish communications goals and objectives

4. Budget Determination

Determine tentative marketing communications budget and allocate the same for promotional spending.

5. Develop Integrated Marketing Communications Program

In this stage, the marketers do the following for all the five components of IMC, viz. Advertising, Direct Sales Promotion, Direct marketing, Personal Selling and Public Relations (PR):

- Set sales promotion objectives
- Determine sales promotion budget
- Determine sales promotion tools
- Develop messages
- Develop sales promotion media strategy

6. Integrate and Implement Marketing Communications Strategies

Marketers at this stage integrate their communication mix and they are as follows:

- Integrate promotional-mix strategies
- Create and produce ads
- Purchase media time, space, etc
- Design and implement direct-marketing programme
- Design and distribute sales promotion materials
- Design and implement public relations/publicity programme
- Design and implement interactive/Internet marketing programme

7. Monitor, Evaluate, and Control Integrated Marketing Communications Programme

- Evaluate promotional program results/effectiveness
- Take measures to control and adjust promotional strategies

(d) Above the Line Marketing Vs Below the Line Marketing

Above The Line (ATL) Marketing represents a theme, that focuses on brand's image building. Below The Line (BTL) Marketing represents sales that focuses on boosting immediate sales revenue. During the economic slowdown, cash flow is an immediate requirement for any company. Cash flow is the life blood of any business. If it slows down or stops, the corporate body suffers. Marketers today understand its importance during the economic slowdown and putting their big bucks in BTL. Under

BTL money would obviously move from (brand building) theme to (sales oriented) schemes[1]. ATL or Above The Line Marketing Communication uses broadcast medium and publish to mass audience. But BTL or Below The Line Marketing Communication focuses on (OOH) Out-Of-Home Advertising Bill Board, Mela Advertising and In-Store Promos. OOH promotion will cost you just peanuts compared to Above the Line Television Ads which costs you ₹ 10 – 12 Crore and 360 Degree promotion could cost ₹ 20 – 25 Crore on an average. Daikin Air-conditioning India Pvt. Ltd., spends heavily on bill-board advertisements, where OOH ads accounting almost 60 – 70% of their marketing expenditure. They have adopted approximately 450 colonies in Delhi NCR and put-up hoarding on the colony gates to spread the brand awareness. LG's Air-Conditioners' Business Head says that the company would involve extensively in BTL marketing using In-Store experience, except Diwali where ATL marketing is used. Reckitt Benckiser hold programmes in Schools and talk to housewives to spread awareness on health and hygiene[2].

In totality, during tough economic times, companies resort to BTL Marketing Promotions which is less expensive compared to ATL Marketing Communications, to boost sales in the short-run.

3. Direct Sales Promotion

(a) Direct Sales Promotion – Meaning
(b) Need for Direct Sales Promotion
(c) Forms of (Direct) Sales Promotion
(d) Developing a sales promotional campaign

(a) Direct Sales Promotion—Meaning

Direct sales promotion is basically a short-term incentive that includes direct and immediate inducement which adds an extra value to the product or a service that persuades or convinces the distributors, dealers and the ultimate consumers to buy the product in a pre-defined period. This leads to increased demand of the company's offerings in a specific period of time.

(b) Need for Direct Sales Promotion

Following are some of the key benefits or need for companies resorting to direct sales promotion:

(1) To introduce new product into the market
(2) To overcome unique and severe competition
(3) To overcome seasonal slump in sales
(4) For getting new sales accounts or for acquiring new customers
(5) For retrieving the lost accounts (customers)
(6) For unloading the accumulated inventory
(7) To support and supplement the sales people's and advertising efforts of the company

---

1 *The Hindu Business Line,* "Waiting in the wings" by Harish Bijoor, CEO, Harish Bijoor Consults Inc.

2 "Brands go for Below-the-line promotions to boost sales", *The Hindu Business Line,* dt. 28-09-2013, pt-5.

(c) Forms of (Direct) Sales Promotion or Direct Sales Promotion Techniques

Following are some of the famous (direct) sales promotional techniques adopted by the market players for promoting the sales of their brands:

(1) Sales promotion letters

(2) Catalogue

(3) POP or POS Displays

(4) Demonstrations

(5) Trade fairs and Exhibitions

(6) Contests

(7) Gifts

(8) Coupons, Installments Payment Offers, Freebies and Price-Offs.

(1) Sales Promotion Letters

They are sent to dealers and customers by the companies. It contains information about the company's offerings along with special promotional offer, often offer's availability restricted to a specific period of time. It reminds and attempts to stimulate the customers to buy their brands. Today, companies resort to e-mail promotional letters to persuade their target market to buy their brands.

(2) Catalogue

It contains all essential information about the company's product offerings. A well designed catalogue contains:

(i) An attractive multi-dimensional image of the product

(ii) Colour variants

(iii) Variety in sizes

(iv) Details on special features or attributes or quality

(v) Quantity

(vi) Price range etc.

(3) POP or POS Displays

POP stands for Point-of-Purchase and POS stands for Point-of-Sales which simply means the retails store. From a customer's viewpoint, a retail store is POP, whereas the same retail outlet is viewed as POS by the Company. Today, innovative and attractive POP displays have become a pre-requisite for any brand's success. Brands today compete aggressively with each other to capture the eye-balls of the customers visiting the retail outlets. POP Displays like posters and stickers are used to attract the attention of the customers and to communicate the special offers of the brands.

Example: When Nestle's Maggi was launched in India, it was sold by keeping in a wire mesh bag which served in two ways, one it saved space in the retail outlet, as it was hung in the ceiling of the store and two, it indeed attracted the customers' attention. Similarly, almost all FMCG brands are offered in sachets, which are hung over the ceiling of the kirana stores or the traditional retail outlets. In fact, companies sponsor the shop banner like what you see in the following exhibit where GSK's Horlicks has sponsored the shop banner.

EXHIBIT 3.4.6 **Point-of-Purchase Display**

http://theforthright.com/wp-content/uploads/2011/08/kirana-shop.jpg	http://www.bloomberg.com/image/it3ZU93bZ9b0.jpg

(4) Demonstrations

When companies launch a new product that is technologically advanced, they resort to demonstration. Most often, companies resort to house-to-house demo by using its sales people. Example: Eureka Forbes Vacuum Cleaners, Water Purifier – Aqua Guard are demonstrated by its sales personnel on door-to-door basis. But some products are hi-tech and costly to make house-to-house demo. In that case, customers are invited to a particular place and then the demonstration of the product is conducted. This is called as School Demonstration.

(5) Trade Fairs and Exhibitions

Whether it is a consumer good or an industrial good, the trade fairs and exhibitions create a direct contact between the prospects (probable buyers or target market) and the company's products.

(6) Contests

Contests are of two types and they are as follows:

(1) Dealers' Contests

(2) Consumers' Contests

(1) *Dealers' Contests:* They are open to dealers only. Always remains a closed affair between the company and its dealers. It is to stimulate sales of the company's offering in a specified period of time.

(2) *Consumers' Contests:* They are open to consumers only. Employees of the company and their relatives are not allowed to compete in the contests. Always remains open and wide open to all so as to attract more customers towards the brand. It is to stimulate sales of the company's offering in a specified period of time.

(7) Gifts

The company would provide free gifts to its dealers, customers and to other important people to create goodwill towards the company and to improve the sales of their brands indirectly.

EXHIBIT 3.4.7 POP Displays of Leading FMCG Brands in India

	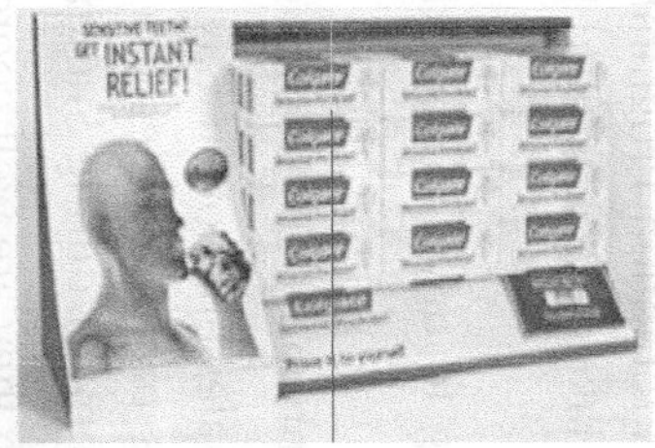	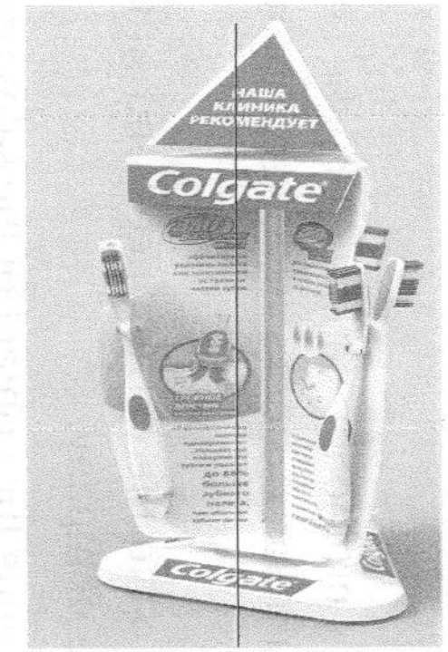	
http://media.cirrusmedia.com.au/BT_Media_Library/pdf/colgate-sensitive-point-of-purchase.jpg	http://s3images.coroflot.com/user_files/individual_files/original_417932_ZDd7b9Wcf7bK0WYqTjlfu3ZcE.jpg	http://s3images.coroflot.com/user_files/individual_files/original_417932_ZDd7b9Wcf7bK0WYqTjlfu3ZcE.jpg	http://www.popon.net/Files/Admin/ARTICLES%202011/ARTICLE-246-PIC-2.jpg

http://www.conceptforum.com.au/images/index/CADBURY%203%20TIER%20CHOCOLATE%20BAR%20DISPLAY.jpg	https://lh3.googleusercontent.com/-1mRhvCGEO2g/UMQcwBDq0hI/AAAAAAAAACE/K6EtYLeOn28/s90-c-k-no/A-1%2BKirana%2BStores	http://images.jdmagicbox.com/jaipur/d1/0141px141.x141.120223121115.m7d1/catalogue/37fa3d222c245fd6cb9c41f6e6d675c6.jpg	http://farm9.staticflickr.com/8189/8447869566_4f192f35f6_z.jpg

(8) Coupons, Instalments Payment Offers, Freebies and Price–Offs

(i) *Discounts Coupons:* It is a certificate that provides reduction in price for consumers on a particular product on repeat purchase. Thus it is done to stimulate repeat purchase of the company's brand. It is quite often distributed through news papers, magazines, placed within the sachets and packages of the products, and delivered through direct mail or email. It is done to introduce a new product into the market and to strengthen the sales of an existing product.

(ii) *Freebies:* Freebies or samples are offered to the prospects in order to persuade them to try their company's product offerings.

(d) Developing a Sales Promotional Campaign

Following are the eight steps involved in developing a sales promotional campaign of a company for promoting its brands:

(1) Identify the basic requirement for developing the sales promotion campaign by the company. Say for instance, it may be for unloading the accumulated stocks or to regain the losing interest of the consumers towards the brand.

(2) Selecting the right promotional programme according to the current need and situation. It is decided based on the available resources of the company.

(3) Enlist the support of the sales people. It involves, briefing the content of the sales promotion programme, the role of sales people in the programme along with their working guides.

(4) Enlist the support of dealers as the success of any Sales Promotion Programme depends upon the support of dealers, where major part of activity takes place around the POPs or Dealer's shops.

(5) Enlist the support of Advertising Agency, which is going to develop the ad campaigns based on the requirements of the company.

(6) Launch and maintain the campaign through advertisement and POP Displays.

(7) Timing of launching a campaign decides its success of the sales promotion. Say for instance, Festival based promotional campaigns like gold jewellers promote sales through special offer on Akshay Trithay in India. Amul Ice Cream's promotion during Summer Season.

(8) The sales promotional campaigns yield better results when they are well coordinated with the other elements or components of promotions like Advertisement, Personal Selling and Publicity through Public Relations.

4. Indirect Sales Promotion or Advertisement

(a) Advertisement – meaning

(b) Why companies need advertisement?

(c) Advertising in India

(d) Various media of advertisement – merits and demerits

(e) Objections towards advertisement

(f) Media Budget

(g) DAGMAR

(h) Media Planning

(a) Advertising

In simple words, advertising is telling and selling!

"Advertising is literal translation of Greek word which means 'to turn' people to an idea. It is a communication process that persuades buyers to act favourably up on any idea, product or service, which then produces a profit to the seller".

Walter E. Vieira,

"Marketing is Business – Insight for 21st Century"

(b) Why Companies/Advertisers Need Advertisement?

Advertising is primarily used by the companies:

- To inform people about new products and services
- To build Brands
- To remind customers about their brand at the right time and place
- To reinforce customer confidence in purchase
- To build corporate Identity
- To help their sales force become more effective
- To give their brand and company a "personality" that makes it unique

Not only companies even the government and autonomous bodies use advertising to:

- Inform people about their policies
- Promote birth control
- Educate the masses on health care
- Prevent panic during natural disasters
- Dispel harmful rumours
- Attract foreign investment

(c) Advertising in India

During the early 1970s and 1980s, DD or Doordarshan was the only Television Channel available in India. Being a national carrier, it had programmes for both urban and rural audiences of India. The revolution, in advertising industry took place in early 1990s. The satellite and Cable TV channels had limited reach, they could target very niche audiences at half the cost. This opened up a new world in terms of quality of production, and content – which, the advertising professional watched with keen interest. In just 15 years time, Indian ad agencies registered success at International Awards like Cannes, AdFest and the New York Festivals made Indian Advertising a sought after profession in India. Today with a high demand for talented individuals, the ad industry of India has evolved into a highly attractive medium, which added value to the quality of television programming in the country and has brought with it a new generation of ideas contributes toward the progress of the nation. Exhibit 3.4.8 shows some of the leading ad agencies operating in India and their International Ad agencies which act as their parent agencies:

EXHIBIT 3.4.8 Leading Ad Agencies in India

S.No	International Ad Agencies	Turnover As on 2002 (in Crores)	Link with Indian Ad Agencies
1.	WPP	1700	HTA, O&M, Contract
2.	Initiative Media	476	Lowe Group
3.	Universal Mc Cann	408	Mc Cann Erickson
4.	FCB	408	FCB Ulka
5.	Starcom	408	Leo Burnett, Ambience, Orchard
6.	Carat	136	–
7.	The Media Edge	340	Rediffusion – DY & R
8.	Mediacom	255	Grey Advertising
9.	Mudra	238	Mudra
10.	Zenith	153	Bates, Saatchi and Saatchi
11.	Madison	153	Madison Communications

Source: The *Hindu Business line*- Catalyst, "when size begets size", dt. 8th August 2002.

(d) Various Media of Advertisement—Merits and Demerits

EXHIBIT 3.4.9 Various Media of Advertisement

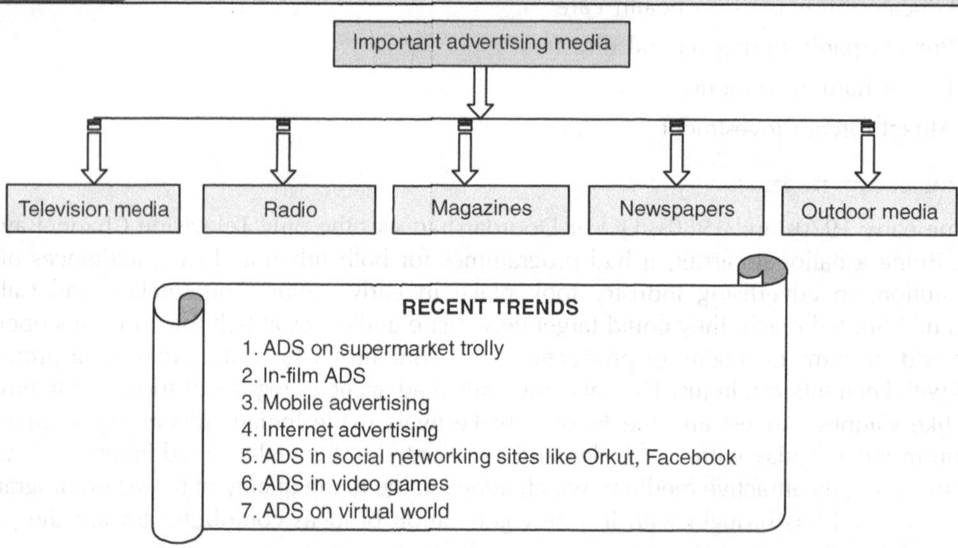

Media-1: Television Advertisement

Merits: It has got Mass coverage, they are Attention getting, always have the Impact of motion and sound, and Can reach illiterates and kids effectively.

Demerits: It has a very Short message life, may become Ineffective in case frequent power cuts, high production cost, and highly cluttered.

Media-2: Radio Advertisement

Merits: It has got the advantage of Local coverage, Low cost advertising, High frequency, Low production cost. Its most important advantage is that it can reach illiterates and kids effectively.

Demerits: It may be Low attention getting, it has a Short message life, Ineffective in case of frequent power cuts if dependent only on power (exception, today almost all basic mobile telephone handsets have FM radio facility), and highly cluttered.

Media-3: Advertisement in Magazines

Merits: It has High reach because of multiple readers, Long message life as the ad can be viewed at any time required. Reproduction of ad is possible.

Demerits: Not effective when the target audiences are illiterates and/or visually challenged.

Media-4: Advertisement in Newspapers

Merits: It has got High reach and coverage, Low cost of advertising; it can be used as coupons for discounts on repeat purchase.

Demerits: It has very short life as today's newspaper is tomorrow's waste paper, Cluttered, Low attention getting, not effective when the target market is of illiterates and visually challenged or small children who cannot read and write.

Media-5: Outdoor Media (Posters, Air Balloons and Bill Boards) Advertisement

Merits: It can be easily noticed, Low cost, High reach if used near traffic signals.

Demerits: They are often location specific, which means if prospective customers do not visit that location, then they would not be able to see the advertisement. Another drawback is its short exposure time.

Understanding the merits and demerits of these famous media channels would help the marketers to decide on their apt media to promote their brands.

(e) Objections Towards Advertisement

The three important objections towards advertisements are as follows:

- Economic Objections
- Social Objections
- Ethical Objections

Economic Objections

Advertising forces people to desire and buy things which in fact are not with-in their means, *e.g.*, Sub-prime Crisis in the USA and Credit Card misuse in almost all sections of the society in India.

Advertisement increases the cost of the product. Ad charges are included in the price which consumer has to pay. An advertisement would brainwash consumer to use a particular brand.

Social Objections

Most of the advertisement contains tall claims where the critical information can be concealed from the target audience. The press is influenced by the advertisers as they provide major revenue for the media such as newspapers, magazines, Radio and TV. Example: EMU farming in Tamil Nadu. Now almost all EMU farms are closed in Tamil Nadu after Government of Tamil Nadu took stringent action against the fraudsters.

Ethical Objections

Advertising appeals people to consume those products that affect their health, *e.g.*, liquor, cigarettes. People with less purchasing power cannot afford to buy products even though ad creates strong need in them. This leads to unethical practices like bribing and stealing which in turn impacts the security of the society.

(f) Media Budget

(i) What is a Media Budget?

(ii) Most widely used methods for setting ad or media budget.

(i) Media Budget

The most important decision made by the advertisers is deciding the media budget. If too little money is spent on advertising, then the sales objective may not be accomplished, which would lead to low profit. If too much of money is spent on advertising, it may lead to low profit or loss due to unnecessary expenditure. Therefore, it is a dilemma faced by the advertiser to judge the amount to be spent on advertising. Media budget is estimating the amount to be spent in media for promotion of a brand.

(ii) Most Widely used Methods for Setting ad or Media Budget

Following are the four widely used methods for setting media budget:

- Percentage (%) of Sales Method
- Objective and Task method
- Competitive Parity Method
- What can the company afford method?
- *Percentage (%) of Sales Method:* The percentage of sales method defines the ad budget as "some predetermined percentage of past or expected sales. This method of estimating the media budget can be understood with the following simple example:

  If a company allocates 5% of anticipated sales to advertising and expects next year sales of a particular brand to be ₹ 50 lakh, then the ad budget will be set as ₹ 2.5 lakh (₹.50,00,000 x 5%). This percentage method is an easiest method that relies on sales. This can be observed from India's FMCG players ad spending for the year 2008 and 2009 in the Exhibit-3.4.10.

EXHIBIT 3.4.10 **Advertising Budget**

Hiking Budgets

	April-Sep 2009		Change over last year	
	Sales (₹ cr)	A&P spend (₹ cr)	Sales %	A&P spend %
Hindustan Unilever	8703	1132	6	31
Dabur India	1591	234	23	47
Marico	1389	176	16	40
GSK Consumer*	964	156	20	57
Colgate Palmolive India	955	141	16	–9
Godrej Consumer	1014	94	43	61
Emami	400	75	58	33
Agro Tech Foods	305	31	–28	63
	15322	**2039**		

*Spends on advertising and promotions from half-yearly results

Source: http://www.blonnet.com/2009/11/09/stories/2009110951610100.htm

As one can observe that the Fast Moving Consumer Goods (FMCGs) majors are setting aside a much larger slice of their sales towards advertising and promotions (A&P) the year 2009 compared the previous year 2008 for the period April to September.

Take the case of Hindustan Unilever. Its advertising and promotion spends in the six months ended September 2009 zoomed 31% to a whopping 1,132 crore, even as its sales grew 6%. Ad spends now account for 13% of the company's sales, sharply up from about 10% last year.

- *Objective and task method:* 2/3rd of the largest companies in the world follow this method. It first looks at the objective set for each activity. And then determines how much money has to be spent for accomplishing each objective. This can be understood with an example:

  Product: HUL's Surf Excel

  Time Period of Promotional Campaign to achieve the objectives: Three Months.

  Objective-1: Create brand awareness among 70% of target audience by repeatedly advertising in newspapers, magazines, Television and Radio.

  Objective-2: Create an urge in the midns of 70% of target audience by communicating the benefits of brand using its features. The message is to be simple which is that it saves two buckets of water at every wash because of Surf's foam-less formula.

Objective-3: Create a positive brand image among 50% of the target audience and brand preference among 40% of the target audience by inviting them to join facebook.com, page of the brand.

Objective-4: Use Discount-Coupons through facebook page of the brand, official website, newspapers, magazines to stimulate the target market to try the company's brand.

Objecive-5: Create trust and confidence on the brand by appointing the right brand ambassador who reflects the personality of the brand and the target audience.

When HUL determines how much to spend for achieving all the above five objectives, it is called as objective and task method.

- *Competitive Parity Method:* It is a method where the advertiser's budget is adjusted in a way, so that it can be compared with the competitors' budget. This method is mostly used by small firms. The logic behind this method is that the collective minds of the advertisers in the industry will generate ad budget somewhat closer to an optimal level.
- *What the company can afford method:* It is a method where the company/advertiser would first allocates for the unavoidable expenditures and then spends a reasonable amount on ads which is affordable to them. Mostly small companies use this method.

(g) DAGMAR—Measuring Advertising Effectiveness

- DAGMAR—An Introduction
- Colley's Communication Process
- Characteristics of sound Communication Objectives

DAGMAR—An Introduction

In 1961, Russell Colley prepared a report for the Association of National Advertisers titled "Defining Advertising Goals for Measured Advertising Results" (DAGMAR).

Colley developed a model for setting advertising objectives and measuring the results of an ad campaign. This model states that the effectiveness of an advertisement must be measured and be measured based on its fulfilling the goals and objectives of the ad campaign. Advertising's job, purely and simply, is to communicate to a defined audience to stimulate an action. Success or failure of an advertisement depends on how well it communicates the desired information to the target audience.

Colley's Communication Process

Under the DAGMAR approach, an advertising goal involves a communications task that is specific and measurable. Colley proposed that the communications task be based on a hierarchical model of the communications process with four stages:

Awareness – making the consumer aware of the existence of the brand or company.

Comprehension – developing an understanding of what the product is and what it will do for the consumer.

Conviction – developing a mental disposition/temperament in the consumer to buy the product.

Action – getting the consumer to purchase the product.

Characteristics of Sound Communication Objectives

Following are the four important characteristics of Colley's DAGMAR Communication Objectives:

(i) Measurable Objective by using Concrete and Measurable Task

(ii) Well-defined Target Audience

(iii) Benchmark and Degree of Change Sought

(iv) Specified Time Period

Let us understand the DAGMAR's Sound Characteristics of Objectives using a chocolate brand.

(i) *Measurable Objective by using Concrete and Measurable Task:* Let us assume that the company's chocolate brand's sales have declined significantly due to a worm controversy. Company understood that to reverse the down-trend, something significant had to be done.

The company developed an entirely new positioning campaign with the following objectives:

- Strengthen the brand's image
- Maximize brand presence
- Broaden the market base beyond traditional consumers.
- Increase sales

(ii) *Well-defined Target Audience:* Another important characteristic of good objectives is a well defined target audience. The primary target audience for a company's product or service may be based on descriptive variables such as geographic, demographics, and psychographics (on which advertising media selection decisions are based) as well as on behavioural variables such as usage rate or benefits sought.

(iii) *Benchmark and Degree of Change Sought:* To set objectives, one must know the target audience's present status concerning response hierarchy variables such as awareness, knowledge, image, attitudes, and intentions and then determine the degree to which consumers must be changed by the advertising campaign. A marketing research study must be conducted to determine prevailing levels of the response.

(iv) *Specified Time Period:* A final consideration in setting advertising objectives is specifying the time period in which they must be accomplished. Appropriate time periods can range from a few days to a year or more, *e.g.,* awareness levels for a brand can be created fairly quickly through an intensive media schedule of widespread, repetitive advertising to the target audience. Repositioning of a product requires a change in consumers' perceptions and takes much more time.

DAGMAR SAMPLE

Offering : Fairness Cream for men / Fair & Lovely – Menz Active.

Target Market : Male, 15–35, single and or married, personal income ₹ 15000+, Modern Lifestyle.

Positioning : World's # 1 Fairness Cream for Men.

Objectives : Convince Fair & Lovely (fairness cream) male users to try Menz Active, Generate–high awareness, generate sales volume, attain atleast 60% of sales from those who are using and intending to use Fair & Lovely.

Budget : ₹ 5 Crore.

Media : For Advertising

- TV Programmes : Prime Time programmes, News and Sports
- TV Channels : National Geographic Channel, Discovery Channel, Sun-TV, Jeya TV, Star Plus, Sony TV, NDTV, CNBC TV18
- Print : Outside – *The New Indian Express, The Hindu*
- Support media : Outdoor (air balloons, Billboards) and PoP displays.
- PR : Sponsoring Male Dressing Style Contests.
- Direct Marketing : Dealers contests to promote sales and Prospects – Create facebook page to get insights on users for feedback for enhancement of brand.

Outcome : To achieve brand recall for atleast 30% in first 45 days and 60% to be completed by completion of campaign, *i.e.* 90 days. To achive a sales target of ₹15 crore, *i.e.* three times of the ad spend.

(h) Media Planning

- Media Planning
- Media Planning Process – How to do it?
- ***Media Planning***

  Media planning is a process of directing (or) communicating a message:

  - To the target audience
  - At an appropriate time and place
  - Through an appropriate medium (or) channels.

  Media planning considers:

  - The target audience whom we are going to communicate?
  - Why, when and where we want to reach them?
  - How often to reach them?
  - How to reach them in a cost effective manner?

  If all the above questions are answered and converted into a written document then it is known as media plan.

- ***Media Planning Process – How to do it?***

  Media planning process explains the step-by-step procedure for preparing a media plan. The steps involved in the media planning are as follows:

  ■ Deciding the target audience

  ■ Deciding the media objectives

  ■ Deciding the appropriate media vehicles to communicate Media budgeting

  ■ Preparing the media schedule

  ■ *Deciding the target audience:* A successful media campaign requires a clear target audience. For this purpose, the advertisers segments the market to know people who have common characteristics who tend to act similarly. This helps them to identify the potential customers and design the message specifically for them.

  ■ *Deciding the media objectives:* Every media plan should have media objectives. This is where Russell Colley's DAGMAR plays a vital role. Define Advertising Goals for Measured Advertising Results.

  D: Define A: Advertising G: Goals M: Measured A: Advertising R: Results

  Ultimately, an ad campaign should assist to attain the marketing objectives. Such media objectives include R: Reach, F: Frequency and M: Message Weight.

  Reach: Total number of target audience exposed to a media vehicle at least once during the given period.

  Frequency: Total number of times an audience is exposed to a media vehicle during the given period.

  Message Weight: It refers to how much total advertising is required to accomplish the reach and frequency objective. The message weight is expressed as (GRP) Gross Rating Points / Gross Impression. GRP measures the total target audience exposed to all media vehicles. GRP is = Reach x Frequency. This can be understood with the following example:

  India's gold haul at Games has viewers hooked to DD

  The Asian Games got the highest number of viewers during the opening ceremony for which around 2.9 crore people tuned in. The opening ceremony also got a peak rating of 4.27 (GRP). The first day of the Games where India won five gold medals got a peak rating of 3.22 with 2.35 crore people tuning in throughout the day. After a slight mid-week slump, on Thursday the ratings again picked up with peak rating at 2.96 and almost 2.4 crore people tuning in[1].

  ■ *Deciding the appropriate media vehicles to communicate:* Media planning involves deciding on Media and Media Vehicle. Media is a channel of communication that carries the message from the advertiser to the target audience. The media can be classified into

[1] The Hindu Business line, Saturday, Oct 09, 2010.

four, Print Media, Broadcast media, Electronic Media (internet), and Mobile Media. The media vehicles are those specific broadcast programmes in TV/Radio or in Print media like *The Hindu, The New Indian Express, India Today* and *Outlook*. Reach data can be obtained from NRS – National Readership Survey, TRP – Television Rating Points and TAM – Television Audience Measurement.

EXHIBIT 3.4.11 TAM Ratings on Six Famous Television Channels in India

Channel	Wk1	Wk2	Wk3	Wk4	Wk5	Wk6	Wk7	Wk8	Wk9	Wk10	Wk11
HBO	0.43	0.31	0.38	0.16	0.10	0.20	0.32	0.49	0.29	0.68	0.46
History	0.10	0.17	0.05	0.07	0.08	0.07	0.08	0.05	0.13	0.06	0.06
PIX	0.15	0.15	0.25	0.20	0.11	0.18	0.08	0.08	0.23	0.11	0.21
Star Movies	0.57	0.70	1.11	0.98	1.19	1.29	1.18	0.43	0.30	0.48	0.54
Zee Café	0.12	0.10	0.10	0.08	0.06	0.10	0.09	0.04	0.09	0.13	0.07
Zee Studio	0.18	0.14	0.20	0.12	0.20	0.11	0.08	0.10	0.08	0.18	0.10

Markets: Six Metros: **Figures:** are TAM ratings from week starting September 10th 2006.

Source: "For a Few Eyeballs More", *Business Today*, dt. 25-02-2007, pg-20

- ***Media Budgeting***

  It helps to know how to accomplish the desired objectives in a cost effective manner. One of the universally used methods is CPM. CPM stands for Cost per Thousand Criterion ("M" —in roman refers to Thousand).

  Let us understand CPM using a simple example, Target market 18–49 years old. Magazine circulation 40,00,000. Circulation to target market 65% (26,00,000 people). Cost per page ₹ 202,000 in case of print media or Cost of ad time per second ₹ 2,02,000, in case of Audio-Visual Media (obtained from the media company).

  Now we need to compute how much the advertiser (the company) has to spend to reach 1000 people (of their target market). CPM = (Media Rate/Total Reach or Circulation) x 1000 (Reach is considered for broadcast media and Circulation for print media)

  Therefore CPM = ₹ 202,000/26,00,000) x 1000 = ₹ 77.69. CPM or Cost Per Thousand helps the marketers/advertisers to compare the cost efficiency of various media and decide the most effective media that is cost effective and gives an optimum reach of the target audience.

- ***Preparing the Media Schedule***

  Media schedule is a report that includes:

  - The media category such as Print, Broadcast, E-Media, & Mobile Media.

- The media vehicles such as specific programmes or editorial sections in magazines and newspapers, Time (in case of broadcast media) or Size of Relay (in case of print media),
- Number of insertions in newspapers and magazines Media Buying – cost of buying 'Space' or 'Time' in media.

  E.g., HUL (formerly HLL) in 2003 spent huge amount and became the biggest advertiser in terms of duration in Setmax Television channel in india during the World Cup Cricket with 29,855 seconds[1].

5. Public Relations (PR)

(i) Public Relations – Meaning and Definition
(ii) History of PR
(iii) Role and objectives of PR
(iv) Public Relations Vs Advertisement
(v) PR Campaign Development or Process
(vi) Managing Business Crisis using PR Campaign

(i) Public Relations – Meaning and Definition

Public Relations (PR) is identifying, establishing, and maintaining a mutually beneficial relationship, between the organisation and various groups of public including the community or communities within which it operates. According to Public Relations Society of America, "Public Relations help the organisation and its public adapt mutually to each other."

(ii) History of PR

The father of PR or Public Relations is Ivy Ledbetter Lee. PR tactics is an aggressive engineering of public perception or opinion. Traditional PR was always soothing and positive. Basically, it was an in-house function which is largely confined to press relations and writing speeches for executives. It is said that traditional PR largely focused on publicity rather than execution of a coordinated campaign with a clear-cut strategy. But today's PR is realistic, admits mistakes and Conveys balanced information. It is more than mere press relations. It plays a vital role in moulding a positive image in the minds of the pubic about the organization, and its brands to create goodwill towards the organisation. It results in sustainable growth, long-range market standing and profitability, The Successor of Ivy Ledbetter Lee, Edwards Bernays was the first person to establish a PR firm.

(iii) Role, Functions and objectives of PR Officer

Role of PR functionality with other departments of the organisation are as follows:

Marketing: Pepsodent toothpaste offered dental insurance, Eureka Forbes sponsored "Pollution Watch" in STAR News.

---

[1] *The Hindu Business Line* dt. 19-03-2003.

Production: TNPL offers eco-friendly notebooks made from Sugarcane wastes (bagasse) where chopping of trees prevented. The trend of Eco-Friendly manufacturing is picking up. Manufacturing of paper cups and paper bags are increasingly seen as a market opportunity.

Human Resources Development: Tata in 1980s built hospitals and schools for its employees' children in Jamshedpur, the steel city.

Finance: PR budget drawn and sanctioned by the finance and accounting department. For instance, Mr. Bill Gates, founder of Microsoft Inc., offered $100 Million to India to combat AIDS.

Following are the functions of a Public Relations Officer in an organisation:

1. To convene press conference to announce new product launch and important corporate news
2. To involve in social and communal activities
3. To donate for social welfare
4. To write articles on company and other social issues
5. To make public announcements and special publications
6. To award scholarships for the education of financially backward students
7. To sponsor well regarded events
8. To distribute corporate brouchers
9. To promote corporate advertising
10. To conduct public opinion poll
11. To mediate between the organisation and its various publics
12. To manage crisis situations.

(iv) Public Relations Vs Advertisement

Public Relations	Advertisements
• Generate positive public opinion to boost up the organisational image	• Focuses only on AIDA (Attention-Interest-Desire-Action) formula to promote the firm's brand
• Uses annual reports, manuals, brouchers, information bulletins, House journals, news letters, and direct mailing	• Uses media and media vehichles such as print, broadcast, mobile and electronic media
• Focuses on the welfare of the stake-holders	• Focuses on the welfare of the target audience only
• Broadened view and covers every individual of the organisation	• A specialised function performed only either by marketing department or ad agency
• PR influences advertisement.	• It is only of the tools of PR

(v) PR Campaign Development or Process

Public Relations process explain the step-by-step procedure for developing a PR Campaign for a organisation. This process can be termed as R-A-C-E.

R-Research – The PR team conducts Focus Group Sessions, Attitudinal Research, and Media Research to determine the exisiting opinion and attitude of the public towards the organisation.

A-Analyse – By analyzing the survey findings, the existing opinion and attitude of the public towards the firm is identified. This can be positive or negative or a mixed one.

C-Create – It is nothing but the planning. Before the firm decides its PR strategy that is to be adopted, the PR team decides the on the target audience and their existing attitude towards the firm. Based on it, the PR team selects a strategy. According to Burson, there are only three strategies and they are as follows:

- Creating a positive opinion
- Re-inforcing an existing positive opinion
- Changing the existing negative opinion to a positive one

Once the strategy is finalised, the PR team decides on what is to be communicated, how or through which media it is to be communicated along with the PR budget.

E-Evaluate – Once the PR plan is designed, it is time for implementation. The performance has to be reviewed in periodical interval after the implementation. In case of any deviation from plan, corrective action should be triggered. All these stages are cyclical in nature as it has to be done throughout the period of existence of the organisaton.

(vi) Managing Business Crisis Using PR Campaign

HUL's fair & Lovely's ad was once banned by the Government stating that it is creating colour discrimination amongst the women fraternity based on All India Democratic Women's Association petition claiming "the ad created complexion prejudices in women"[1]. Immediately, HUL (formerly HLL) established "Fair & Lovely Foundation" with a tagline "Taking you to a brighter future". It published an print ad stating "WANTED – Women who want their world to extend beyond the four walls of home" where it aimed to offer economic independence to the Indian Women fraternity through education, career guidance and scholarship.

In August 2003, When Coca-Cola and Pepsi got caught in Pesticide Residue Case raised by Centre for Science and Environment, in India, both came together to fight against the claim of presence of pesticide residue in their carbonated soft drinks. Pepsi India's Chairperson, Rajiv Bakshi, himself appeared in an ad campaign saying "Your Pepsi is Absolutely Safe" and Coca-Cola's ad campaign with the message "I have 100% confidence that Coca-Cola is Absolutely Safe" with its brand ambassador, Bollywood Star, Aamir Khan.

---

[1] *The Hindu Business Line*, "Fairness Cream ads acquire darker hue", dt. 04-03-2003.

EXHIBIT 3.4.12 **Coca-Cola's PR Campaign to Create a Positive Image Towards the Brand**

Source: http://1.bp.blogspot.com/-kSNq2cDyLqg/UHGaRGz1n9I/AAAAAAAAAIA/tISdEjWgEXc/s1600/coca-cola-billboard-india.jpg

6. Personal Selling – The Art of Salesmanship

(a) Personal Selling and Salesmanship
(b) AIDAS Formula – The Success Mantra
(c) Qualities of a Successful Sales Person
(d) Types of Sales Persons
(e) Duties and Responsibilities of a Sales Person
(f) Functions of a Sales Manager

(a) Personal Selling and Salesmanship

Promotion and sales by sales persons is called as personal selling. The sales persons are also called as Client Relationship Executives and Sales Executives. Life Insurance Corporation of India's strength is its insurance advisors who are sales persons. The sales persons are employed by the organisations to promote brands and to create demand for the company offerings (products and services) in order to increase sales.

The art of selling is called as salesmanship and not only includes the art of sales but also the art of serving the customers after the sales had taken place, say for instance, the LIC's Insurance Advisors assisting their clients in remittance of Insurance Premiums, arranging for loan facility against the insurance policy cover on client's request and so on.

According to W.G. Carter, "Salesmanship is an attempt to induce people to buy goods". According to National Association of Marketing Teachers of America, Salesmanship is, "the ability to persuade people to buy goods or services at a profit to seller and benefit to buyer."

In totality, a salesperson's job is to persuade or convince the prospective buyer to buy the offerings of the company by explaining the benefits of owning the same to the customer and thereby increase the sales of the company.

(b) AIDAS Formula – The Success Mantra

Any sales person to succeed in the market would follow AIDAS formula. The expansion of the Success formula is as follows:

- ***A–Attention:*** The sales person must invite the *Attention* of the prospect towards the company offerings.
- ***I–Interest:*** Developing the interest in the minds of the prospect about the product and service offerings
- ***D–Desire:*** Then, must create desire in the minds of the prospect to buy the offering.
- ***A–Action:*** Convert the desire into Purchase Action
- ***S–Satisfaction:*** Strive for customer satisfaction continually through after-sales services which would eventually end-up in repeat purchase. All these five stages explain how a person is targeted as a prospect and converted into a customer or consumer.

(c) Qualities of a Successful Sales Person

Following are the characteristics or qualities of a successful sales people:

1. The sales persons should be neat in appearance and healthy
2. They have good imagination, alertness and patience
3. They are self-confident and have good manners
4. They are reliable for any task assignment and are honest in nature
5. They show the intention to learn new things and are ready to re-learn in order to update themselves
6. They have complete knowledge about their company and their rivals
7. They have thorough knowledge about the company offerings and rival brands
8. They have good knowledge about the customers
9. Follow AIDA formula
10. They are tactful
11. They have clarity in voice
12. They have very good memory power. This helps to remember customers by name, remember key dates like their date of birth (helps to build emotional relationship with clients) and their previously served requirement to serve them better.

(d) Types of Sales Persons

Following are the six types of sales persons operating the organisation:

(a) Creative Sales Person (b) Service Sales Person
(c) Detail Sales Person (d) Manufacturer's Sales Person
(e) Wholesaler's Sales Person (f) Retailer's Sales Person

(a) **Creative Sales Person:** Creative sales person is also called as missionary sales person. Creative sales person is used for creating demand for the company's offerings among the customers. Their job is to develop a sales territory.

(b) **Service Sales Person:** These sales persons are specifically used for selling intangible products like insurance, shares, travel or tourism and software programmes.

(c) **Detail Sales Person:** The detail sales persons are also called as merchandising sales person. They use their in-depth knowledge or details of the company's products and services to convince a group of customers. Hence their job is called as 'Detail Selling'. For instance, a medical representative of a pharmaceutical company convincing the doctors to prescribe the company's medicines by listing out its benefits in detail.

(d) **Manufacturer's Sales Person:** The sales persons who get directly appointed, controlled, and paid by the manufacturer are called as manufacturer's sales persons.

(e) **Wholesaler's Sales Person:** The sales persons who get directly appointed, controlled, and paid by the wholesaler are called as wholesaler's sales persons.

(f) **Retailer's Sales Person:** The sales persons who get directly appointed, controlled, and paid by the retailer are called as retailer's sales persons. Those sales persons who are assigned with the field work are called as outdoor sales persons and those who operates inside the store are called as Indoor or Counter Sales persons.

(e) Duties and Responsibilities of a Sales Person

Following are the core duties and responsibilities of a sales person:

(1) Developing the demand and sales volume in the assigned territory.

(2) Establishing wholesaler and assist the dealer in moving the product smoothly in the assigned territory.

(3) Regularly meet the retailers and take the orders of purchase

(4) Establishing good connection between the company and the retailers in the sales territory

(5) Collection of money from the retailers on credit sales made and assisting the wholesaler remitting the same to the company.

(6) Collect market information continually and update them with the sales manager to track the changes taking place in the sales territory.

(f) Functions of a Sales Manager

A sales person, based on performance and experience, becomes a sales manager. Following are the functions of a sales manager:

(1) Optimize lead generation programmes

(2) Align the marketing activities with sales

(3) Align the sales team structure

(4) Analyse the customer buying process to understand the prevailing tastes and preferences

(5) Enhance the access to relevant information of customers to implement Customer Relationship Management package with the assistance of software successfully

(6) Enhance the sales team communication

(7) Revise sales channel strategy

(8) Revise compensation programme

The above points are not exhaustive but only indicative. New roles may evolve as per the changing and demanding market environment.

7. Latest Trends in Promotional Techniques

Customers today are bombarded with traditional advertising and have become resistant and unaffected by it. Which means it is time for the dynamic marketing team to change the way they market. Hence marketers have started experimenting with various non-traditional promotional techniques which are as follows:

(i) Ambush Marketing
(ii) 360 Degree Promotion
(iii) Guerilla Marketing
(iv) Surrogate Advertising
(v) Scam Advertising

(i) Ambush Marketing

Ambush attack is a war tactic; the word 'ambush' refers to hiding in a bush in order to surprise the enemies. Ambush marketing, a term first coined by marketing guru Jerry Welsh. It is a marketing tactic, which gained prominence globally in 1980s. When an unofficial sponsor associates his promotional campaign with an event without paying a fee and surprises the official sponsor, then it is known as ambush marketing. To be more specific, an unofficial sponsor attempts to steal the attention of the viewers and gain benefits by imaginatively exploiting the exclusive association with an event of a main sponsor, astonishingly, without breaking any laws, then it is known as ambush marketing. This ambush marketing can be classified into onsite and on-media and they are as follows:

Onsite Ambush Marketing

It occurs at the event itself or at the area surrounding. For instance, Pepsi hot-air balloon were seen above SHARJAH, on the day of coca-cola cup final.

On-Media Ambush Marketing

Media ambush marketing would occur through sponsorships of spots, scrolls, logo positions and so on, on the media used to cover the event, generally in TV, radio or press. For example, though 1996 cricket world cup was officially sponsored by Coca-Cola, Pepsi stole the limelight with the tagline "Nothing official about it". Similarly, in 2010, P&G "Mystery Shampoo" campaign for Pantene was with the tagline, "The Mystery Shampoo that is world's No.1 hair care brand" got ambushed by HUL's Dove Shampoo, with its tagline "There is no mystery – Dove is No.1"[1].

Why Companies Involve in Ambush Marketing?

Why would companies wish to spend such sizeable sums for ambush marketing? The obvious rationale for underwriting such sponsorships is to achieve audience awareness and image enhancement. This form of sponsorship permits marketing communicators to talk more directly to particular market segments in a manner that may be more efficient and less costly than traditional media advertising.

Therefore, following are found to be reasons for ambush marketing:

(i) To increase the turnover by stealing the attention of the viewers simultaneously undermining the branding efforts of the rival players.

(ii) To establish brand awareness and occupy the mind space of the target market in a very short span of time.

(iii) To get maximum Return on Investment by exploiting the official sponsor's association with the special event.

Ambush marketing is both illegal and unethical. But marketing analysts say that it would be almost impossible to stop ambush marketing, which directly affects the free flow of ideas.

EXHIBIT 3.4.13 Ambush Marketing

Source for first picture:

1. Pepsi Ambush Coca-Cola: http://marketingbloggers.in/wp-content/uploads/2012/08/Nothing-Official.jpg
2. HUL' Dove shampoo ambush P&G's Pantene Shampoo.

Source for second picture:

1. "Ambushes a war tactic" by Shunu Sen, *The Hindu Business Line dt.* Thursday, Sep 05, 2002.
2. "All About Ambushes", by Neha Kaushik, *The Hindu Business Line dt.* Sep 05, 2002.

[1] *The Economic Times*, dt. 30-07-2010, pg-4.

(ii) Guerilla Marketing—Punk Marketing

The term 'Guerilla Marketing' was Coined by Jay Conrad Levinson. It comes under the concept of Punk marketing. Punk marketing is about having fresh ideas. Guerilla Marketing is defined as "Unconventional marketing intended to get maximum results from minimal resources." It's all about coming up with a truly unique idea for very little cash and converting any exposure you get into sales. When you do that, one would often come out with things, which are distinctive and attention-getting that generates word-of-mouth spread of news at social spots.

The Guerilla Marketing and Advertising Campaigns focus on creating a buzz around a product or service; it's then passed on by word of mouth as people talk about it in Social Spots like pubs, beaches and parks. When one successfully implements guerilla marketing into the marketing plan, the cost per lead will considerably gets reduced while the quality of the traffic will spectacularly increase.

EXHIBIT 3.4.14 Guerilla Marketing

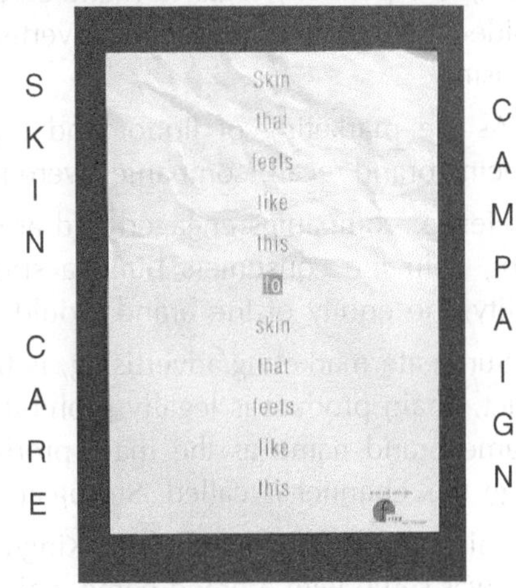

EXHIBIT 3.4.15 Interesting Samples of Guerilla Marketing

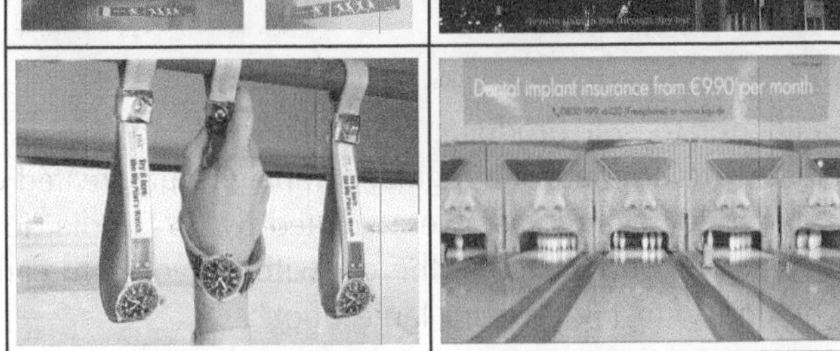

Source:
www.6pins Forums.htm
http://ezinearticles.com/?Guerilla-Marketing:-4-Ways-To-Generate-More-Traffic-Next-Week&id=43480.
http://www.gmarketing.com/

(iii) Surrogate Advertising

In India, it is perfectly legal to manufacture liquor and cigarettes or beedis and sell them at every roadside stall but it is illegal to advertise it. And that is precisely why marketers use surrogate advertising.

As the marketing of liquor and cigarette are not legally acceptable, with an objective of enhancing brand recall, companies were forced to look at innovative ways for building their brands.

Hence, companies engaged and are engaging in 'surrogate advertising'. These surrogate ads, in turn, help the consumers build a strong equity of the parent brand, and with the enhanced visibility, the equity of the brand would definitely become higher.

Surrogate marketing/advertising, is the one where a product which is different from the main product, (main product is legally prohibited from promotion) that is advertised and promoted with the same brand name as the main product. The product is called as 'surrogate' and advertising through this channel is called 'Surrogate advertising'.

This can be understood with Kingfisher brand promotion. One can factually notice that the airline was setup with a brand name, colour and logo style that was same as their liquor brand they own. Today United Breweries' has a legitimate airlines business 'Kingfisher'. They even promote their brand in the name of 'King Fisher' mineral water. Many of these liquor and cigarette companies also involve in sports sponsorship. Say for instance, UB Group's IPL Bangalore franchise 'Royal Challengers' has been named after its premium whiskey brand 'Royal Challenge'.

EXHIBIT 3.4.16 Surrogate Advertising

Source: *The Hindu Business Line*, "What's Surrogate about advertising" by Ramesh Narayan, Thursday, Mar 28, 2008.

(iv) Scam Advertising

Scam ads are those ads that are created not to sell products or services, but to win awards in international advertising contests. ads that were not part of a regular campaign but, created only for entry in advertising awards shows. In March 2013, three ads were created by JWT India, for Ford's small car Figo, the ads highlighted the spacious boot space of the car with provocative caricatures with the tagline "Leave your worries behind with Figo's extra large boot".

EXHIBIT 3.4.17 **Scam Advertisement**

Source: CNBC TV 18, Scam ads: Here's why Ford, JWT India are in a mess, dt. Mar 28, 2013

One ad shows women tied and tossed into the boot with former Italian Prime Minister Silvio Berlusconi. In another, Paris Hilton, appearing in the same scenario with the Kardarshian sisters and in the third F1 driver Michael Schumacher putting in trash his rivals in the trunk. This led to a negative publicity around the brand. Hence, the client (Ford) and the agency (JWT India) swung into damage control. Ford India released an official statement saying that the posters were contrary to the standards of professionalism and decency and thier agency partners. Together with their partners, they were reviewing approval and oversight processes to help ensure nothing like this ever happens again in future.

(v) Comparative Advertising

Comparative advertising can be termed as the war for supremacy between brands that compete for the same pie of market. Comparative advertising is a promotional campaign either in print or

EXHIBIT 3.4.18 **Comparative Advertisement**

RIN Vs TIDE	COMPLAN Vs HORLICKS

Vs.

Source:

1. http://articles.economictimes.indiatimes.com/2012-02-25/news/31099752_1_hul-s-rin-detergent-brand-laundry-brand
2. http://www.thehindubusinessline.com/todays-paper/tp-brandline/whos-the-whitest-of-them-all/article1010817.ece
3. http://www.bestmediainfo.com/wp-content/uploads/2011/07/goair-kingfisher.jpg

electronic media where the rivals compare their brands' attributes directly or indirectly, in order to out-smart one another in a specific market. late 2008, the makers of Horlicks, GlaxoSmithKline Consumer Healthcare (GSK), and the makers of Complan, Heinz India (Heinz), came out with advertisements that directly compared the brands using the competitor brand's trademarks. Rin Vs. Tide directly competed with their price points. Classic Comparative ads carried out by the airlines major of India.

The advantage of comparative advertising is that it improves the quality of information available to consumers, thus enabling them to make more informed decisions relating to a choice between competing products/services by demonstrating the merits of comparable products. However, there is no point in using comparison unless there is genuine superiority.

8. Regulation of Advertisements and Sales Promotion

Advertisements in India are governed and regulated by "The Advertising Agencies Association of India (AAAI)". The role of AAAI in regulation of ads in India is as follows:

(i) To benefit Indian consumers and protect their interests by helping ensure that advertising is honest and in good taste.

(ii) To benefit Indian advertisers by promoting their sales, and increasing their profitability.

(iii) To establish sound business practices between advertisers and advertising agencies and other various media organizations.

(iv) To co-operate with the government in promoting its social objectives and nation-building.

(v) To question advertising that is wasteful and extravagant (exaggerated).

(vi) To encourage the interest of the youth in the business of communication, to assist in educating and training programmes.

(vii) To sustaining the prestige of the advertising profession.

(viii) To establish a forum where representatives of advertisers, agencies, media and Government can meet and examine problems of mutual interest.

(ix) To co-operate with government bodies in discussion of such matters as taxes, radio & TV advertising, legislation, political campaign advertising, controls on pharmaceuticals, tobacco or liquor advertising.

(x) To serve as a spokesman against unwarranted attacks or restrictions on advertising.

Apart from AAAI, the Department of Consumer Affairs, Government of India publicise on creating awareness on false promotional campaigns among the Indian public.

EXHIBIT 3.4.19 **Ad Campaign for Awareness Towards False Advertisement**

ADVERTISING AGENCIES ASSOCIATION OF INDIA

CASE-8: Cadbury's Worm Infestation Controversy

Cadbury ropes in Big B as brand envoy

Source: http://economictimes.indiatimes.com/thumb/msid-19191202,width-640,resizemode-4/cadbury-dairy-milk.jpg

Cadbury has a 70% market share in chocolates. Cadbury Dairy Milk chocolate has a market share of 30%. "Daily 2.7 million chocolate bars are sold, of these 1 million bars are Cadbury Dairy Milk," Sanjay Purohit, General Manager – Marketing, said.

Following the warm controversy, the company carried out quality checks at its facilities as well as its C&F warehouses and distributor warehouses and found products free of infestation. "Our quality control goes beyond the factory gate to the distributors, but our control over the retail chain does diminish," he said adding that Cadbury products are sold across 650,000 outlets.

"Improper storage and its consequences is not unique to Cadbury. Every food items is affected. Unfortunately, though there is adequate legislation, ensuring compliance at the retail level is impossible," he said.

In the aftermath of the controversy, the company launched Project Vishwas, a retail education programme under which 190,000 retailers in key States were covered. The program entailed generating awareness and providing assistance in improving storage quality. Cadbury suffered major impact in sales in Maharashtra and Kerala. These States account for 20–23% of the total sales[1].

In a bid to prevent any incidence of infestation, Cadbury has introduced a double packaging for its 13 gm ₹ 5 Cadbury Dairy Milk chocolate, its flagship brand. The chocolate is wrapped in aluminium foil and enclosed in a polyflow pack, which is sealed on all sides. The larger Cadbury Dairy Milk packs will come in poly-coated aluminium foil, which will be heat-sealed and then wrapped in the branded outer package. Both these are first ever in chocolate packaging in India.

[1] http://www.thehindubusinessline.in/2004/01/08/stories/2004010800690600.htm

The new packaging is going to add to the company's cost of production to the extent of 12 – 15%. But at the current juncture, Cadbury does not plan to raise the price of its products. "Our margins could be under pressure, but we are hoping to ramp up volumes, thereby neutralise the cost increase," Puri said. The new ₹ 5 pack of Cadbury Dairy Milk chocolate bar has been rolled out in Maharashtra and will be rolled out nationally in three weeks, officials said. The new packaging is being introduced for its moulded chocolates.

The capital expenditure of setting up new machinery is to the tune of ₹ 12 – 15 crore. Bachchan has been signed on as the brand ambassador for a period of two years, during which period he will endorse and promote Cadbury chocolates. On queries about Bachchan endorsing far too many products, Puri said that he has a universal appeal cutting across ages.

CASE DISCUSSION

1. Why do you think Cadbury's faced the worm controversy issue? Who is to be blamed for this mess?
2. What was the impact of this controversy on the brand image of Cadbury's?
3. What are the measures taken by Cadbury's to recover its brand image in the market place? Do you agree with the solutions of the company to overcome the worm infection controversy?
4. As a PR officer, what measures would you take apart from the measures already taken by the company?

CASE-9: The Success Story of Cafe

Coffee culture began in the country on the backbone of Udupi hotel coffees and coffees that were offered by the many restaurants and Darshinis in the big and small cities alike. These were basic coffees. Even bad coffees. But they served the populace well. They offered a hot beverage that packed coffee and chicory in it. Chicory for strength and coffee for flavour and aroma. This backbone set the pace for early coffee consumption in a country that had a pathetic per capita consumption of 54 gm per person per year in South India and all of 1.2 gm per person per year in the rest of India.

Then in came Café Coffee Day (CCD) in 1996. The cyberwave was in and this cybercafé which offered good coffee in an air-conditioned set-up was a big hit. Others followed, even as CCD took its time to ramp up. In came Barista and modernised the format even more and added youth-zing with its guitar to pick up and play, Pictionary box to play with, Scrabble and more. The café sought to position itself as a youth hangout. An alternative to the college canteen, the movie theatre, the park outside and 'addas' of every other kind. Young people thronged the café and a café culture emerged. The café became a place to meet, a place to hang out, and even a place to sit and watch others. The café today has emerged as a place where lots happens – dates, people watching, music, messaging and more. I am sure a lot of romance as well. And many culminate in marriages, just as many culminate in break-ups that are nursed with more cups of steaming latté. Both ways, coffee wins. You drink it when you are happy and you drink it when you are sad!

The café is today a crucible of young India. Young India as it evolves from its cocooned environment to a more open and frothy future. As frothy as the cappuccino cream one licks off a tasty cup of coffee. Coffee is fast becoming a preferred drink of the young and the ones on the go. It is emerging as a centre point around which a lot revolves for the young and young at heart. And that's coffee culture. In the future we will have jazz cafés, pop cafés, trance cafés. Possibly, cine-cafés in our cities and many more.

Discussion Questions

1. What are the reasons paved way for modern Coffee Retailers to establish a strong foothold in India?
2. List down the Key Success Factors that would influence the successful launch of coffee café in your home town.
3. What would be your USP to differentiate your café from your rivals? Develop a media campaign.

CASE-10: Comparative Advertisement – A Brand Building Tool or an Unethical Business Practice

Comparative advertising is on the rise in the FMCG category with the latest Rin versus Tide commercial based on comparing 'whiteness', being aired extensively across prime time on television since last weekend. Hindustan Unilever has been facing a threat to its market share across all categories and detergents are currently one of the most affected categories in its portfolio. In fact, with consumers downtrading heavily, HUL has been dropping prices on select packs of Rin and Surf Excel since January this year, but that move has been not been enough to stem the fall in shares.

According to Gopal Vittal, Executive Director, Home & Personal Care, HUL, "There has been a pressure on shares but the maximum shares have been hit in the detergent category where consumers have been downtrading. But now we are seeing a gradual recovery in shares." In spite of HUL's volume shares growing sequentially by one per cent in the laundry segment during the December quarter, overall it faced a 2.4 per cent decline in share in the soaps and detergents during the same quarter. Today its value share in the ₹ 12,000-crore detergent category stands at 34.6 per cent with brands such as Surf Excel Blue, Surf Excel, Rin and Wheel. According to The Nielsen Company, in January, the value shares of Tide (8.8 per cent) was almost double that of Rin (4.8 per cent). While last year in January of 2009 the gap between the two brands was less when Tide enjoyed an 8 per cent value share and Rin was behind at 5.1 per cent value share.

To combat the fall in shares, HUL in January did drop prices of Rin Powder (1kg) from ₹ 70 to ₹ 50. In its latest ad, the price cut is being prominently displayed (₹ 25 for 500 gm) for the Rin Pack while Tide Naturals is pegged at ₹ 20 for 500 gm. Considering both the FMCG companies are on the board of the Advertising Standards Council of India (ASCI), it is P&G that has been more responsible in its advertising compared to HUL, claim industry observers. According to an ASCI official, the last time the two companies got into a spat of this kind was in 2004 when the comparative advertising was based on the whiteness proposition where the competitor's brand was blurred. "But at that time the case went against HUL, as it had to withdraw its ad," said this official. According to ASCI, comparative advertising is permissible as long as it is backed by scientific evidence. ASCI has already written to HUL based on the complaint received from two consumers and HUL has been given 15 days to back its ad by 'scientific justification' for its latest Rin commercial, as per the legal requirement mandated by ASCI. Rin commercial is in line with the advertising code followed by the industry. "The claim is factual, accurate and substantiated as it is based on laboratory tests done through globally accepted protocols in independent third party laboratories," an HUL spokesperson said. A P&G spokesperson, on the other hand, said, "We are aware of the disparaging advertisement on air against Tide Naturals and have filed a case against the same. The matter is currently being heard in the court and we are not in a position to comment on the outcome."

Discussion Questions

1. Why do advertisers involve in Comparative advertising?
2. Is it a tactical war for building a brand or an unethical business practice? Justify your view.
3. Will it affect the image of the brands that are involving in comparative advertising?

CASE-11: Complan Vs. Horlicks

In recent times one of the spots to come up was the new Horlicks commercial. It was a piece of aggressive comparative advertising, with Horlicks dissing its competitor Complan—the usual sneaky ways of showing similar packs while intoning about "other rival products" was given a go-by as a couple of boys and their mothers indulged in gleeful one-upmanship over who had made a smarter decision. The Complan boy said his health drink had 23 nutrients, and the Horlicks boy said, hah, mine has that too. The Complan boy asserted that his drink made him taller, while the Horlicks boy replied, hah, mine makes me taller, stronger, sharper. The Complan Mom says it cost her ₹ 170 while the Horlicks kid says, huh, ours cost only ₹ 131. The Complan kid looks jubilant at Complan being higher on something—thus revealing, perhaps, his lack of sharpness? The Complan Mom looks annoyed and just to rub it in, a billboard of Horlicks floats past.

"Are they allowed making comments like this about another product?" The makers of Complan had indeed sought a stay on airing of the television commercial, only to be told by the Judge, "We are discussing the health of children here and if such ads are taken seriously, then as per claims made by the companies, children consuming these products should be growing taller and taller." Sure enough, a print ad of Complan was released—presumably a TV spot will follow—which explained how milk protein (Complan) was better than inferior protein from the kind of sources used by inferior health drinks and urged parents not to compromise on health. I am sure that the battle of the health drinks is not over and we will see some ping-pong games between the two.

Discussion Questions

1. Why do advertisers involve in Comparative advertising?
2. Is it a tactical war for building a brand or an unethical business practice? Justify your view.
3. Will it affect the image of the brands that are involving in comparative advertising?

CASE-12: Toyota Suv Recall – A Never Ending Dilemma

In 2008, Toyota made a record profit of $ 16.5 billion. A year later, the economic crisis saw it record its first loss in 50 years ($4.4 billion). Now just when things were beginning to look up. It's getting battered again, after being forced to recall millions of vehicles. Toyota's problems have given GM and other companies an opening, particularly in the US, its largest market. For instance, players like GM, Ford started offering customers $1000 to trade Toyota and buy one of their vehicles. Not surprisingly, the company's sales for January fell 16% while its rivals did much better. It looks like Toyota will have to conduct refresher course in Kaizen (continuous improvement), its core principle.

January 2010 Sales Growth in the US.

Company	Sales Growth %
Toyota	-16%
GM	14
Ford	25

1. Identify the key issue faced by Toyota Motors in the U.S. Markets.
2. Develop a promotional Strategy to recover the brand image of Toyota Motors and sales in the U.S. Markets.

Dear Students, your strategy will have to discuss on following issues:

1. The objective of the PR campaign
2. Who will you rope in as your brand ambassador and why?
3. Create a tagline to reinforce the quality of Toyota Motors.
4. Will your offer any special sales incentives like freebies or free service checkup etc?
5. How long will the campaign last for?
6. Which media and media vehicle will you choose and why?
7. How much will you spend for this campaign and what is the logic behind it?
8. How will you measure the effectiveness of your campaign?

LEARNING EXERCISES

1. Get the List of leading Indian Brands and their brand values from www.milwardbrown.com, and compare it with last three years' ranking data.
2. Get the List of Top-10 Global Brands and their brand values from "Top 100 most valuable global brands 2011 - BrandZ" and compare them with their last three years ranking data.
3. Find which sectoral-brand occupies the top slot both in Indian Brands and Global Brands. Check whether there is any change in the sector/brands during the last three years.
4. Choose an FMCG product of your choice and draft a Distribution Channel Strategy.
5. Develop a Distribution Channel Strategy for Perishable goods like fruits, flowers and Vegetables.
6. Develop your own Channel Design (blueprint) for Mumbai Dabbawallas to operate the same business in your city or town.

❑❑❑

Chapter 4

OVERVIEW OF BUYER BEHAVIOUR, MARKETING RESEARCH AND MARKETING OF INDUSTRIAL PRODUCTS AND MARKETING OF SERVICES

Chapter Objectives

After studying this chapter, you should be able to learn the following:

4.1. Role of Buyer Behaviour in Marketing

4.2. Marketing Research

4.3. Marketing of Services

4.4. Marketing of Industrial Products

UNIT 4.1: ROLE OF BUYER BEHAVIOUR IN MARKETING

(a) Why Study Buyer Behaviour

The sellers' market has disappeared and buyers' market has come up. This led to a paradigm shift of the manufacturers' attention from product to consumer. The evolution of marketing concept from a mere selling concept to a consumer-oriented marketing has resulted in buyer behaviour becoming an independent discipline. The growth of consumerism and consumer legislation emphasizes the importance that is given to the consumer.

EXHIBIT 4.1.1 Individual Buyer Consumer Behaviour

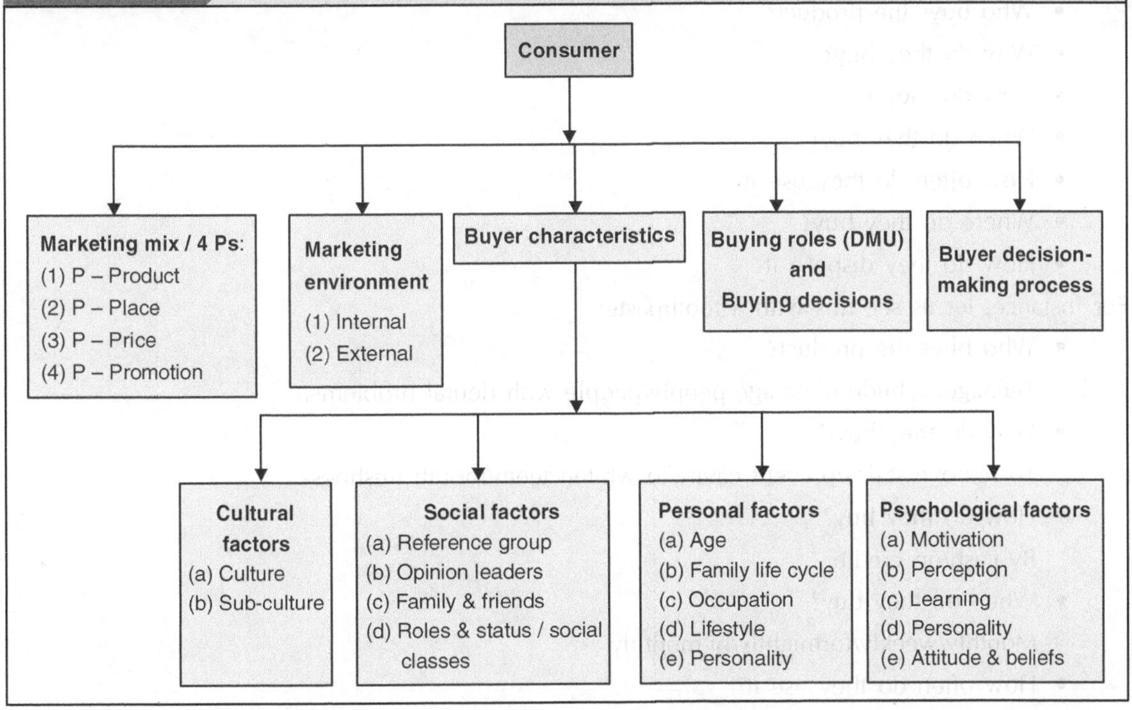

Consumer behaviour is a study of how individuals make decision to spend their available resources (time, money and effort) or consumption related aspects (What they buy? When they buy? How they buy?). The heterogeneity among people makes understanding consumer behaviour a challenging task to marketers. Hence, marketers felt the need to obtain an in-depth knowledge of consumers' buying behaviour. Finally, this knowledge acted as an imperative tool in the hands of marketers to forecast the future buying behaviour of customers and devise marketing strategies in order to create long-term customer relationship.

An important component of the marketing process is to understand why a customer or buyer makes a purchase. Without such an understanding, businesses will find it hard to respond to the customer's needs and wants. Marketing theory traditionally splits the study of buyer or customer behaviour into two broad groups for analysis:

- Personal Consumers
- Industrial Buyers/Consumers

Personal Consumers

Personal consumers are those who purchase items for their personal consumption. Industrial buyers are those who purchase items for resale and not for own use. Businesses now spend considerable time and money trying to learn about what makes customers to buy their products.

The questions they try to understand are:

- Who buys the product?
- Why do they buy?
- How do they buy?
- When do they buy?
- How often do they use it?
- Where do they buy?
- How do they dispose it?

For instance, let us see this with a toothpaste:

- Who buys the product?
  Teenagers/children/old-age people/people with dental problems.
- Why do they buy?
  To remove stains/prevent cavity/to whiten teeth/mouth freshness.
- How do they buy?
  By cash/on credit.
- When do they buy?
  Monthly/weekly/fortnightly/bi-monthly
- How often do they use it?
  Morning/after food/before bed-time
- Where do they buy?
  Super market/nearby mom-&-pop retail store/drug store
- How do they dispose it?
  Dustbin/fire them into ashes.

For a marketing manager, the challenge is to understand how customers might respond to the different elements of the marketing mix that are presented to them. If a marketing manager can understand these customer responses better than the competition, then it is a potentially major source of competitive advantage.

(b) Customer vs. Consumer

A customer is the one who buys a product and a consumer is the one who uses the product. Since he brings an end to the product by consuming/using it, he/she is also called as end-user or the consumer. A consumer can always be a customer but a customer need not always be a consumer. Say for instance, your father takes you to a shop, buy coke and drink it by making you to watch. Here, your father is both customer and consumer. Assume that your father offers you the coke. In this case your father is the buyer/customer and you are the consumer.

Customers can be classified into two:

- Individual Customers/Buyers.
- Industrial Customers/Buyers.

Individual Customers

Individual Customers are those who buy goods and services for own use or personal household use.

Industrial Customers

Industrial Customers are those who buy goods for resale and not for own use.

Why One must Understand the Difference between the Customer and a Consumer?

In some cases, it is essential for the marketers to understand the difference between the customer and a consumer. Say for instance in the case of kids diapers, infant foods, the consumer is the child but the customer is the mother who has got the deciding authority to buy the product. One can also remember the advertisement of GSK's Horlicks and Heinz's Complan, where both mother and children are used in advertisement. We knew that the customers are mothers and consumers are children. So who should we target? Obviously, it is the mother, who makes the purchase decision on behalf of the children.

(c) Consumer Behaviour – Definition

Consumer behaviour can be defined as, "the study of individuals, groups, or organizations and the process they use to select, secure, use and dispose-off products, services, experiences, or ideas, to satisfy needs and the impact that these processes have on consumer and society."

(d) Understanding Individual Buyer Behaviour

To market their offerings, marketers must understand buyer behaviour. To understand buyer behaviour, they have to learn the factors influencing purchase decision of the prospects, customer decision-making process, people influencing buyer behaviour and how a new offering of a company is accepted by the target market using diffusion of innovation.

1. Factors Influencing Purchase Decision

Following are the factors that decide the characteristics of the buyer behaviour and influence purchase action:

(i) Cultural factors (culture and sub-culture)

(ii) Social factors (reference groups, family members and friends, social roles and status)

(iii) Personal factors (age, family life cycle, occupation, lifestyle and personality)

(iv) Psychological Factors (motivation, perception, learning and attitude)

EXHIBIT 4.1.2 **Factors Influencing Purchase Decision**

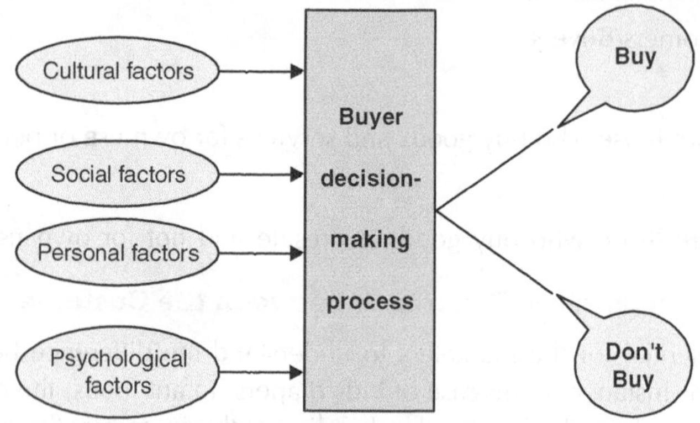

(i) Cultural Factors

Culture in the study of buyer behaviour includes knowledge, belief, moral values, morale (self-esteem/self respect), law, customs and all other habits acquired by person as a member of society and are transmitted from generation to generation within that society which serves to guide and direct the behaviour of all members of that society. Howard and Sheth have defined culture as "A selective, manmade way of responding to experience, a set of behavioural pattern".

Culture is learned through the following three ways:

1. *Formal learning:* Parents and elders teach children the proper way to behave. For instance, you have been taught that you need to study well to be successful and happy in life.
2. *Informal learning:* We learn by imitating the behaviour of our parents, friends, or by watching TV and film actors in action
3. *Technical learning:* Instructions are given about the specific method by which certain things to be done such as painting, dancing and singing.

Characteristics of Culture: Following are the characteristics of culture:

1. Culture is learned.
2. Culture regulates society – Norms, standards of behaviour, rewards and punishments.
3. Culture makes life more efficient.
4. All members follow same norms.
5. Culture is adaptive.
6. Culture is environmental.
7. Multiple cultures are nested hierarchically.
8. Culture also determines what is acceptable with advertising.
9. Culture determines what people wear, eat, reside and travel.

Cultural values in India are good health, education, respect for age and seniority. But in our culture, today, time scarcity is a growing problem, which implies a change in eating habits which has led to mushrooming of fast foods in India. Some of the key changes in our culture in India are:

Convenience: as more and more women are joining the work force there is an increasing demand for products that help lighten and relieve the daily household chores, and make life more convenient. This is reflected in the soaring sale of washing machines, microwaves, pressure cookers, mixer grinders, food processors and frozen food.

Education: People in our society today wish to acquire relevant education and skills that would help improve their career prospects. This is evident from the fact that so many professional, career oriented educational centers are coming up, and still they cannot seem to meet the demand. As a specific instance count the number of institutions offering courses and training in computers that has opened in your city.

Physical appearance: Today, physical fitness, good health and smart appearances are on premium today. Slimming centers and beauty parlours are mushrooming in all major cities of the country. Cosmetics for both women and men are being sold in increasing numbers. Even exclusive shops are retailing designer clothes. Skin care products like Fair & Lovely and Fairever are moving fast in the market.

Materialism: There is a very definite shift in the people's cultural value from spiritualism towards materialism. We are spending more money than ever before on acquiring products such as air-conditioners, cars and DVD players, which adds to our physical comfort as well as status.

Culture and Colours: Different countries attach different meanings to colours. Colours have different interpretations. A list of colours and their interpretations are given below:

Pink: Associated with a female, and blue with the male in the US, whereas it is just the opposite in Holland.

White: Symbol of mourning or death in the Far East and China, but happiness, purity and peace in the United States and India.

Purple: Associated with death in many Latin American countries.

Blue: Symbolises feminity in Holland and masculinity in the United States, Sweden and India.

Red: Colour for brides and children in India. Sign of masculinity in the UK and France, negative in Nigeria, Germany and positive in Denmark, Rumania and Argentina.

Yellow: Sign of death in Mexico, infidelity in France, celebrations in many countries including India.

White lilies: Suggestion of death in England.

Sub-culture: A sub-culture is an identifiable distinct, cultural group, which, has its own belief, values and customs that set them apart from other members of the same society in which they operate. Sub-culture categories are:

Nationality: Indian, Srilanka, Pakistan

Religion: Hinduism, Islam, Christianity.

Age: Young, middle-aged, elderly

Sex: Male, Female

Occupation: Farmer, teacher, business

Geographic regions: South India, North-Eastern India.

Coca Cola is sold all over the world. Procter & Gamble and other companies give cross-cultural training to their employees. By making cross-cultural mistakes, many companies have difficulty in pushing their products for example: Kellog's could not succeed in the beginning stage, when it launched milk based corn breakfast in India, as the country's dining habits differ significantly in each state in India.

(ii) Social Factors

The social factors that influence buyer behaviour for purchase action are reference group, social roles and status. The family, friendship groups, formal social groups and consumer action groups. All of them are called as reference group. Reference group refers to any person or a group that serves as a frame of reference for individuals in their purchase decisions.

The Family: An individual's family and relatives are the most important groups to influence one's purchase decisions. The family has a greater extent of influence on the establishment of a wide range of values, attitudes, and behaviour. Example, family members play a vital role in deciding or selecting bridal wears, necklace, automobile, consumer electronics and family excursion or pleasure trips.

Friendship groups: Friendship groups are informal groups because they are, usually unstructured and lack specific authority levels. Consumers are more likely to seek information from those friends they feel have values or outlooks and personality, similar to their own.

Formal social groups: A person joins a formal social group to fulfill specific goals such as making new friends, meeting 'important' people or promoting a specific cause. Example: Lions' Club Membership and All India Management Association membership.

Consumer Action Group: Consumer action group has emerged in response to the consumerist movement. This type of consumer group has become increasingly visible since the 1960s and has been able to influence marketing practices of both manufacturers and retailers. They are organized to address and correct a specific consumer abuse or exploitation.

Social Classes: Social class can be defined as the division of members of a society into a hierarchial distinct status, classes and assumed that Persons within a given social class tend to behave more alike. Generally the social classes or status of people are classified into three broad categories:

S.No	Social Class	Status	Factors affecting Social class
1.	Low Income Class	Low	Lower level occupation with no authority, less income, and no education or minimum education, *e.g.*, labour class.
2.	Middle Class	Medium	Graduates, or postgraduates, work as managers of companies with authority, drawing handsome salary of which certain amount can be saved and invested. For example, executives or middle level managers of companies.
3.	Upper Class	High	Authoritative person, drawing handsome salary, very often professionally qualified, working in a very senior position or a person born into a rich family, with a good background of education.

(iii) Personal Factors

Following are the four important personal factors that influence the buyer behaviour:

(a) Age

(b) Occupation

(c) Lifestyle

(d) Personality

In fact, all the above can be better understood using FLC or Family Life Cycle. Family Life Cycle explains the family pattern at various stages of a person's life and the consumer behaviour associated with it at each stage. Following schedule explains the FLC and the buyer behaviour.

S.No.	FLC Stage	Family Type	Economic Situation	Buyer Behaviour
(a)	Bachelor	Young and single	Earning good salary. No financial commitment	Two wheeler, fastfood and vacation with friends
(b)	Parenthood	Young – Just Married and attained parenthood	Good financial position but less savings	Gold jewellery for wife, infant food, diapers and toys for kid
(c)	Post-Parenthood	Grownup children	Financial position improve. Chance of wife working for additional income and savings	Buy home, home decoration, buy car, buy electronic and electrical appliances, family vacation package
(d)	Dissolution	Retired and lone surviving	Good financial position	Not interested in spending Buy medicines and Spiritual tours

(iv) Psychological Factors

Motivation, perception, learning, and attitude constitute the psychology (mind) of an individual that influence purchase action.

Motivation and Buyer Behaviour—Maslow's Hierarchy of Needs—To Understand the Buyer Needs: To understand how motivation influence the buyer behaviour, marketers need to understand Abraham Maslow's Hierarchy of needs. Understanding consumer behaviour helps the markets to target his/her target customer groups clearly. Consumer behaviour is influenced by needs. To understand the consumer behaviour, the marketers must understand the underlying needs of human beings. Abraham Maslow propounded five levels of human needs which are as follows:

1. *Physiological needs:* It refers to the basic requirements for human survival, *e.g.* food, sleep and water.
2. *Safety Needs:* It refers to a place that protects the human beings from predators and elements.
3. *Social Needs:* It is a stage where there will be a sense of belonging and affection. People join together as friends.

EXHIBIT 4.1.3 Abraham Maslow's Hierarchy of Needs

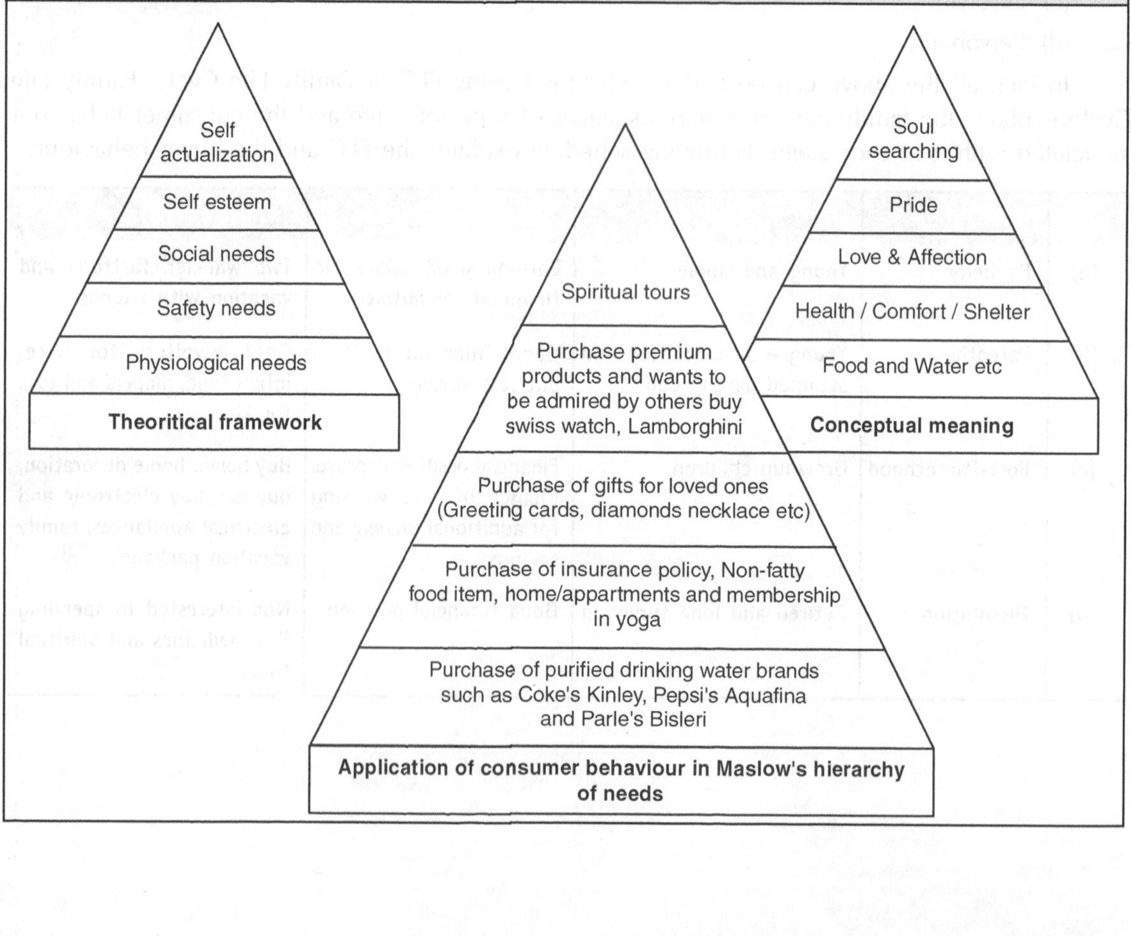

4. *Self-Esteem:* Only a few people attain this stage. People get satisfied and get appreciated for their achievement. Example: getting recognized by people for writing an award winning book.
5. *Self-Actualization:* Only a very few people attain this stage. Example: Sachin Tendulkar, got self-actualized for being the first sports person to get the Bharat Ratna award.

Attitude and Buyer Behaviour: An Attitude is a person's enduring or long-term favourable or unfavourable emotional feeling based on beliefs and evaluations toward some object or idea (that leads to purchase action). People have attitude towards almost everything, religion, politics, clothes, music, food etc. Company tries either to fit their offerings into existing attitudes or to try to change people's attitude towards the company's offering.

Why Study Attitude?: Mostly marketers believe and operate under the assumption that ***"favourable attitude of a person towards a brand leads to purchase decision and action"***. It is found that attitude does leads to behaviour, *i.e.,* purchase action. Fishbein describes the element of attitude as TACT.

T = Target
A = Action
C = Context
T = Time

Let's see this with an example: "Buying an imported American car from Ford this weekend".

T = Target = An imported American car.
A = Action = Buying
C = Context = Ford
T = Time = Weekend.

How buyer behaviour is influenced by attitude?: Evaluations of salient (most important) beliefs constitute the overall attitude of a person. For instance, let's take 7Up, a carbonated soft drink. A person who is thirsty first identifies the salient belief of 7Up that it has no caffeine in it. Then by evaluation he finds that since it does not have caffeine, it is not hazardous to health. This makes him to buy the 7Up. There are two types of attitude that influence an individual in purchase decision:

(1) Positive Attitude
(2) Negative Attitude

(1) *Positive Attitude:* Positive Attitude is a person's enduring or long-term favorable emotional feeling based on ***beliefs*** and ***evaluations*** toward some object or idea that leads to ***purchase action.***

Example: A person think of having 7Up to quench his thirst.

Person's Salient ***Beliefs*** - 7Up has no caffeine
Evaluation - No caffeine – No harm to health
Action - Purchase/consumption

(2) *Negative Attitude*: Negative attitude is a person's enduring or long-term unfavourable emotional feeling based on ***beliefs*** and ***evaluation*** towards some object or idea that leads to ***purchase action of competing brand.***

Example: A person has two choice Coke and 7Up to quench his thirst.

Person's Salient Beliefs - Coke has caffeine/7Up don't.

Evaluation - Coke has caffeine – harmful to health and 7Up has no caffeine – not harmful to health.

Action - Purchase 7Up and Ignore Coke.

Exceptions

There are exceptions to above rule. Certain behaviour can not be predicted accurately from attitudes because it is difficult to predict the buyer behaviour when the alternatives are very similar and the individual has positive attitude towards all the alternative brands.

Example: If an individual feels (attitude) that both Coke and Pepsi has got similar taste and knows that both of them contains caffeine, then it becomes difficult for marketers to predict which brand is going to be purchased by the customer.

2. Customer Decision-Making Process/Individual Buying Process

As Peter F. Drucker said, all marketing activities revolve around customers. It starts and ends with customers. Hence, there is no business without customers. Therefore, important part of the marketing process is to understand why and how a customer or buyer makes a purchase. Without such an understanding, businesses would find it hard to respond to the customer's needs and wants. Therefore, marketers need to understand the processes that their customers go through when making a purchase decision. The consumer decision-making process involves series of related and sequential stages of activities. The process begins with the discovery and recognition of an unsatisfied need or want. It becomes a drive. Consumer begins search for information. This search gives rise to various alternatives and finally the purchase decision is made. Then buyer evaluates the post purchase behaviour to know the level of satisfaction. The process is explained in the Exhibit 4.1.4.

EXHIBIT 4.1.4 **Customer Decision-Making Process**

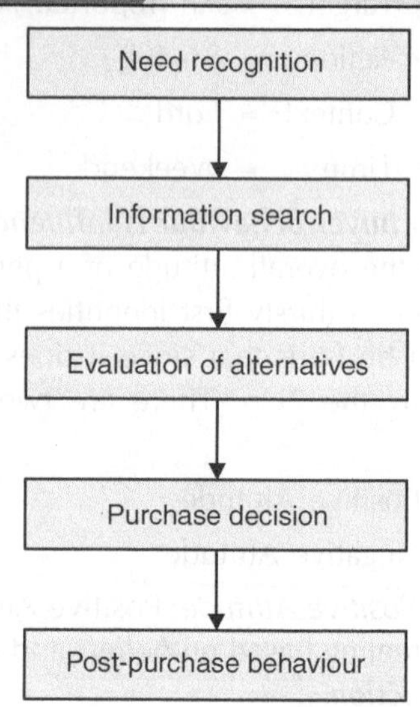

Following are the five stages involved in buyer's purchase decision making process:

1. ***Need recognition:*** In the first stage the buyer realize unsatisfied needs. The customer's knowledge on how to satisfy the needs will be limited as he is unaware of the products

or services that can satisfy his/her needs. For instance, a person wants to reach Mumbai from Delhi in 3 hours. Now he recognizes/identify that he needs a quick transport facility to reach Mumbai.

2. ***Information search:*** The customer's identified needs can be satisfied only when desired product is known and also easily available. Different products are available in the market, but consumer must know which product or brand gives him maximum satisfaction. And for that the person has to search out for relevant information of the product, brand or location. Consumers tend to use many sources for information to satisfy their needs and wants *e.g.*, neighbours, friends and family. Marketers should find ways to make customers aware of the company's offerings. Marketers today provide relevant information through advertisements, retailers, dealers, packaging and sales promotion, and window displaying.

   Mass media like newspapers, radio, and television provide information. Nowadays internet has become an important and reliable source of information where, latest, reliable and adequate information are provided by the company. For example: He searches for seat vacancy in Indian Airlines, Air India, Air Deccan, King Fisher in the official websites of the airlines

3. ***Evaluation of alternatives:*** This is a critical stage in the process of buying. Following are important elements in the process of alternatives evaluation.
   - A product is viewed as a bundle of attributes. These attributes or features are used for evaluating products or brands.
   - Factors like corporate image, brand image, country of manufacturing, and after-sales service also become critical in evaluation.

   Marketers should understand the importance of these factors to the consumers while manufacturing and marketing their products. For example, the passenger who has to reach Mumbai in 3 hours will check for price, time of departure and class of all airlines service provider.

4. ***Purchase decision:*** Based on the evaluation, consumers understand the pros and cons of alternative products or brands in the market. A positive attitude will get developed towards the product that has the most value (benefits). This attitude towards the brand influences a decision as to buy or not to buy. Thus the prospective buyer heads towards the final selection. In addition to all the above factors, situational factors like finance options, loan interest rate, dealer terms, falling prices etc., are also considered.

   For example, the passenger will decide now, by which carrier to go and what is the mode of payment for the air ticket, viz. by cash/credit card/debit card.

5. ***Post-Purchase behaviour:*** This post-purchase behaviour of consumers is more important for a marketer as consumers gets brand preference only when that brand lives up to their expectations. If the needs and wants of the consumers are satisfied then it will lead to a brand preference that influence repeats purchase.

Marketers realize that a satisfied buyer is a silent advertisement. But, if the used brand does not yield desired satisfaction, then it will create a negative feeling and that will lead to negative attitude towards brand, which could influence brand switching. This phenomenon is called **cognitive dissonance**. In fact, the consumers after using the product would have a confusion on whether the product or the service consumed by them have satisfied their needs and wants. This period of confusion is described as buyer remorse or post purchase dissonance or cognitive dissonance. Marketers try to use this phenomenon to attract users of other brands to their brands.

For example,

Case-1: If the passengers successfully reach the destination in time, then he would be a satisfied customer and will subsequently prefer to travel by that particular carrier. They will also spread their satisfaction through word-of-mouth to the friends, colleagues and family members which would create new customers for the airline carrier. This would end-up not only in customer retention but also acquisition of new customers.

Case-2: Suppose if there is a flight delay due to unwanted circumstances, and if not treated by the company workers properly, then it would lead to a greater dissatisfaction that ends up in lost customers for the airlines. Because these dissatisfied customers would spread their dissatisfaction through word-of-mouth to the friends, colleagues and family members which would affect the brand image and the business as a whole.

A word of caution: Marketers should not assume that the buying process is a straight line. It is cautioned that it is highly incorrect to assume that all buying process to begin with awareness and go through all the stages in linear progression and end up in repeat purchase.

3. People Influencing the Buyer (DMUs)

Most often, purchase decision of an individual is influenced by many people. These people are called as DMUs or Decision Making Units. The people comprising DMUs are as follows:

- Initiator
- Influencer
- Decider
- Buyer
- User

- **Initiator:** A person who is the first to suggest or think of buying a product or a service is the initiator. For instance, a father could suggest his son or daughter to buy a two-wheeler to travel to school. Here the father is the initiator
- **Influencer:** A person whose advice would influence the buyer to take a final decision is the influencer. The mechanic, the two-wheeler showroom sales representative, family members, friends are the influencers. These people are called as reference group.
- **Decider:** The person who decides what to buy? When to buy? Where to buy? & how to buy? is the decider. Here the son/daughter is the decider.
- **Buyer:** One who buys or purchases the product is the buyer. Since the son/daughter is school going child, it the father who has the financial capacity to buy the product. Hence the father is the buyer.
- **User:** One who consumes or uses the product is the user. Hence user is also called as consumer or end-user. Here, the school going son/daughter is the user of the two-wheeler.

4. Diffusion of Innovation

Diffusion of innovation explains how consumers accept new offerings (products and services). According to L.G. Schiffman, "diffusion of innovation is a process by which, acceptance of innovation is spread by communication to members of the target market over a period of time."

Diffusion refers to consumer adoption. Innovation refers to converting a new concept or idea into a tangible product offering or an intangible service offering. An innovation is said to be successful, if a new product or a service becomes feasible and gains commercial acceptability in the market. Now, it is time for marketers to learn how diffusion of innovation takes place *i.e.,* The Diffusion of Innovation Process and The Various types of New Product Adopters.

(i) Diffusion of Innovation Process.

(ii) Various types of New Product Adopters.

(i) Diffusion of Innovation Process

There are five stages in the diffusion of innovation process. They are as follows:

(a) Awareness stage
(b) Interest stage
(c) Evaluation stage
(d) Trial stage
(e) Adoption stage

(a) *Awareness stage:* In this stage, the prospective customers comes to know about the company offering and become aware of it through their friends, neighbours, co-workers and other commercial sources.

(b) *Interest stage:* In this stage, the individuals or the prospects gets stimulated and an interest gets developed in the prospects mind to gather more information regarding the company's offering such as its utility, performance, durability, price etc. from their reliable sources.

(c) *Evaluation stage:* By using the gathered information, the prospects would start evaluating the worthiness of owning the new offering of the company. In short, the prospects would check in what way the offering would be useful to them and based on the outcome of the evaluation, they would decide on whether to buy the new product or ignore it as a whole.

(d) *Trial stage:* Once the evaluation of the worthiness of the new offering is over, the prospects would mentally get prepared themselves to try out the new product on small scale. This is where sample sachets come into picture. The prospects would first experiment by trying the new offering.

(e) *Adoption stage:* After using the new offering on trial basis, the consumers, if satisfied, would go for full fledge usage of the new product or the service that has been offered. Since they feel that it is suitable and comfortable for them for continuous consumption, they start adopting the habit of using it on regular basis.

(ii) Various types of New Product Adopters

As we have learnt how a new product or a service is accepted or adopted by the prospects in the Diffusion of Innovation Process, we now learn the various types of adopters prevailing in the market.

They are as follows:

(a) Innovators
(b) Early adaptors
(c) Early majority
(d) Late majority
(e) Laggards

(a) *Innovators:* After being aware of the new offering, in general it has been found that only 2.5% of total customer market seek more information on the new product and try it out. Hence they are called as pioneers or innovators. They are always open to new ideas. These people are always willing to experiment by trying out new products. They are often found to highly educated and follow a life style of high social class in status.

(b) *Early adaptors (Opinion Leaders):* The early adaptors are the next 13.5% buyers who adopt new offerings. These people do not plunge into buying the new offering as soon as they are launched in the market. They do try out new offerings quite early but only after a careful gathering and verification of information about the products from the reliable sources. Often these early adaptors are seen as opinion leaders in their social circle or community. Since they posses high social respect, they are treated as social leaders of a society or community who can influence the decision making of a large section of the society.

(c) *Early majority:* The early majority are the next 34% of the buyers who show willingness to accept the new product offering. These people are found to be thoughtful, shrewd, and will not get easily swayed by the promises made by the new product. These people wait and watch to learn the experience from the early adaptors, before trying out the new product. This today happen via facebook.com and other leading social networking sites. This is infact one of the key reasons for all leading brands in India to establish their exclusive facebook.com or other social media sites or pages. These people are of middle class, have reasonable education, occupation and income.

(d) *Late majority:* The late majority are the next 34% of buyers who adopt the new offering of the company. These people are highly conservative and do not respond any change immediately. Their acceptance of new product depends upon the favourable public opinion towards the product. As they are very skeptical in nature, they would adopt or accept a new product or a service only after a majority of people have tried it and accepted it. They are characterised as people with limited education, possess average social status and draw a limited salary which in turn results in limited purchasing power.

(e) *Laggards:* Laggards comprises of the remaining16% of the total market. They get this title as they lag behind others in accepting new offerings. This is because, they exhibit a lot of deliberation, caution and suspicion before buying a new product. These people will adopt the new innovative product simply because the new product has eliminated the traditional product from the market.

(e) Customer Value

The fundamental idea behind marketing is the idea that an organization will create something as value to a group of customers who, in turn, will be willing to pay the perceived right price. 'Value' in marketing simply means 'benefit' that customers obtain from the purchase of the company's offerings. This value is also called as 'Utility'. Value can be created in a number of different ways. Say for instance, the customer value for Complan (health food drink) buyers is that they are offered with a Complete Planned Food for the growth of their children and incase of Horlicks, it makes the consumer Taller, Stronger and Smarter. The two fundamental classification of customer value are Tangible value and Intangible value.

EXHIBIT 4.1.5 Customer Value

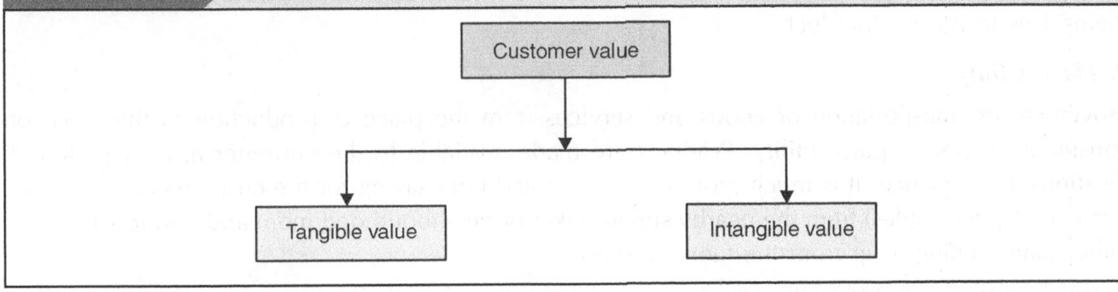

Tangible customer value: Firms make products whose tangible value is supplemented by services and direct sales promotion activities. Tangible value takes place in retail business when a manufacturer offers a freebie to the regular customers as thanks giving. Example, Godrej offering Cinthol Deo Spray free with Cinthol Combo Pack.

Intangible customer value: An intangible value could take place in a Personal Computer (PC) business. A computer manufacturer provides a computer loaded with software and provides a warranty, technical support, and software updates at free cost of time for a limited period of time. It should be noted that value (benefits/usefulness/utility) must be examined from the point of view of the customer. Some customer segments value certain product attributes more than others.

Simply put, the customer segment has to think that the benefits received by them are greater than the sacrifice made by them (usually in terms of money), this is called as 'Value for Money'.

EXHIBIT 4.1.6 Forms of Customer Value/Utility

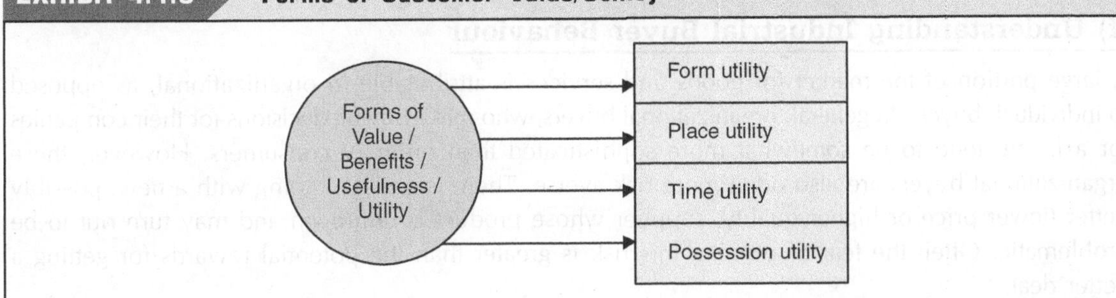

The marketing process involves ways that value can be created for the customer. They are:

1. Form Utility
2. Place Utility
3. Time Utility
4. Time Utility

1. Form Utility

Development of new products brings form utility. It is the one where a product is made available to the consumer in some form that is more useful than any commodities (components) that are used to create it.

For example, A customer would benefit (value) from buying a chair rather than the commodities (raw materials) such as wood and other components used to create the chair. *Exception:* but now-a-days, in the Netherlands and in some European countries, consumers prefer (DYK) 'Do-It-Yourself' Kit. It is the one where, consumers buy the product in a disassembled form and put them together themselves to make a product.

2. Place Utility

Movement or transportation of goods and services from the place of production to the place of consumption creates place utility. Products are made available to the customer at their preferred locations. For instance, it is much more convenient and time saving for the customers to buy food items (fruits, vegetables) from the nearby supermarket or neighbourhood mom and pop retail outlets rather than picking it up from the farmers' places.

3. Time Utility

Storage of goods from the time of production till the time of consumption creates time utility. It is all about making the products available when they are needed by the customer. Examples, woolen sweaters are made throughout the year but stored and made available to the customers only during the winter season. Similarly, perishable goods like vegetables, fruits and milk are kept in cold storage till they are sold in the market.

4. Possession Utility

Transfer of title/ownership of goods and services from seller to buyer results in possession utility. The idea is that the consumer can go to one store and obtain a large assortment (variety/collection) of goods from different manufacturers during one shopping occasion. It facilitates buyers to become owners of variety of products, *e.g.,* Super malls and hypermarkets such as Tesco of UK and 'Wal-Mart' of USA, Big Bazaar of India.

(f) Understanding Industrial Buyer Behaviour

A large portion of the market for goods and services is attributable to organizational, as opposed to individual, buyers. In general, organizational buyers, who make buying decisions for their companies for a living, tend to be somewhat more sophisticated than ordinary consumers. However, these organizational buyers are also often more risk averse. There is a risk in going with a new, possibly better (lower price or higher quality) supplier whose product is unproven and may turn out to be problematic. Often the fear of running this risk is greater than the potential rewards for getting a better deal.

In the old days, it used to be said that "well bought goods are half sold". This attitude is beginning to soften a bit today as firms face increasing pressures to cut costs. But it is important to realize that one must not compromise on quality as the market would react immediately by avoiding the products and services that are not fulfilling the requirements of the buyers.

The industrial buyers are resellers. They act as either wholesalers or retailers who buy from one organization and resell to some other entity. For example, large grocery chains sometimes buy products directly from the manufacturer and resell them to end-consumers. Wholesalers may also sell to retailers who in turn sell to consumers.

Even companies act as industrial buyers. Producers buy raw materials from sub-manufacturers/ suppliers to create a finished product. For example, computer manufacturers buy hard drives, motherboards, cases, monitors, keyboards, and other components from sub-manufacturers rather than manufacture the components themselves, and put them together to create a finished product. Organizational buying usually involves more people than individual buying. Often, many people are involved in making decisions as to

- Whether to buy now or later?
- What to buy?
- How much to buy?
- From whom to buy?
- At what cost?

Say for instance, if a company wants to construct a quarters for its employees, then an engineer would make a specification based on the project requirement, which may be approved by a manager, and the final purchase will be made by a purchase specialists who spends all their time finding the best deal on the goods that the organization needs.

Often, such long purchase processes can cause long delays. In the government, rules are often especially stringent, *e.g.* vendors of stationeries have to meet lots of specifications laid down by the government. In many cases, government buyers are also heavily bound to go with the lowest price through auction or bidding which is called as tender or reverse auction. Even if it is obvious that a higher priced vendor will offer a superior product, it may be difficult to accept that bid.

Following are the steps involved in Industrial Buying Behaviour in Indian Context

1. Recognition of a need
2. Confirmation of the need
3. Agreement on specifications
4. Recommendations as to supplier
5. Purchase authorization and
6. Placing of the order.

Buying centre: The department that takes responsibility for the purchase of industrial goods or the raw materials is called as buying center. The participants in the buying process can be described in terms of their roles in the buying process. These roles have been defined as initiators, users, buyers, deciders, influencers, and gatekeepers.

Initiators – define the buying situation and start the buying process

Users – actually use the product

Buyers – can commit the organization to spend money

Deciders – have the authority to choose among potential product offerings and vendors
Influencers – add information or constraints in the buying process
Gatekeepers – can control the flow of information into the buying process

Everybody in the industrial buying process is called as Buying Decision-Making Unit (DMU) and is often called the buying center.

UNIT 4.2: MARKETING RESEARCH

(A) Marketing Research

Marketing research is a process of systematic gathering, rewarding and analysis of data on problems related to marketing of products and services.

The goal of marketing research is to provide the facts and direction, to the marketing manager to make their important marketing decisions. Marketing research is a research on the elements of the marketing mix, competitors, markets, and the customers as a whole.

(B) Definitions of Marketing Research

"Marketing research is the function that links the consumer, customer, and public to the marketer through information – information used to identify and define marketing opportunities and problems; generate, refine, and evaluate marketing actions; monitor marketing performance; and improve understanding of marketing as a process. Marketing research specifies the information required to address these issues, designs the methods for collecting information, manages and implements the data collection process, analyzes, and communicates the findings and their implications."

American Marketing Association—
Official Definition of Marketing Research

"Marketing research is about researching the whole of a company's marketing process."

—Palmer (2000)

(C) Types of Marketing Research

All forms of marketing research can be classified as either problem-identification research or as a problem-solving research. In other words, ***Exploratory research*** provides insights into and comprehension of an issue or situation. ***Conclusive research*** draws conclusions: the results of the study can be generalized to the whole population.

A company collects ***Primary Research*** for its own purposes. When data are collected from the prospective customers for the very first time directly by the researcher then it is called as primary research. This contrasts with ***Secondary Research***: research published previously and usually by someone else. Secondary research costs far less than primary research, but seldom (rarely) meet the exact needs of the researcher/company.

Following are the types of marketing research techniques conducted by the corporate players for marketing their product and service offerings:

Test Marketing: A small-scale product launch used to determine the likely acceptance of the product when it is introduced into a wider market

Concept Testing: To determine if consumers consider a concept useful that satisfy their specific needs and wants.

Store Audits: It is conducted to determine whether retail stores provide adequate service to the customers.

Demand Estimation: It is undertaken to determine the approximate level of demand for the product.

Mystery Shopping: An employee of the company conducting the research contacts a salesperson and indicates they are shopping for the product they sell without revealing his identity that he is from the same company that makes and sells the product. Then they record the entire experience. This method is often used for quality control or for researching competitor's products.

Sales Forecasting: It is carried out to determine the expected level of sales in a particular future period.

Customer Satisfaction Studies: Exit interviews or surveys that determine a customer's level of satisfaction with the quality of the transaction.

Distribution Channel Audits: To assess distributors' and retailers' attitudes toward a product, brand, or company.

Price Elasticity Testing: To determine how sensitive customers are to price changes.

Segmentation Research: To determine the demographic, psychographic, and behavioural characteristics of potential buyers.

Consumer Decision Process Research: To determine what motivates people to buy, when, how much, how frequently, they buy, how do they use them and how do they dispose it off.

Positioning Research: How does the target market see the brand relative to competitors? What does the brand stand for?

Brand Name Testing: What do consumers feel about the names of the products?

Brand Equity Research: How favourably do consumers view the brand?

(D) Marketing Research Process

Marketing research is conducted using a systematic approach. They are as follows:

1. Problem Identification & Objective Setting
2. Formulation of Research Design
3. Formulation of Sample Design
4. Data Collection
5. Data Analysis & Interpretation
6. Reporting

1. Problem Identification

In the first stage of the marketing research, the researchers have to decide on what they are going to investigate. In order to know this, they gain in-depth knowledge on the particular subject, which they intend to investigate.

To gain sufficient knowledge on the selected subject, the researcher can do the following:

- Review (study) all the literature related to the subject
- Undergo critical evaluation of previous studies done on the same subject
- Discuss with knowledgeable persons

Once the researchers are able to get complete knowledge on the selected subject, they will be able to formulate the marketing problem clearly and precisely which can then be translated into a marketing research objective. For example,

S.No.	Research Problem	Research Question	Research Objective
1.	Advertisement and product price	Does a TV ad campaign boost the image of a company affect its product price?	To identify whether a TV ad campaign of a company can influence its image and its product prices

2. Formulation of Research Design

In the second stage, the researcher should select suitable research design from the options: (i) Exploratory research design (ii) Conclusive research design. A research design is a Blue Print or procedure for conducting a research study.

(i) *Exploratory Research* is the one which is used for developing a hypothesis/an assumption/ statement which may or may not be proved.

(ii) *Conclusive Research* is used for solving the developed hypothesis/problem. It reveals the cause and effect relationship and is more formal method compared to exploratory.

At the end of this stage, the researchers should have selected an appropriate research design and also have specified the reason & merits of using such research design in their study.

3. Formulation of Sample Design

In the 3rd stage, the researcher has to decide on the sample design. Following are the key sample design decision to be made by the researcher:

(i) Nature & Size of the Universe or Population

(ii) The Size of the Sample

(iii) The Sample Frame and Sampling Unit/Element

(iv) The Sampling Technique

'Population' or 'Universe' refers to the aggregate of all items, sharing some common set of characteristics, *i.e.* total number of people who share a set of common characteristics. 'Sample' refers to the respondents who are parts of the population and who represent the population. 'Sample size' refers to number of respondents from whom the primary data are to be collected. When the data are collected from 30 or less than 30 respondents ($n <= 30$), then the sample size is small. When the data are collected from more than 30 respondents ($n > 30$) then the sample size is large. Sample frame refers to a predetermined set of rules for selecting the sample respondents. Sampling units/elements refer to the type of respondents who are selected as sample from the universe or population. The sampling technique refers to the method used for selecting the sample respondents from the population.

At the end of this stage, the researchers should have specified the reason for selecting the above said aspects and also the merits of using them in the study.

4. Data Collection

In the 4th stage, the researcher has to decide on the following:

(i) Sources of data, viz. primary data or secondary data or both.

(ii) Primary data collection tool/method, viz. questionnaire, interview schedule, mail survey and telephone interview.

(iii) Data collection technique, viz. survey, observation or focus groups

The researcher should also decide on the following:

(i) Number of field workers used for collecting the required data

(ii) How they are selected, trained and supervised

(iii) How their work was verified

The researcher will have to give reason for selecting the particular data collection method and also state the merit of using it in the study.

5. Data Analysis and Interpretation

Once the data are collected, they are neatly and logically tabulated. Tabulation of data can be:

(i) Univariate data tabulation. (Single variable: Age, Gender)

(ii) Bi-Variate data tabulation (Two variable)

(iii) Multivariate data tabulation (More than two variables)

The researcher can use the following tools for data analysis and interpretation:

(i) Graphs and Charts

(ii) Statistical tools

(iii) Test statistics for testing hypotheses

By analyzing the data, interpretations (explanations) and findings are made by the researcher. The findings are the basis for conclusion, which would be the answer for the problem, which was framed by the researcher in the initial stage of the study.

6. Reporting

This is the final stage where all the above said stages are neatly recorded and documented in a report form, which is to be submitted on or before a pre-specified period of time.

Conclusion

Thus, marketing research process is the one where the problem faced by marketing manager is translated into a market research problem in the form of questions that gives the information that is required by the marketing manager to make the appropriate marketing decision.

(E) Application of Marketing Research/Preparation of Marketing Research Report

This unit deals with designing a research report. Following are the contents of a typical marketing research report:

1. Title Page
2. Table of Contents
3. Forward or Introduction
4. Statement of Objectives
5. Research Methodology
6. Data Analysis and Interpretation
7. Limitations
8. Findings
9. Conclusion and Suggestions
10. Appendix

1. Title Page

The title page indicates the subject or study title, the (date) period during which the report is prepared, by whom the report is prepared and for whom the report has been prepared.

2. Table of Contents

It shows various chapters of the study and also the list of charts, graphs etc. included in the study.

3. Foreword or Introduction

This section gives the background of the problem (*i.e.* how and when it came into existence), importance of the problem, various dimensions of the problem, and whether any previous research was done on the same subject/problem. Some times one may also include the company profile and product profile depending on the business situational requirement.

4. Statement of Objectives

This section shows the ultimate objectives/problems for undertaking a particular study. It should be as brief as possible. Some times it is possible to classify the objective of the study into primary and secondary objective.

5. Methodology

This section describes the research procedure. It includes the following details:

(a) Research design

(b) Data collection method

(c) Sampling

(d) Field work

(e) Data analysis and interpretation

(a) Research Design

This section describes whether the research study is based on exploratory or conclusive. The researcher should specify the reason for selecting a particular research design along with the merits of using the same.

(b) Data Collection Method

In this section, the researcher should declare the source of data collection *i.e.,* primary data or secondary data or both. The researcher should also specify the data collection method employed. And most importantly, the researcher should specify the reason for selecting a particular data collection method.

(c) Sampling

In this section, the researcher has to give the following details:

1. Nature of the universe/population and its size
2. The exact sample size
3. The exact sample units/elements and sample frame
4. Method employed for determining the sample size and sample units are to be specified
5. Finally the researcher should specify the reason for selecting the particular sampling technique

(d) Field Work

This section describes about the following:

1. Number of field workers used for collecting data from the respondents
2. How they were selected, trained and supervised?
3. How their work was verified?

6. Data Analysis and Interpretation

This section explains about the various tools used for analysis of data such as test statistics, statistical tools, graphs, charts and mathematical tools.

7. Limitations

Every project has limitations. Specifying the limitations will show the readers, how carefully the research has been done by the researcher. Moreover, it will help the decision makers to realize the impact of such limitation over the findings or conclusions.

8. Findings

Findings are the results of the study. The researcher should present the findings with reference to the specific objectives of the research study.

9. Conclusions and Suggestions

Conclusions should be drawn with direct reference to the objectives of the study. The reader should be able to read the objectives, turn to the conclusion section and find specific conclusions relative to each objective. While it is always necessary to present the conclusion, it may not always be possible for the researcher to offer suggestions or recommendations. Hence it's not compulsory to offer suggestions or recommendations.

10. Appendix

The purpose of appendix is to provide a place for those report items, which, do not fit in the research report as they are too detailed or too special. Some of such report items are:

- Copies of forms and questionnaire used
- Details of sample with validation
- Bibliography
- Special tables those are not included in the findings

UNIT 4.3: MARKETING OF SERVICES

(a) Service

Service is an intangible offering of a service provider which might satisfy the needs and wants of the customers or clients. For instance, a person buying an anti-virus pack for protecting his computer from potential virus and worm attacks.

(b) Service—Definitions

According to Philip Kotler and Stanley, "A service is any activity or benefit that a party can offer to another party, essentially intangible, does not result in ownership of anything, its production may not may not be tied to a product."

(c) Differences between a service and a product

S.No.	Product	S.No.	Service
1.	A product is produced	1.	A service is performed
2.	A product is tangible	2.	A service is intangible
3.	Ownership is possible	3.	Ownership is impossible

4.	A product can be stored or inventoried	4.	A service cannot be stored or inventoried
5.	Production & consumption need not be made simultaneously	5.	Production & consumption should be made simultaneously
6.	A product can be standardized	6.	A service cannot be standardized
7.	Easy to measure in quantity	7.	Not easy to measure in quantity or value
8.	A product is first produced and then stored, sold and finally consumed	8.	Service is first sold and then produced and consumed simultaneously

(d) Characteristics of Services

The characteristics of a service can be termed as VIIP

V – Variability

I – Intangibility

I – Inseparability

P – Perishability

V – Variability

As needs and wants change from person to person, from place to place, and from time to time, no service can be standardized and is variable in nature. Example: Doctor's treatment to patient cannot be standardized as the patient has to be treated as per his/her disease. Business fraternity from various industries meet a management consultant with their own issues faced in their specific industry where the consultant can not suggest standardized suggestions or advices to resolve the problems. Similarly, an Income Tax Auditor can not offer standardized guidance to his/her clients as they may be individuals or corporate.

I – Intangibility

A service is intangible as it can't be physically touched, seen or tasted. For instance, booking train or air ticket online, placing an order to buy books online and E-Banking services.

I – Inseparability

Since a service is intangible, it can not be stored. Therefore, a service is first sold, and then produced and consumed simultaneously. Thus, production and consumption of a service is considered to be inseparable. Example: watching a movie in a cinema theatre, where the tickets are first sold, and then a movie is screened (produced) and watched (consumed) simultaneously by the audiences. In an hospital, the patient has to be with the doctor where the affected person can be tested and diagnosed and prescribed with relevant medicine. Here, both the doctor and the patient cannot be separated and medication be offered. One can also take Medical Operation as an example for inseparability where both the doctor and patient have to be in the same place, the operation theatre.

P – Perishability

A service is perishable in the sense that it can't be stored or restored. Say for instance if you miss to reach the cinema theatre on time, or in time, then you would miss some scenes in the beginning which can't be viewed at that point of time. Similarly, A service is can not be restored. For example, a bad hair cut by a hair dresser can not be restored and when a patient die due to wrong operation by a doctor will also justify that a service is perishable in nature.

(e) 7Ps of Service Marketing Mix—Expanded Services Marketing Mix

Following are the services marketing mix:

(i) P – Service Product

(ii) P – Place

(iii) P – Price

(iv) P – Promotion

(v) P – People

(vi) P – Process

(vii) P – Physical Evidence

(i) Service Product

Anything that is intangible and offered into the market for satisfying the needs and wants of the people is a service product. A service product is a bundle of offering. In case of service product, experiences are offered. Example, Direct-To-Home Television Entertainment service providers Tata Sky, Dish TV, Videocon DTH, Reliance DTH, Sun Direct, Airtel DTH provides Television Channels as a Pack such as family pack, sports pack, kids pack and south pack.

(ii) Place

Place in services marketing deals with two key factors and they are Location and Channel of Distribution. Location in services explains how interaction between the service provider and the customer takes place. There are three kinds of interaction that can take place between the service provider and the customer. They are as follows:

- The customer goes to the service provider. Example, Hotels, Restaurants, Banks.
- The service provider goes to the customer. For instance, Laundry services, Cable TV services
- The customer and the service provider transact business at arm's length. Example: internet banking, online airline and railway ticket bookings.

Channels of distribution or channel in service marketing explains how a service is taken to the customers and sold to them or how a service is delivered to the customers. In a service business, channel of distribution involves three people, viz. the service provider, intermediaries, and the customers. Today commercial banks in India are offering the banking services to its customers through internet e-banking and mobile banking services where intermediaries (employees) are eliminated. ICICI's Insurance arm offers insurance through internet where intermediaries are eliminated.

(iii) Price

Price is the exchange value of a service product. Since a service is intangible and cannot be measured in numbers or quantity, it becomes difficult to fix price for a service. Say for instance, the life insurance premium for 25 years old man is less compared to a person aged 50 years, as the chance of mortality increases along with the increase in age.

(iv) Promotion

The service provider use ISMC or Integrated Services Marketing Communication Mix, viz. direct sales promotion, indirect sales promotion or advertising, public relations, personal selling and direct marketing for promoting their service offerings in the market.

(v) People

People include all the people in the service process. They are called as internal and external customers. The internal customers are the employees. These internal customers or employees play the role of front-end and back-end employees. Front-end employees have direct contact with the customers, example, the reception employees in hotel and the chef, maintenance section employees are called back-end employees.

(vi) Process

Process refers to the service delivery mechanism. Service providers use blueprint, to define the service process which represents the flow of activities diagrammatically.

(vii) Physical Evidence

Physical evidence refers to the environment where the service is offered and the equipments used for offering the service.

In marketing of products, only 4Ps (Product, Place, Price and Promotion) are present in the marketing mix. But in service marketing, it is further extended by three components, viz. people, process and physical evidence. Marketers use these 7Ps to market their service offerings to the target market.

UNIT 4.4: MARKETING OF INDUSTRIAL PRODUCTS

Following are the basics for marketing of industrial products in the market:

1. Make the branding relevant to the industrial buyer's profitability
2. Understand the role of the Buying Centre in the organizational (or) industrial buying process
3. Make the value proposition of the brand relevant to the DMUs and the company's requirements
4. Adapt corporate branding approach
5. Build the corporate brand using brand intangibles
6. Build brand's sales revenue using brand communications

1. Make the Branding Relevant to the Industrial Buyer's Profitability

Your industrial product must have a core competency which would make your business entity distinct from others. This core competency must be translated into industrial buyer's benefits in the value-chain. In simple words, your industrial brand must offer superior value or benefits to the chosen target market or the industrial buyers. This value must be positioned in the industrial brand's communication in the target market minds, the industrial buyers.

2. Understand the Role of the Buying Centre in the Industrial Buying Process

Use the market research and gatekeepers to identify the people involved in the buying centre or the (DMUs) Decision Making Units, and what role do they occupy in the DMU. This will definitely help the organisation to define the industrial good's attributes in accordance with the criteria put forward by the DMUs or the buying centre of the organisation.

3. Make the Value Proposition of the Brand Relevant to the DMUs and the Company's Requirements

Once the DMUs and their company's requirements are identified, these requirements are to be injected into the brand as its value proposition to make the industrial brand relevant to the industrial buyer or the buying centre of the organisation.

4. Adapt Corporate Branding Approach

As far as branding of industrial product is concerned, it is advisable to adapt corporate branding strategy where the brand communication address two key concerns, viz. the credibility and reliability. In other words, promote trustworthiness and consistency in quality and delivery.

5. Build the Corporate Brand Using Brand Intangibles

The industrial brand has to build its credibility and reputation by banking up on its expertise knowledge, trustworthiness, and ease of doing business. By this way, the industrial buyer will start treating the company as its value-cum-strategic partner rather than a mere supplier of raw materials.

6. Build Brand's Sales Revenue Using Brand Communications

The company manufacturing the industrial brand should build and enhance the sales revenue of the brand using effective industrial communication techniques which are as follows:

- Media Advertising (TV, radio, newspaper, magazines)
- Trade Journal Advertising
- Directories and Yellow Pages
- Direct Mail
- Brochures and Sales Literature
- Audio-Visual Presentation Tapes
- Giveaways
- Sponsorship or Event Marketing
- Exhibitions, Trade Shows, and Conventions
- Publicity or Public Relations

In industrial brand communication, one need to understand the following:

(i) Industrial brand communication budgets are usually smaller compared to the consumer brand marketing.

(ii) Mass media will not provide extensive reach and availability for industrial brands. Hence, specialised media such as industry trade shows, educational activities, and professional journals may be most effective in reaching specific industrial market segments.

(iii) Training, compensation and incentives must be employed to keep the sales department engaged in the long-run.

CASE-1: Why Nokia Money was Axed?

In 2012, Nokia decided to exit its mobile money business. Nokia shut down its service in just two years after it was launched was debated in India. The decision by the Finnish handset maker made many to get baffled as it happened at a time when all the analyst projections showed that financial services on mobile is set for a phenomenal growth over the next two years. Just before one month of Nokia shutting down its business there were at least six new launches of mobile money services by various market players including leading players like Mastercard, Visa, Airtel and HDFC Bank.

According to Tavess Research, 'mobile money' as a business in emerging markets like the Middle East, Asia, and Africa are expected to cross 1 billion users by 2015, with India accounting for more than 100 million subscribers. Nokia clearly had its potential market as India in mind when it launched the service in 2010. So what made them to shut down its business in just two year since its commencement?

The main problem is, mobile payment, which is an extremely service based business to sustain. In two years, Nokia had managed to sign up 1.2 million customers. Of these, one million users were Yes Bank and Union Bank customers using their banks' platform for mobile money transactions and about 2 lakh subscribers were using the standalone Nokia Money service. It was getting less than 50,000 new customers a month. Nokia has roughly 2 lakh retail outlets across the country, which translates into one customer signing up a store a month. It is clear that adoption (refer diffusion of innovation in this chapter) was slower than Nokia had expected, particularly considering the size of the Indian population and the low banking penetration in the country, says a report.

When one compares Nokia's performance to other players in the market, we get to see a clearer picture. For instance, M-Pesa in Kenya. In two years since its launch in 2007, it had 6.5 million users. NTT DOCOMO of Japan is another player which has had success in mobile payments services with its mobile wallet services. In India, Bharti Airtel managed to acquire 50,000 subscribers in Maharashtra alone within the first 10 days of launching Airtel Money. But not many have been able to crack this business and those who have succeeded are all mobile telecom operators and not the mobile handset makers.

Why Nokia could not Succeed?

That's because mobile operators have been able to have better control over the 'mobile money' business by offering a far more efficient model. To be more specific, they deal well with cash flow as their retailers are already handling money for recharging pre-paid cards and post-paid billing. Secondly, the mobile telecom operators like Airtel owns the customers as subscribers and hence can offer more conveniences to the subscribers such as a single bill for mobile payment transactions and telephone calls at the end of month. They can even recharge their DTH connection at ease at arm's length. A handset maker would not find it easier to match this and that's the reason why none of the other major device makers have entered this market[1].

Discussion Questions

1. Did Nokia do the right thing by exiting its mobile money business in just two years, without waiting patiently till its business broke even?
2. What have you found as the reason for Nokia exiting its mobile money business?
3. What would have you been done if you were the strategic decision maker of Nokia's mobile money business? Justify.

LEARNING EXERCISES

1. Apply the 7Ps of Services Marketing Mix in Nokia's Mobile Money Business.
2. Apply the characteristics of services on Movie Mall located in your place and explain how you would overcome the challenges derived out of the service characteristics.
3. Go to Tyre Company or Automobile Spares manufacturing company and prepare a write-up on Industrial Buying Centre and Industrial Branding.
4. Go to a mall or super market in your town. Find out the most preferred tea brand of customers visiting the mall or the super market by observing their behaviour.

❑❑❑

[1] Source: Based on "Why Nokia Money was axed?" By THOMAS K THOMAS, the hindu-businessline http://www.thehindubusinessline.com/features/eworld/article3007049.ece

Chapter 5

MARKETING STRATEGIES

Chapter Objectives

After studying this chapter, you should be able to understand the following:

5.1. Marketing Strategy

5.2. Michael E. Porter's Generic Strategy/Business Selection Strategy

5.3. Market Selection Strategies

5.4. Market Entry Strategies

5.5. Product Life Cycle Strategy

5.6. Product Stretching Strategies

5.7. Market Attack Strategies

5.8. Customer Relationship Management

UNIT 5.1: MARKETING STRATEGY

What is Marketing Strategy?

Marketing strategy is a plan or policy of a company that involves a tactical line of attack that is either pro-active or reactive against the rival companies or market players.

Why Learn Marketing Strategy?

Marketers' foremost job would be to select the right business to succeed in the market. For this, the marketers use Michael E. Porter's Generic Strategy. Then they must select the best profitable and sustainable market segment. For this purpose they shall refer to market selection strategies such as

(a) Michael E. Porter's five forces model—A Strategic Market Analysis Tool.

(b) Bottom of the Pyramid.

(c) Blue Ocean and Red Ocean Strategies.

(d) Niche Market Strategy.

Once the marketers have chosen the right market segment to enter, they must opt for the appropriate market entry strategy to launch their new offerings, which can be early entry, parity entry or late entry. When a new product is launched into the market, it goes through various (stages) market scenarios during its life and the marketers must know how to manage the sales and market-share without falling during these stages. This strategy is called as Product Life Cycle Strategy. Any multi-business firm needs to decide on which business to expand with additional investment, which one has to be maintained without any additional investment and which one is to be phased out. For this purpose, marketers use BCG Matrix. No matter in which market the marketers operate, they have to face their rival sooner or later. In order to outsmart the rivals in the market place, they need to understand the product stretching strategies and market attack strategies.

This chapter discusses on all the above strategies in detail with Indian examples so as to help the readers understand the same and attempt applying them while marketing their offerings in today's hyper-competitive environment.

UNIT 5.2: MICHAEL E. PORTER'S GENERIC BUSINESS SELECTION STRATEGY

During 1980s, Michael E. Porter came out with his Generic Strategies, which includes three main strategic options open to the organisation for achieving a sustainable competitive advantage in the market. In fact, it helps any corporate player on what grounds it is intending to compete in the market. The three strategic business options are cost leadership, differentiation, and niche focus.

(i) Cost Leadership

The corporate entity which focuses on the low cost leadership produces the product offerings at the lowest possible cost to become the market leader. Since, the cost advantage is the key focus, the company aggressively attempts to shave-off the superfluous costs in every element of the value chain or the business process.

Example: Tata Steel, Indian Steel Major, is the world's low-cost and high quality steel producer in the world. World's cheapest artificial limbs are made in Jaipur, India, and world's cheapest eye care services are offered at Aravind Eye Hospital, Madurai in Tamil Nadu, India.

(ii) Differentiation

Organisations would focus on adding values or benefits that generates higher price and better margins. In order to add value, company focuses on differentiating its offerings from its rival players using USP or Unique Selling Proposition (Unique attributes of the products). To capitalise on the benefits of using USP, the company needs to segment the markets and target the specific markets to succeed in it.

Example: Khazana, India's leading jeweller uses its low wastages in jewellery making as its USP in its promotional campaign in order to differentiate it from its rivals.

(iii) Niche Focus

In this strategic option, the business house would focus on small market segments that are negligible interest to the major players. This strategy is often used by smaller firms. Since the market size is small, the company follows premium pricing strategy in order to see attractive profit margins. It is not feasible for the niche player to be a 'Low-Cost' producer as it cannot achieve Economies of Scale (cost reduction over a period of time due to large scale production).

EXHIBIT 5.2.1 Michael E. Porter's Generic Strategy

Kalyan jewellers its variety as its USP.

Khazana's offering with no wastage in making of jeweler used as its USP.

Tanishq's special edition gold coins to commemorate the carnatic singer M.S. Subbulakshmi, a classic example of niche focus.

Example: Tanishq, India's leading Jewellery retailer launched a special edition of gold coins to commemorate the Legendary Carnatic Singer M.S.Subbulakshmi, targeting Carnatic Musicians and Fans. In Feb'13 launched jewellery collection for working women.

UNIT 5.3: STRATEGIC MARKET ANALYSIS

(a) Michael E. Porter's Five Forces Model
(b) Bottom of the Pyramid/Rural Marketing

(c) Blue Ocean and Red Ocean Strategies

(d) Niche Market Strategy

(A) Michael E. Porter's Five Forces Model

Classic strategist Michael E. Porter postulated one of the best strategies in 1979 in his Harvard Business Review article entitled "How Competitive Forces Shape Strategy", (Mar-Apr 1979) for staying competitive in the hyper competitive market. He set out a framework for business and marketing managers to assess their companies' overall competitive environment and the relative risks associated with, a particular industry. This framework is known as the "Five Forces Model". The "Five Forces" describe the opportunities and threats in a market faced by the corporate entity which would eventually decide the company's competitive advantage in an industry.

Let us understand the role of Five Forces Model by Application of Michael E. Porter's Strategic Analysis Tool in Jewellery Retailing in India. Some of the major players in India are Tanishq, Nathella, Sree Kumaran Thanga Maligai, Vummidi Bangaru Jewellers, Thangamayil, Jos Alukkas Jewellery, Kirtilal Kalidas & Co., L K S Gold House P Ltd, Malabar gold and diamonds, Kalyan Jewellers, Original Kerala Jewellers, K P Jewellery & Gems, Sumangali Jewellers, Prince Jewellery, Khazana Jewellery, NAC Jewellers, Lalitha jewellery, G.R. Thanga Maligai Jewellery, Saravana Stores Thanga Maligai, Tata Gold Plus etc.

The five forces that determine the success or failure of a jewellery retailing business in India are as follows:

1. Competitive rivalry amongst existing firms
2. Threat of new entrants
3. Threat of substitute products
4. Bargaining power of customers
5. Bargaining power of suppliers

1. Competitive Rivalry amongst Existing Firms

Today's jewellery retailing in India expose that a large number of established players are competing with local players. While the big players compete on Quality, Designs and Fixed Price Tag with Minimal Wastages, the small players compete on competitive price but don't focus on wastage reduction. In order to increase footfalls and sales in their (POS-Point of Sales) Showrooms, jewellers resort to heavy advertisement using (ESP) Emotional Selling Proposition and (USP) Unique Selling Proposition.

2. Threat of New Entrants

In this analysis, as a marketer, one would analyse threat from new entrants. The new entrants may find it difficult to enter into the market due to key reasons such as high investment costs, no brand image (customer trust not available) in the initial stage. The barriers to exit are very high in this industry as selling all gold at once and exiting the business is not feasible. The new entrant is a late entrant, hence cannot compete with established players due to not having economies of scale and learning curve which are indeed the two (CSF) Critical Success Factors to outsmart the rival players in the market. The Government of India's moves have also been not in favour of new entrants. Govt. on 23rd Jan'13 raised the import duty on gold to 6% which increases the price of the gold further. By October 2013, the import duty of Gold jewellery raised to 15%. Government of India wants to fix a cap on gold import as it affects the country's ballooning[1] current account deficit. Gold purchases are one of the biggest contributors to India's current account deficit which hit a record $US22.3 billion ($A21.3 billion), or 5.4 per cent of GDP, in the July-September quarter of 2013, as imports outpaced exports. RBI has asked the commercial banks to not to offer loans for buying gold since 19th November 2012. All The above discussed aspects clearly shows that there is no green signal for the New Retailers to Enter the Golden Arena. This means, the threat of new entrants is very low.

3. Threat of Substitute Products

The threat of substitutes depends on the relative price and performance of the competing products and on customers' willingness to consider substitutes. Alternative to Gold investment are Silver, Platinum, Diamond, ETF Gold, Gold Saving Schemes by jewellers, Gold MF, Gold Coins offered by Banks, Post Office and corporate like Reliance, Gold Bars and Land (Real Estate). This clearly indicates that Threat of Substitutes is high.

4. Bargaining Power of Customers

Customers have little or moderate bargaining power regarding price when they shop at luxury stores. Moreover, customers could not bargain in those stores where fixed price tag is utilized to attract customers. Example: Kalyan jewellers promoting transparency in pricing policy using brand ambassador Mr. Prabhu, South Indian Actor & Fixed Price Tag. In general, bargaining power is high in small jewellery stores and moderate or almost nil in well established premium stores.

5. Bargaining Power of Suppliers

Gold price is determined by Bullion Market in England. The industry has only a few skilled workers where the wastages ('sedaram' in Tamil) will be less while making ornaments by them. Since the world economic condition is volatile, the price of gold is moving upwards day after day as demand for safe investment increases. The wastages in ornament making can be reduced if machines are used. But the power shortage in South India, especially, in Tamil Nadu ruins such option. Thus the bargaining power of suppliers is indeed high.

Analysis Outcome

Based on above analysis the marketers can decide on entering into the jewellery market. The question arising now would be is whether a small jeweller should enter the market now or procrastinate such decision? The answer is 'Yes!' it must enter now. There is no meaning in being just KING OF GOOD TIMES. If one can sail during tough times, he can succeed in any business cycle.

---

[1] http://timesofindia.indiatimes.com/city/jaipur/Rajasthans-traders-cheer-hike-in-import-duty-on-jewellery/articleshow/22904691.cms

Marketing Strategies for Small Jewellers

Following marketing strategies are pursued by key players in the jewellery retail market in India:

- Stop Mass Marketing and Segment the Market and address specific market requirements. For instance, Tanishq launched jewllery for working women.
- Acquire Quality/Hallmark Certification from BIS—to instill confidence and trust in the minds of the consumers on your brand.
- Bring Transparency in business operations. For instance, Kalyan jewellers do this by following Fixed Price Tag strategy.
- Use digital board on the Window Display of the Showroom that indicates daily prices of gold, *e.g.,* Tata Gold Plus Showroom.
- Promote Trust using Quality—Hallmark – BIS, less wastages and Fixed Price Tag – Transparency.
- Advertise on Gold Savings Scheme where you would accept savings from small depositors and give them back gold jewellery on a special price, provided ornaments are made out of the gold savings maintained with you.
- Exchange Offer: Bank/post offices don't buy back gold coins sold by them. Hence, Jewellers draft a clear scheme to improve their business. Jewellers can do so based on a scheme where they buy gold jewellery out of it.
- CSR Initiative: Associate with social welfare organization and donating a part of profit for it.
- Product Offerings: Promoting Platinum and Silver jewelers as fashion jewelers, promoting gold and diamond studded belts, footware, wrist watches etc.

(B) Bottom of the Pyramid/Rural Marketing

Prof. CK.Prahalad, Michigan University, USA, promulgated a strategy "Bottom of the Pyramid", in the year 2004 in his research publication entitled "Fortune at the Bottom of the Pyramid". Usually business entities target only the middle-class and higher income groups for selling their offerings. Often, they tend to ignore the poorer section of the society, as they do not have the requisite purchasing power and even if they posses it, the profit margin was seen as peanuts for them across the globe.

But, Prof. CK.Prahalad, one of the top-10 business thinkers of the world boldly postulated the "Bottom of the Pyramid" strategy which today, every organisation is viewing it as an opportunity for sustainable growth.

World Resources Institute, located in Washington, USA, one of the world's famous socio-economic research centre, classified people of this world based on their population and annual income.

They are as follows:

- *Rich*: There are 50 crores people in the world who earns more than US$20,000 annually.
- *Middle-Class*: There are 200 crores people in the world who earns in the range of US$3260 and US$20,000 annually.
- *The Poor:* There are 400 crores people in the world who earn up to US$3260 annually.

EXHIBIT 5.3.1 Bottom of the Pyramid

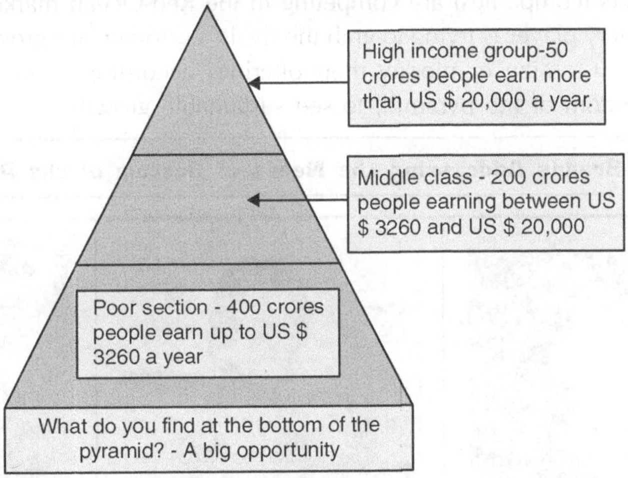

The above information on population and their corresponding income were mapped and it came out in the form of a pyramid.

As one can find 400 crores people at the bottom of the pyramid with the earning capacity of US$3260 per annum, Prof. CK.Prahalad found a huge scope for business opportunity at this point. Thus he convinced the corporate houses that they must focus on all the three layers of the pyramid to attain sustainable growth or long-lasting growth.

Application of Bottom of the Pyramid Strategy in the Indian Markets

This strategy was adopted in India way back in 1959, when HLL (now HUL) faced stiff competition from NIRMA washing powder. In 1959, HLL's Surf, a washing powder, was dominating the market as the market leader. It was offered for ₹13 per kilo gram. At that point of time, it was affordable only for the top of the pyramid (the rich) to buy surf. But Ahmadabad based Mr.Kasan Bhai Patel offered Nirma for just ₹ 3 per kg. Mr. Kasan Bhai Patel made his company ₹ 100 crore business.

During 1980s, HUL (formerly HLL) was offering shampoos only in 100 ml and 200 ml bottles where the price would range from ₹ 10 to ₹ 20. Again, bottom of the pyramid ignored, due to low profit margins. Mr. Chinni Krishnan from Tamil nadu, offered Velvet shampoo in 5 ml. Mr. C.K. Renganathan of Kavin Care offered Chick Shampoo in sachets for just 50 paise per sachet. Now-a-days one cannot see any branded products without sachets.

Coca-Cola in 1990s offered Mini Coke at a price point of ₹ 5 with its ad campaign "Paanch Matlab Coca-Cola" (₹ 5 means Coca-Cola). Britannia and ITC's Sunfeast were offered for ₹ 5 packs.

In the year 2013, Godrej offered mini refrigerators branded "chotukool" for just ₹ 3250 targeting rural India where the need is to principally to store milk, curd, cooked food and cool water. These light weight mini- refrigerators weighing only 7.8 kg are distributed through Indian Post Office[1]. World's cheapest tablet brand Aakash tablets cost just ₹ 2499.

---

[1] http://articles.economictimes.indiatimes.com/2011-05-20/news/29565146_1_indian-consumer-godrej-refrigerator **and** http://www.thehindu.com/business/companies/post-offices-to-market-coolers/article2461929.ece

What should Marketers Learn from the Bottom of the Pyramid?

Today almost all players (companies) are competing in the Red-Ocean market (severely competed market place) where every player is trying to grab the rivals' customers for growth. Instead, marketers can change lane and customize or modify their offerings according to the buying capacity and requirements of the bottom of the pyramid, to see sustainable growth.

EXHIBIT 5.3.2 Brands Addressing the Needs of Bottom of the Pyramid

Vs

Source:

Coke: http://www.afaqs.com/news/news_story_grfx/2009/23835_1.jpg

paanch matlab Coca-Cola: http://www.livemint.com/r/LiveMint/Period1/2009/12/25/Photos/0d04ce8d-e090-45e5-9d35-8474603f520c.jpg

Nirma: http://www.eurobrandsindia.com/blog/wp-content/uploads/2011/07/nirma-detergent-pwd.jpg

Surf: http://3.bp.blogspot.com/_E-KyFEBON7g/SHdnJrgfceI/AAAAAAAAAGY/XKTTvBikxWk/s400/surf.gif

Aakash: http://androsym.com/wp-content/uploads/2011/12/Aakash-Tablet-Ncarry.jpg

Godrej's mini refrigerators: http://www.thehindu.com/multimedia/dynamic/00784/CB17_CHOTUKOOL_784363e.jpg

(C) Blue Ocean and Red Ocean Strategies

From the beginning of industrial era, companies have been engaged in competition over the long lasting profitable growth. They have battled for their own market share through Economies of Scale, differentiation and niche focus. But in today's 21st century hyper competitive business environment, these competitive strategies alone may not be the way to create sustained growth. A market universe is composed of two sorts of oceans (markets)—Red oceans and Blue oceans. Red oceans represent all the industries already existing in the market space. Blue oceans denote all the untapped market space.

Competing within a market space where severe competition exist and trying to steal the customers from rival players is red ocean strategy. As a result, products and brands become commodities and cut throat competition turns the ocean bloody (Red Ocean). It leads to less opportunity for growth that is both profitable and rapid. Blue oceans, in contrast, is creating and developing an uncontested market space that makes the competition irrelevant. It leads to demand creation, and the opportunity for highly profitable growth. In blue oceans, competition is irrelevant as the rules of the game are waiting to be set. It will always be important to swim successfully in the red ocean by out-competing rivals. Hence, corporate entities focused on competition based red ocean strategies *i.e.,* how to compete skillfully in red waters (cluttered market) by being a low cost competitor or differentiation or niche focus, and benchmarking the rivals best business practices.

Red oceans does matter and be a fact of business life. But with, supply-exceeding demand in more industries, and players competing with each other for a share of shrinking markets, to achieve sustained performance, companies need to go beyond this. Which means, to seize new profit and growth opportunities, they also need to create blue oceans.

W.Chan Kim and Renee Mauborgne, Professors of Strategy and International Management at INSEAD conducted a study of 150 strategic moves spanning more than a hundred years and 30 industries. The authors argue that lasting success comes not from battling competitors but from creating "blue oceans"—the untapped new market spaces, which is ripe for growth. As per the authors, such strategic moves, are called as **"Value Innovation"**. It means to create a strong boost in value that often render rivals obsolete for more than a decade.

Thus to outsmart rivals, companies today follows Blue Ocean Strategy to make the competition irrelevant[1]. For instance, Sir Richard Branson's Virgin Atlantic, offers space tourism where none of the rival literally exists[2].

---

[1] www.valuebasedmanagement.net.

[2] http://www.engadget.com/2013/04/29/virgin-galactic-spaceshiptwo-commercial-space-plane-first-test-flight/

EXHIBIT 5.3.3 Virgin Galactic

The world's first commercial spaceline owned by Sir Richard Branson's Virgin Group and Abu Dhabi's Aabar Investments PJC

Source: http://www.ttrweekly.com/site/wp-content/uploads/2013/05/inside-no-101.jpg

(D) Niche Market Strategy

1. Niche Market

Niche market refers to a small well designed market segment (customer-group) with high purchasing power, which may be a negligible interest to the major players as they tend to overlook this small group of customers' needs for addressing the larger-size market segments. Say for instance, in many parts of India, obesity has become a major problem. If all the textile majors focus only on standard sizes of Shirts and Trousers, that it called as mass market. If any textile major focuses on the size of the obese people, it is the niche market. If airlines are going to have standard seat size for all the travelers, then it is mass marketing strategy, if an airline offers larger sized seats for obese passengers, then it is niche marketing strategy. Some of the successful niche brands in India are Royal Enfield Bullet Bikes, M&M's Electric Car – REVA etc.

2. Features of a Niche Market

Following are the key features of niche marketing:

1. The niche market player or the company should make clear market segmentation, targeting and positioning.
2. Niche market or customers must have high purchasing power

3. Market size or Number of customers in the niche market must be of sufficient size.
4. Niche market must have future growth potential.
5. The niche market must be a negligible interest to the major players.
6. The player or the company targeting niche market must have a specialized skills and resources to serve the niche in a superior fashion.
7. Once niche market need not continue to be a niche market in the long-run, which means that if found profitable, major players could start focusing on it.
8. To retain its market-share the player or the company must continually create niche businesses and explore new niches in the available cluttered market.

In totality, being a niche marketer is all about, "it is better to be a king of small territory rather than being a minister in a larger territory."

UNIT 5.4: MARKET ENTRY STRATEGIES

Product Commercialization

Product commercialization is the final stage of New Product Development. It involves full fledge manufacturing and marketing of the new product. Marketers at this stage, have to deal with market entry decision.

Marketers in this stage focus on following 3 key issues:

- Situational analysis of market entry.
- Strategic importance of the entry decision.
- Formulating the time for market entry.

Market Entry Decision and Market Entry Strategies

In today's hyper-competitive market, the market entry decision is said to be a crucial one as it involves careful analysis of market factors. There is a direct relationship between market entry decision and long-term competitive advantage.

Various types of market entry:

(i) Early Entry
(ii) Parity or Parallel Entry
(iii) Late Entry

(i) Early Entry

It is generally believed that the early entry would pave way for competitive advantage. It helps the early entrant to build bottle necks or barriers so as to defend the market share, against the rivals. Early entry barriers can be of economies of scale (cost advantage acquired due to large scale production), experience curve effect (learning curve effect), continuous enhancement in production and technology etc.

This strategy helps the market player (company), to build strong loyal customer base that would influence others to buy the company's offerings (products and services). In short, early entrants would be able to occupy the customer minds and set industry standards as there would be no competitors at this stage.

(ii) Parity or Parallel Entry

When a company launches its offerings in a market, marketing rivals will simultaneously launch their brands, in the same market. It is a face-to-face competition. It is useful when the market is characterised by proliferation (rapid launch of brands in a very short span of time) of brands. It can also be used as an offensive strategy in a multi-product market scenario.

(iii) Late Entry

It refers to the postponement of launch of a product in the market for long-term competitive advantage. It is done so as to wait until the market opportunity grows to an attractive size. The most important advantage of this strategy is that the late entrant can always learn from the early entrant which leads to lower cost of innovation, altering the product decision, lower market rejection risk and more precise market and marketing research results. Furthermore, the tastes and preference of the market can be known, which helps to modify and improve the quality or features (attributes) of the product accordingly. Say for instance, HUL's effort has helped its followers like ITC to market its offerings in rural market, as it is smoothened by it.

Conclusion

Based on the above market entry strategies, a company shall enter into a market with its new product offering.

UNIT 5.5: PRODUCT LIFE CYCLE STRATEGY

(a) Why Learn Product Life Cycle?
(b) Stages in Product Life Cycle

(a) Why Learn Product Life Cycle?

As a marketing manager or sales manager, one must first know the purpose of learning the concept of PLC or Product Life Cycle Strategy. It is understood that every product offering of the company has a limited life. The product's sales pass through different stages in the market. Usually, there are four stages in PLC (we will discuss the fifth stage in the PLC stages section). They are as follows:

(i) Initial or Product Introduction (in the market) Stage.
(ii) Growth Stage.
(iii) Maturity Stage.
(iv) Decline Stage.

EXHIBIT 5.5.1 **Product Life Cycle**

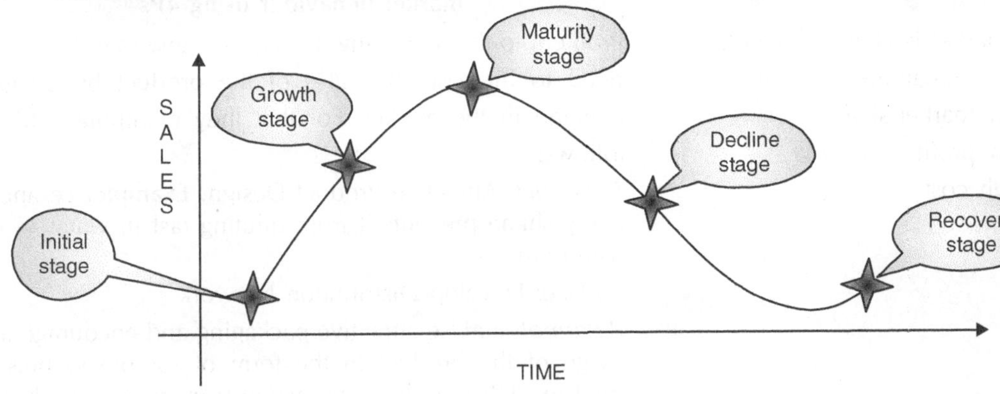

Sales, market share and profits increase and decrease in these four stages. At every stage of the PLC, the market is characterized by certain market behaviour. Thus the marketing manager must address the changes that take place in the market behaviour by suitable marketing strategies. One must understand that a product launched (introduced) in the market need not pass through all the above cited four stages in the sequential order and furthermore, the product entering and exiting any of the above stages cannot be timed.

(b) Stages in Product Life Cycle

Several models of Product Life Cycle have been promulgated over the years by the management gurus and they are as follows:

(a) **1973:** Mr.Fox – Pre-commercialization, Introduction, Growth, Maturity and Decline.

(b) **1974:** Wasson – Market development, Rapid growth, Competitive turbulence, Saturation or Maturity and Decline

(c) **1984:** Anderson and Zeithaml – Introduction, Growth, Maturity and Decline.

(d) **1998:** Hill and Jones – Embryonic, Growth, Shakeout, Maturity, Decline.

Before we enter into the stages of PLC or Product Life Cycle, one must clearly understand the purpose of learning it. The purpose is to make the marketing manager to have a marketing strategy to manage the market's behaviour during the four stages of Product Life Cycle by manipulating the 4Ps or the marketing mix. Following are the five stages in Product Life Cycle:

(i) Initial or Product Introduction (in the market) Stage.

(ii) Growth Stage.

(iii) Maturity Stage.

(iv) Decline Stage.

(v) Recovery Stage.

(i) Initial or Product Introduction (in the market) Stage

Market behaviour	Marketing strategy to address market behaviour using 4Ps
The market is characterized by • Low demand = low sales • Low market share • Low profit • High cost	Problem to the marketing managers is low sale. Now they need to increase the sales of the product by creating demand in the market. For that they manipulate 4Ps as follows: *P-Product:* Attractive Product Design. **Example:** Lesancy's curvy shape prevents it from diluting fast in water in the bathroom. *P-Place:* Develop Distribution Network *P-Promotion:* Use attractive packaging and encourage trial usage of the product in the form of sample sachets as freebie. Ultimately, use promotion to create brand awareness among the target market. *P-Price:* Follow innovation oriented pricing such as skimming price or penetrating price or affordable premium price like Tata Nano.

(ii) Growth Stage

Market behaviour	Marketing strategy to address market behaviour using 4Ps
The market is characterized by the following behaviour • Demand/Sales increase • Market share increase • Profit increase • As your company makes sound profit, you will start facing competition from existing and new players of the industry.	Now, Problem to the marketing managers is competition. Now they need to increase the sales of the product by creating demand in the market by instilling brand preference. For that they manipulate 4Ps as follows: *P-Product:* Launch varieties in product such as taste, colour, flavour, fragrance etc. ***Example*** HUL in 1990s launched Lesancy, a curvy-shaped bathing soap which prevented it from diluting fast in water in the bathroom. *P-Place:* Enhance the Distribution Network to the nook and corner of the market. *P-Promotion:* Use attractive and suitable brand ambassador to outsmart the competitors and offer freebies to stick to your brand. Ultimately, the marketing manager's campaign must focus on brand preference. *P-Price:* Follow competition oriented pricing such as Discount price or Premium price or parity/parallel price. Premium Pricing is to position the brand as superior than rivals, discount pricing is to attract new customers and retain existing customers and parity pricing is to show the market that it equals the market leader.

(iii) Maturity Stage

Market behaviour	Marketing strategy to address market behaviour using 4Ps
The market is characterized by the following behaviour • Demand/Sales saturates • Severe Competition • Marketing Cost Increase so as outsmart the competition • Profit shrunk • Due to the demand-supply mismatch (demand is less than the supply as they receive enough supply from several players), dealers start dictating on terms of trade and profit margins.	Problem to the marketing managers is stagnant sales and keener competition. Now they need to increase the sales of the product by creating demand in the market. For that they manipulate 4Ps as follows: *P-Product:* Offer the existing product to a new market or promote a new application of the existing product. *P-Promotion:* Develop campaigns using the (USP) Unique Selling Proposition and (ESP) Emotional Selling Proposition to differentiate the brand from the rivals. *P-Price:* Follow competition oriented pricing such as Discount price or Premium price or parity/parallel price.

(iv) Decline Stage

Market behaviour	Marketing strategy to address market behaviour using 4Ps
• Due to availability of technologically advanced products, change in tastes and preferences of the customers Demand and sales fell to rock bottom • Low market share • Low profit • High cost	Problem to the marketing managers is falling sales and keener competition. Now they need to increase the sales of the product by creating demand in the market. For that they do any of the following: *P-Product:* Time to sell or phase-out the product or re-launch the product with more values (benefits). *P-Promotion:* Develop campaigns using the (USP) Unique Selling Proposition and (ESP) Emotional Selling Proposition to clearly communicate the value additions of the re-launched brand. Example: New Horlicks relaunched in different flavours and for different markets like Junior Horlicks, Mother Horlicks, Horlicks Lite etc. *P-Price:* Follow competition oriented pricing such as Discount price or Premium price or parity / parallel price.

(v) Recovery

The fifth stage, 'Recovery stage' is the outcome of implementing strategy to overcome the Decline Stage of the product, where the product sales and market share recovers from the decline and profit starts rising again.

Conclusion

The marketing managers must realize that in the introduction stage, the new product is launched in a market with intense marketing efforts using 4Ps or marketing mix for establishing a clear identity and brand awareness in the market. In the growth stage the marketers see sales of the product offering increasing and competitors entering the market. To overcome this competition the marketers develop marketing strategy for vendor engagement and customer engagement for repeat purchase.

In the maturity stage, weak rivals leave the market, sales volume becomes stagnant. At this stage, only the loyal customers buy the brand. In the final decline stage, the sales of the brand declines dramatically, due to economic slowdown, new fashion trend, arrival of better technology, change in tastes and preferences of the consumers. In all the above stages, the marketing managers must know how to tackle competition and make the brand profitable and sustainable in the market. This is what is learned in PLC strategy.

EXHIBIT 5.6.1 BCG Matrix Strategy

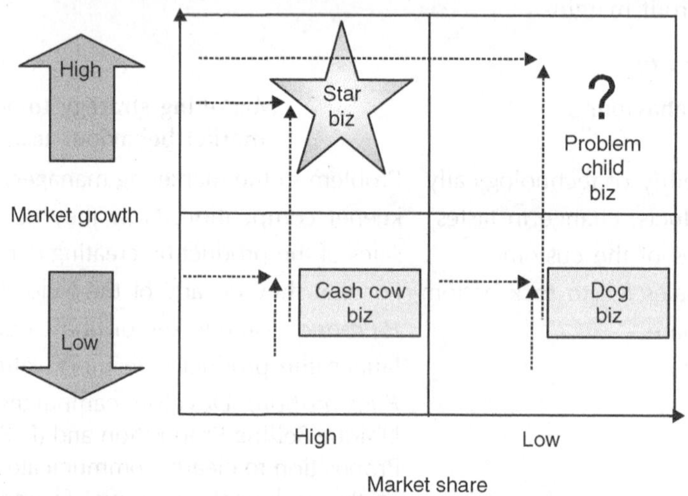

If you find any difficulty to understand the above diagram, refer to the following one to understand the concept clearly:

Assume you have got 4 businesses viz. A, B, C and D. the market share shows the competitive position of your business in the market and is always expressed as percentage. The growth rate would obviously in percentage.

Business-A: It has got 5% (high) market share and 5% (high) growth rate in sales or sales revenue. Hence it is your star business.

Business-B: It has got 1% (low) market share and 1% (low) growth rate in sales or sales revenue. Hence it is your dog business.

Business-C: It has got 4% (high) market share and 2% (low) growth rate in sales or sales revenue. Hence it is your cash cow business.

Business-D: It has got 2% (low) market share and 4% (high) growth rate in sales or sales revenue. Hence it is your Question Mark or Problem child business.

Now map the following data in X-Axis and Y-Axis as shown below, and you will get the exact picture as diagram shown earlier.

EXHIBIT 5.6.2 **BCG Matrix Strategy-Simplified**

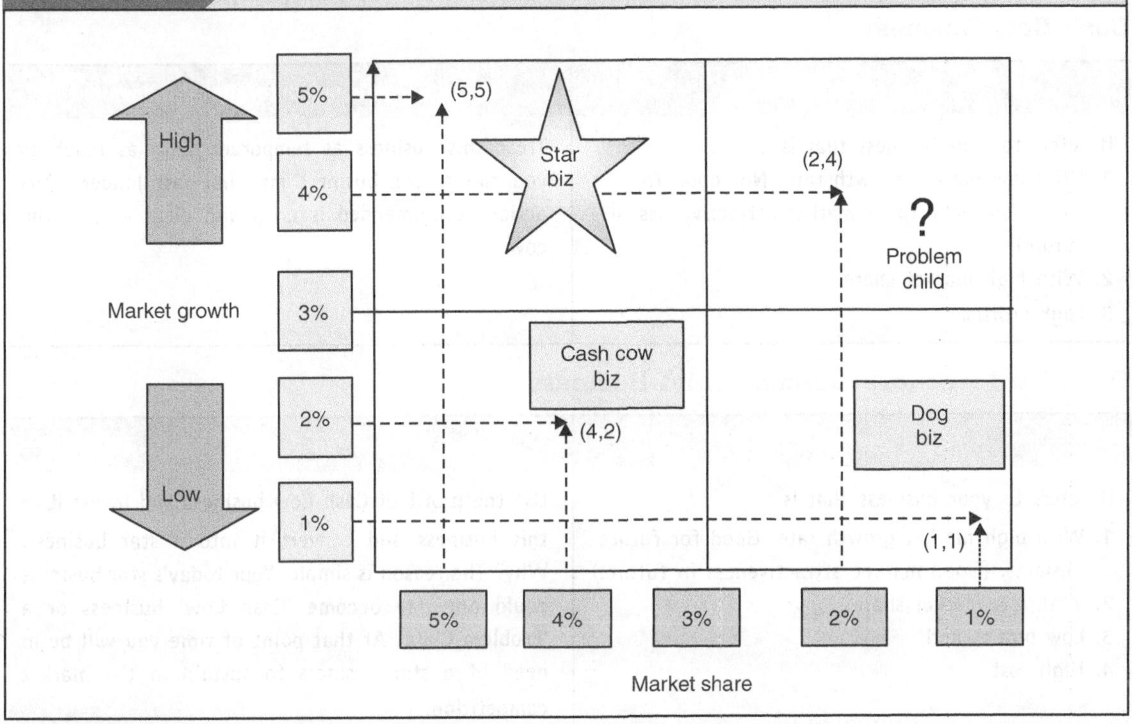

Star Business

Business Scenario	Action Recommended to the Management
It refers to your business that is 1. With high market growth rate (market attractiveness) 2. With high market share 3. High profits and 4. Low cost.	Assume yourself a movie producer (the movies market or industry) and let your business be Amitabh Bachchan, a super star by whom you can make profit. Thus Cash the Star: Earn a good amount of profit from this business.

Dog Business

Business Scenario	Action Recommended to the Management
It refers to your business that is 1. With low market growth rate. Not good for future business. (poor market attractiveness) 2. With low market share. 3. Low profits and high cost.	This business is going to drag you down. All your earlier investments had become wasted. Hence it is wise to divest or sell this business. The strategy is clear – Get rid of the dog.

Cash Cow Business

Business Scenario	Action Recommended to the Management
It refers to your business that is 1. With low market growth rate. Not good for future business. (poor market attractiveness in future) 2. With high market share. 3. High profits.	Treat this business as temporary. Earn as much as you can as the business may not last longer. Thus action recommended is crisp and clear – milk the cow.

Question Mark (or) Problem Child Business

Business Scenario	Action Recommended to the Management
It refers to your business that is 1. With high market growth rate. Good for future business. (Good market attractiveness in future.) 2. With low market share 3. Low profits and 4. High cost.	Use the profit of Cash Cow business and invest it in this business and convert it into a star business. Why? The reason is simple. Your today's star business could one day become 'Cash Cow' business or a 'Problem Child'. At that point of time you will be in need of a star business to sustain in the market competition.

UNIT 5.6: PRODUCT STRETCHING STRATEGIES

Following are the three product stretching strategies adapted by the marketers to outsmart the rival players and they are as follows:

(i) Upward Stretching

(ii) Downward Stretching

(iii) Two-way Stretching

(i) Upward Stretching

In this situation, the company would be operating at the lower-end of the market. The higher profit margin stimulates the company to choose this up-ward stretching strategy. When a company introduces a new product with a high price, it is known as upward stretching. Adoption of this strategy involves a huge risk as it could backfire if not properly planned and executed. Two issues to be addressed on upward stretching are as follows:

- Has the company got the infrastructure to produce the product offering for the high-end or premium market?
- Can the company produce superior quality products for the premium market?

For instance, HUL was offering Lifebuoy and moved upwards by offering Lifebuoy Gold and Lifebuoy liquid soap in 1990s.

(ii) Downward Stretching

In this situation, the company would be operating in the premium market and offers a new product with a low price, this strategy is known as downward stretching. A company would choose this strategy due to slow growth in the premium market and severe competition from rivals. One major risk of downward stretching is that the customers and prospect might think that the company is attempting to offer inferior quality products which leads to fall in brand image. For instance, P&G was operating in the premium market segment with Ariel dertergent. It moved to the lower-end of the market by offering 'Green Ariel'.

(iii) Two–way stretching

In this scenario, the company will be operating in the middle-end market. The scope of earning high profit margins influences the company to choose the two-way stretching strategy. When a company does both upward and downward stretching simultaneously, it is known as two-way stretching.

Example: ITC's Ashoka group of Hotels follow this strategy. It targets the premium market (upward stretching) by extending its services with its Elite Five Star Hotel and downward stretching with its Ashoka Yatri Nivas. TVS was offering only mopeds in the initial stage, now it offers TVS Star for ₹ 38500 by downward stretching and TVS Apache RTR 180 for ₹ 85,135 by upward stretching simultaneously.

UNIT 5.7: MARKET ATTACK STRATEGIES

Market Players today compete with each other so as to garner their pie of market share and to retain them. Marketers adopt any of the following market attack strategies:

1. Frontal attack.
2. Flank attack.
3. Encirclement attack.
4. By-Pass attack.
5. Guerilla attack.

1. Frontal Attack

When a company or market player directly attacks the opponents' strengths, it is called as Frontal Attack. It is done by matching the opponents' price, advertising, and distribution. In general, the player with greater resources wins. For instance, Horlicks Vs. Complan, Pepsi Vs. Coca-Cola etc. The most apt example would be HUL Rin's open challenge to its rival brands with tagline "Rin Ke Safedi Se Jeetoge? No Chance" (Can you win Rin's Brightness Challenge? No Chance). Sometimes, a modified frontal attack is practiced where all the aspects of the company's product are offered something more than the rival's offering. HUL Vs P&G (Rin Vs Tide): HUL's frontal attack on P&G by reducing its price along with a free Rin bar.

EXHIBIT 5.8.1 Frontal Attack Strategy

Source:

Rin Challenge: http://www.afaqs.com/news/news_story_grfx/2010/26742_2_big.jpg

Tide Vs Rin: http://3.bp.blogspot.com/-JaFoPIZa8P4/T2Akx-szq0I/AAAAAAAAATo/fEDLaV57aKE/s1600/getimage.dll.png

Horlicks Vs. Complan: http://www.siliconindia.com:81/news/newsimages/special/7E69sifc.jpeg

2. Flank Attack

When a company or market player directly attacks the opponents' small weaknesses, it is called as Flank Attack. Challenger identifies the weaker areas in the offering of the company or rival player such as product design, price, advertising, and distribution and attacks those areas. Example: When Titan was the market leader for watches in India, Timex watches launched a complete range of plastic watches that offered a refreshing product alternative to the market particularly to the youth market (18 to 35 age group) and was able to achieve a staggering sales volume of 2 million watches in just two years, a figure that Titan took more than five years to reach.

3. Encirclement Attack

When a company or market player directly attacks the opponents' big weaknesses, it is called as Encirclement Attack. Challenger identifies the important areas in the offerings of the company or rival player such as price, advertising, and distribution and attacks those areas. It is an offensive strategy done on several fronts. In short, the challenger offers everything that is offered by the opponent and goes even beyond that to capture the, market share. Say for instance, Nirma attacked HUL's (formerly HLL) Surf in early 1980s on price and quantity front in 1959, where Surf was priced at ₹13 per kilo gram and Nirma was offered for just ₹ 3 per kg.

4. By-Pass Attack

When a company launches a completely new product by diversifying the product range to outsmart the rival players, it is called as by-pass attack. Coca-Cola India at one point of time launched its famous tea brand Georgia instead of competing only in carbonated soft drinks against its rival Pepsi India.

5. Guerilla Attack

Attack on narrow (smaller) territory of the rival player is called as guerilla attack. The challenger attacks the market leader by using price discounts, offering cheap or premium products, offering a variety of products, improving existing pre-sales and post-sales services etc. to enhance its market share. Furthermore, guerrilla attacks are not restricted to marketing. Legal action such as law suits can be used to restrict competitor's growth. The key to success is that it has to be unpredictable to the rivals and must have the ability to destroy and deplete resources of rivals, such as time and finance. Say for instance, Bajaj's quadricycle small car opposed by key Indian automobile majors.

EXHIBIT 5.8.2 **Guerilla Attack Strategy**

The quadricycle conundrum

For	Against
Subject to meeting govt standards, will be a better option than three-wheelers, which undergo no such tests	Due to low cost, could result in an increase in the number of vehicles on the road if volumes not regulated
Could reduce the country's fuel import bill as vehicle can run 35 km/litre	Lack safety technologies such as crumple zones, airbags and anti-lock brakes
Half the carbon emissions of other four-wheelers at 60 grams of carbon per km	Only an intra-city vehicle, could pose a traffic hazard if used on highways

Source:

Bajaj Quadircycle: http://www.zigwheels.com/news-features/news/quadricycles-like-bajaj-re60-finally-get-govt-nod/16439/

http://www.thehindubusinessline.com/multimedia/dynamic/01464/bl23_newPg1Graphic_1464551g.jpg

UNIT 5.8: CUSTOMER RELATIONSHIP MANAGEMENT

(a) Why Learn CRM?

All marketers want to have a close relationship with their customers. But it is quite difficult to establish a close emotional relationship and maintain it consistently in today complicated business world. Why is it complicated? The reasons are as follows:

1. Customer decision making process is not in a systematic order or linear progression. It has now become dynamic.
2. Today the market is proliferated with brands.
3. Customers are literally bombarded with brands through all medias of promotion. But customers are less attentive.
4. Today, internet has empowered the customers. Customers collect brand experience from social networking sites, collect their required information from the official website of the brand and simultaneously compare the offering's features with the competing brands along with their prices.

EXHIBIT 5.9.1 Customer Relationship Management

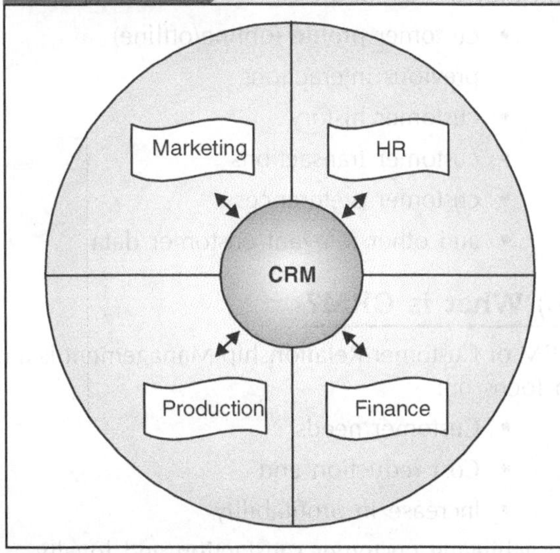

As an outcome, traditional marketing has become outdated. This has compelled marketers to search for new techniques so as to collect deeper insights on buyer behaviour and identify the key trends along with their tastes and preferences to influence their purchase action.

In simple words, marketers today observe the Customer Behaviour by studying the Customer Life Cycle. The CLC or Customer Life Cycle includes awareness, trial, consideration, purchase and repeat purchase. This system is called as CRM or Customer Relationship Management. Every marketer must understand that the stage of Customer Life Cycle may not take place in the above cited sequential order always.

Say for instance, a customer might enter a Nokia Showroom to buy a specific model of smart phone. All customers shall not be generalised. The customer might be a novice or beginner looking for information and guidance to buy smart phone or a tech-savvy customer who had already collected all the information from blogs, official website of the brand etc.

Can the retailer treat both the customer equally and spend the same amount of time in providing layman's explanation about the product's attributes to both the customers? The answer is obvious. The two of the prospects requires two different marketing approaches. To be more specific, the beginner may be provided with detailed demo, aggressive sales promotion, and in-store POP displays might be useful to close the deal. The same may not be required for the tech-savvy prospect to close the deal successfully by the retailer.

We understood that the marketers use Customer Life Cycle Stages to study the buyer behaviour to formulate their marketing strategy in accordance with the changing tastes and preference of the prospects and this system is called as CRM or Customer Relationship Management. Now it is time to learn the key information that is used by the marketing managers for making their marketing programmes relevant to the target market. This information is put forward by Mr. Mitch Lieberman, and they are as follows:

- customer profile (online/offline)
- previous interactions
- customer history
- customer transactions
- customer preferences
- and other relevant customer data

(b) What is CRM?

CRM or Customer Relationship Management is a company-wide business strategy which is designed to focus on:

- Customer needs
- Cost reduction and
- Increase in profitability

by achieving customer satisfaction and loyalty.

CRM helps to collect information of customers from both inside and outside the organisation, which helps the employees (the internal customers) to satisfy the customers' (the external customers') needs and wants based on their tastes and preferences.

(c) Advantages of Implementing CRM in the Organisation

Following are the key benefits (merits or advantages or purposes) of establishing CRM in an organisation:

1. CRM helps to gain insight on buyer behaviour and it leads to improved customer service.
2. It leads to efficiency in customer care and services.
3. It promotes cross-selling and up-selling. Both cross-selling and up-selling are sales strategies where the seller will provide opportunities to the prospects to purchase related products or services, often for the sole purpose of making a larger sale.
   (a) **Cross Selling:** *When a customer approaches a commercial bank to invest ₹ 50,000 as Fixed Deposit, and if the Client Relationship Executive suggests the customer to look into other investment options like Mutual Funds and Gold Coins, it is called as Cross-Selling.*
   (b) **Up-Selling:** *When Toshiba offers extended warranty period for an additional 1 year or 2 years warranty extension for an additional cost, along with the standard warranty period, it is called as Up-Selling. 1 year additional warranty costs ₹ 2,999 and 2 years' additional warranty costs ₹ 4,999 respectively. This offer is additional to the standard warranty which is offered at free of cost for the first one year from the date of purchase.*

4. It helps to improve the 'Deal Close Rate'.
5. It helps to streamline the marketing programme with sales activities.
6. It helps to attain effective customer profiling, which facilitates effective targeting, which prevents spill-over effect.
7. It helps to optimize sales promotion costs.
8. It helps to increase the overall profitability of the organisation.
9. It reduces cost to acquire new customers.
10. It increases customer satisfaction, which results in customer loyalty.
11. It increases revenue per customer.
12. It reduces cost of selling.
13. It increases the returns on relationship.
14. It reduces the cost to deliver or serve the customers.
15. It increases the competitive advantage of the company.
16. It reduces the time to serve the customers.
17. It increases the number of consumers.
18. It increases the retention rate.
19. It increases the customer value.

All the above benefits are acquired by the company by using a CRM software package. The information collected and processed are presented to the marketing managers for facilitating sound marketing decisions. The module that facilitates this function is called as Marketing Information System (MIS). Some of the major Information Technology players offering CRM software package with their market share and revenue are presented for learners convenience in the following Exhibit-5.9.2.

EXHIBIT 5.9.2 **CRM Software Vendors' Worldwide Revenue***

Company	2008 Revenue	2008 Market Share	2007 Revenue	2007 Market Share	Growth Rate (%) 2007–2008
SAP	2055	22.5	2072	25.5	-0.8
Oracle	1.475	16.1	1.320	16.2	11.8
Salesforce.com	965	10.6	676	8.3	42.7
Microsoft	581	6.4	332	4.1	75
Amdocs	451	4.9	419	5.2	7.6
Others	3620	39.6	3311	40.7	9.3

Note: * Revenue: Estimated Revenue in Millions of US Dollars

Source: Gartner, 2009

(d) Challenges in Implementing CRM Strategy in the Organisation

Following are key challenges in implementing CRM as a strategy in an organisation:

(i) Convincing the staff.

(ii) Identifying the process to be re-engineered.

(iii) Obtain relevant customer information.

(iv) Automation of data and process.

(v) Deciding the time frame for CRM implementation.

(vi) Cost of CRM technology.

(i) Convincing the Staff

The first and the foremost hurdle in implementing CRM strategy in the organisation would be to convince the employees that change is good and it will definitely benefit them.

(ii) Identifying the Process to be Re-engineered

Once the employees are convinced with the benefits of CRM, the next challenge would be identifying the business process by analysing it and decide which area of business needs to be re-engineered.

(iii) Obtain Relevant Customer Information

CRM is a strategy which would provide the organisational managers with a lot of data on customers. From all these collected data, the company managers must decide on the relevant information and the way it is to be used (how the relevant data or information are to be used) to make sensible business decisions.

(iv) Automation of Data and Process

The forth challenge in implementing CRM strategy is to automate the CRM process. It needs a CRM software package. The challenge is to select the right technology to automate the required process.

(v) Deciding the Time Frame for CRM Implementation

The fifth challenge is to decide the time frame for implementation of CRM strategy with the help of a CRM software package. The time frame for implementation is influenced by the type of data, size of the company, training required for using or operating the CRM module etc.

(vii) Cost of CRM Technology

Companies have to spend a huge amount of money for acquiring a CRM software package. The cost of CRM technology not only includes the cost of the software but also the training cost of employees to the module. High cost of CRM package prevents small and medium enterprises from accessing the benefits of CRM package.

(e) CRM – Process (or) Stages in CRM Process

CRM Process encompasses the entire spectrum of activities starting from customer segmentation to acquisition and profitable retention. Each of these activities demand a very strong operational process, which is effectively integrated with business intelligence.

Every marketing manager has to understand that the CRM is not mere technology but a comprehensive, customer-centric approach to an organisation's philosophy of dealing with its customers.

EXHIBIT 5.9.3 Customer Relationship Management Process

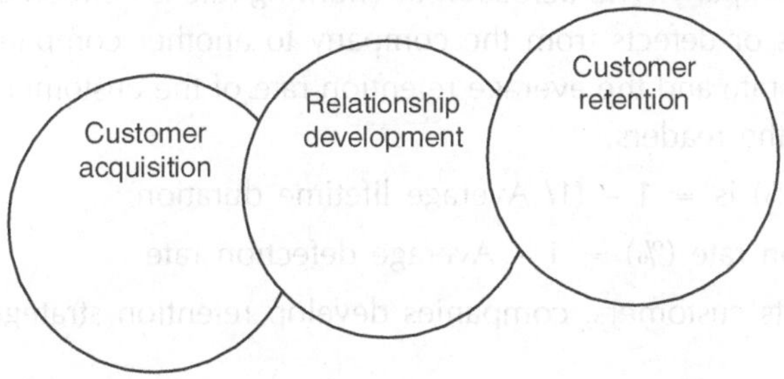

Following are the three phases or stages involved in the CRM process:

(i) Stage-1: Customer Acquisition

(ii) Stage-2: Customer Development

(iii) Stage-3: Customer Retention

(i) Stage-1: Customer Acquisition

In this stage, the companies offer new schemes to attract new customers or prospects to buy their brands. Say for instance, Shri.Dhirubhai Ambani's Reliance Telecom offered CDMA handset with talk time for just ₹ 500 as its introductory offer.

(ii) Stage-2: Customer Development

In this stage, the company engages the acquired customers by special offers so as to make them spend more on their offerings. Say for instance, Godrej Consumer Product's Cinthol. The offer is buy two Cinthol soaps (combo pack) and get one pen free.

(iii) Stage-3: Customer Retention

In this 3rd phase of CRM process, the company develops strategies to prevent its customers switching to its rival brands. Customer retention is possible only when the company attempts to create Customer Life Time Value by maintaining an emotional bond with the existing customers. It is very important to retain the existing customers as the cost of acquisition is higher than the retention. This can be understood well in the mobile telecom market. After implementing MNP or Mobile Number Portability (a scheme to switch mobile telecom service providers at a nominal charge without changing the telephone number already allotted by the service provider), many existing customers of telecom players switched to competitively priced service providers. On this backdrop, Harsh Goenka, Chairperson, RPG Enterprises, Kolkata, India commented as following:

"In the cellular business, it costs five times more to acquire a customer. It is the same in every business. Retaining this customer is the critical first step for success.[1]"

Customer Retention and Customer Defection are like two sides of the same coin. Retention rate can be defined as the average likelihood for customer's repeat purchase of product or service offering from the same company. The defection or churning rate is defined as the average likelihood that a customer switches or defects from the company to another company. Thus the formula for calculating the retention rate and the average retention rate of the customer are given below for the better understanding of the readers.

- Retention rate (%) is = 1 – (1/ Average lifetime duration)
- Average retention rate (%) = 1 – Average defection rate

In order to retain its customers, companies develop retention strategies.

(f) Components of CRM Process

EXHIBIT 5.9.4 Components of Customer Relationship Management

Operational Areas	Components				
Marketing	Customer Value	Customer Segmentation	Customer Behaviour Analysis and Prediction	Customer Retention	Customer Loyalty
Sales	Customer Account Management	Cross-Selling and Up-Selling	Sales Force Automation		
Service and Support	Customer Contact or Service Centre	Quality Management	Customer Satisfaction Measurement		
Information Technology	Hardware and Software	Database Management like Cloud Computing	Data Warehousing	Data Mining	Security Systems

The above Exhibit 5.9.4 shows the components of CRM process in an organisation. The operational areas of the company are Marketing, Sales, Service and Support and Information Technology. The components of marketing are Customer Value, Customer Segmentation, Customer Behaviour Analysis and Prediction, Customer Retention and Customer Loyalty.

[1] Journal of Services Research, Volume 3, Number 2 (October 2003-March 2004)

The components of sales (operational) area are Customer Account Management, Cross-Selling and Up-Selling and Sales Force Automation. The components of Service and Support are Customer Contact or Service Centre (Call Centre), Quality Management, and Customer Satisfaction Measurement. Finally, the components of Information Technology are Hardware and Software, Data Warehousing and Database Management like Cloud Computing, Data Mining and Security Systems.

(g) Customer Centric Organisation – CRM Strategy Implementation Model

Customer Centric Organisation is an organisation which revolves around customers. Mr. Payne and Frow developed a CRM process which depicts how an organisation operates as a customer centric one. These authors proposed a strategic framework for customer relationship management (CRM) which helps broaden the understanding of CRM and its role in enhancing customers' value and, as a result, shareholder value. The Customer Centric Organisational model as shown in Exhibit 5.9.5 has two main components:

(1) Five Key core cross-functional CRM processes and
(2) Four Key CRM implementation elements.

EXHIBIT 5.9.5 Customer Centric Organisational Model—CRM Implementation Strategy

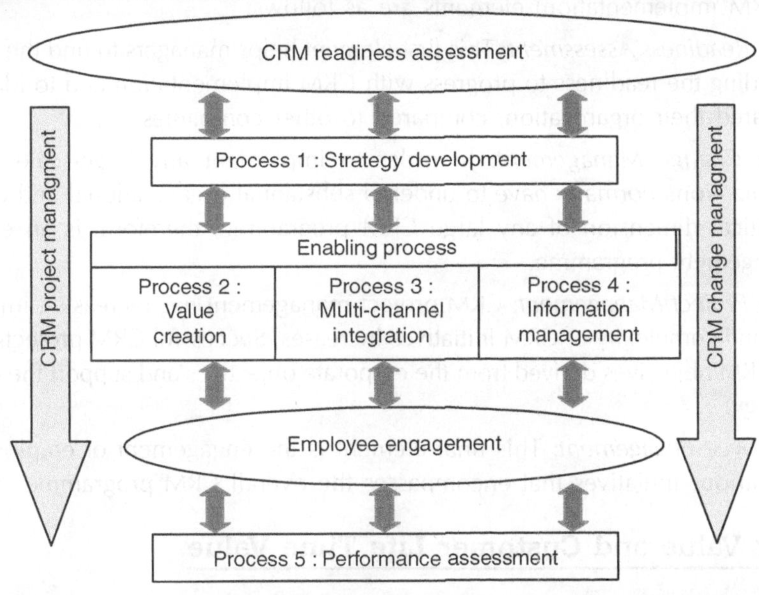

Source: CRM Strategy and Implementation Model, Payne and Frow, 2006.

The model contains five key cross-functional CRM processes viz. strategy development, value creation, multi-channel integration, information management, and performance assessment. It also contains four key CRM implementation elements viz. CRM readiness assessment, CRM change management, CRM project management, and employee engagement.

(1) Five Key Core Cross-Functional CRM Processes

(i) *Strategy Development Process*: The process defines the overall objectives and structure or the parameters for the organization's CRM activities. The process focuses on the organization's business strategy by keeping customers as its base.

(ii) *Value Creation Process:* It involves taking the outputs of the strategy development process and building a program that delivers value or benefits to the customers.

(iii) *Multi-Channel Integration Process*: This process involves managing every contact point between the customer and the company. Also, creating better ways for customers to experience the company's customised or tailor-made offerings.

(iv) *Information Management Process*: This process is the engine that drives CRM activities. It involves IT systems which includes organization's hardware, software, analytical tools; and front-office and back-office applications.

(v) *Performance Assessment Process*: This final process ensures that the organization' strategic CRM objectives are being delivered and that key factors that guides future improvement are identified.

(2) Four Key CRM Implementation Elements

The four key (CRM implementation) elements are as follows:

(i) *CRM Readiness Assessment:* This first element helps managers to find the overall position regarding the readiness to progress with CRM implementation and to identify how well prepared their organization, compared to other companies.

(ii) *CRM Change Management:* In order to implement any large-scale CRM software, organizations *normally have* to undergo substantial organizational and cultural change. A critical dimension of any large CRM programme, therefore, is an effective change management programme.

(iii) *CRM Project Management*: CRM project management has increasing importance as the size and complexity of CRM initiatives increases. Successful CRM projects deliver against the CRM objectives derived from the corporate objectives and support the overall business strategy.

(iv) *Employee Engagement*: This final element is the engagement of employees to support the various initiatives that encompasses the overall CRM programme.

(h) Customer Value and Customer Life Time Value

Customer Value

The fundamental idea behind marketing is that an organisation will create some value to a group of customers. The customers in turn will be willing to pay the perceived right price for the company's offerings. Value in marketing simply means, 'Benefits', which a customer would obtain from the product or service purchased. This customer value is also called as 'Utility' or 'Usefulness'.

This customer value can be classified into two:

(1) Tangible Customer Value

(2) Intangible Customer Value

(1) *Tangible Customer Value:* Tangible Customer Value or benefits would take place in tangible product retail business. Say for instance, a retailer or the manufacturer offering a freebie to the regular customers as thanks giving.

(2) *Intangible Customer Value:* Intangible Customer Value or benefits would take place in intangible service retail business. Say for instance, when a computer is sold, it would be pre-loaded with an operating system, anti-virus pack, free updates, technical support and warranty service.

Customer Perceived Value

Marketers must know not just customer value but also the Customer Perceived Value. Customer Perceived Value means the opinions of the customers towards the value or benefits of the product or service that are to be purchased. In simple words, it refers to the expected customer benefits. It is very important for marketers to note that the customer value must be examined from the customer viewpoint and not from the company's viewpoint. Ultimately, knowing the expected value or benefits from the view point of the customer (Customer Perceived Value), will help the marketers to price their offering more accurately. It influences the pricing decision as the customers will be willing to spend more, when they feel that the benefits received by them are greater than their sacrifices such as time, money and efforts spent to buy the company's offerings.

Customer Life Time Value

Companies are becoming increasingly aware of the many potential benefits provided by CRM. Some potential benefits of CRM are as follows:

(1) Increased customer retention and loyalty

(2) Higher customer profitability

(3) Creation value for the customer

(4) Customization of products and services

(5) Lower price, higher quality products and services[1]

When evaluating customer profitability, marketers are often reminded of the Alfredo Pareto's 80:20 rule (80% of the profits are produced by top 20% of profitable customers and 80% of the costs are produced by top 20% of unprofitable customers). The core parts of CRM activities are understanding customers' profitability and retain profitable customers. To capitalise on the full profit potentials of customers, many companies have tried to measure and use customer value in their management activities. Therefore, many firms assess their customers' value and build strategies to retain profitable customers in long-term. Emergence of Customer Relationship Management (CRM) concept highlighted the existence of different customers; hence companies started giving attention

[1] Jutla, Craig, & Bodorik, 2001 ; Stone, Woodcock, & Wilson, 1996

to how customers perceive value added services. CRM relies upon the acquisition of customer needs and desires with particular relevance to customer satisfaction which, in turn, leads to long-term relationship. This is called as Customer Life Time Value.

Conclusion

CRM is an approach helps for better, quicker and more successful organizing of any business interactions with its customers based on a cutting-edge technology and customer-centric foundation. It is an entire discipline, not a single activity. Customer relationship management allows businesses to execute relationship marketing at an enterprise-wide level, where every employee of the organisation is involved in the CRM Process.

CASE 1: Role of CRM in Insurance Industry in India

In recent times, Insurers in India have started adopting a customer-centric approach that helps them improve productivity and customer intimacy while better equipping agents, brokers, and service representatives to improve the customer experience. A well-defined and executed customer relationship management (CRM) strategy will help the insurance company and its brokers focus on key vitals that impact costs, premiums, new business, and renewal rates. Since 2010 the life insurance industry in India has undergone dramatic changes[1]. The regulator continually works on creating an environment where insurance is seen as a long-term investment, the products are transparent and customer-friendly, and the players are continually encouraged to take steps to streamline their costs. A new channel of distribution bancassurance, picked up pace in India. Thus insurers with strong bancassurance tie-ups are expected to do better in the coming years. Relatively low-cost channels and technology-driven means to access customers will also drive volumes in the future.

Customer service and retention will become the CSF or Critical Success Factor. As markets have evolved and consumer needs have grown more complex, the distribution model for life insurance has gradually shifted from a product-push to an advisory model. An advisory approach based on a clear understanding of investors' individual needs and risk appetites which are possible only by maintaining close relationship with the customers. Service standards, need based selling, and customer retentions will become key differentiators.

The future is expected to be enormously positive for customers where service standards of Insurance companies will become more and more customer-centric. Companies are expected to offer several unique offerings in the coming years targeting at the different customer segments in line with emerging needs of special customers like child, women, youth, etc. "With increased standardization in products, customer service delivery is poised to be a key differentiator in the life insurance industry. The entire management of the customer life cycle—starting from initiation and policy issuance to maintenance (premium payment reminders, fund switches, customer feedback) and finally claims (release of the claim amount) will become the main reason why customers will choose one insurance company over the other[2]" says Glenn Williams is the CEO, Bharti AXA Life Insurance Co. Ltd.

---

[1] http://economictimes.indiatimes.com/opinion/guest-writer/customer-centricity-for-insurance/articleshow/7199398.cms

[2] http://www.livemint.com/2010/11/01203044/Customer-centricity-should-be.html

A 360° CUSTOMER CENTRIC CRM APPROACH IN INSURANCE INDUSTRY

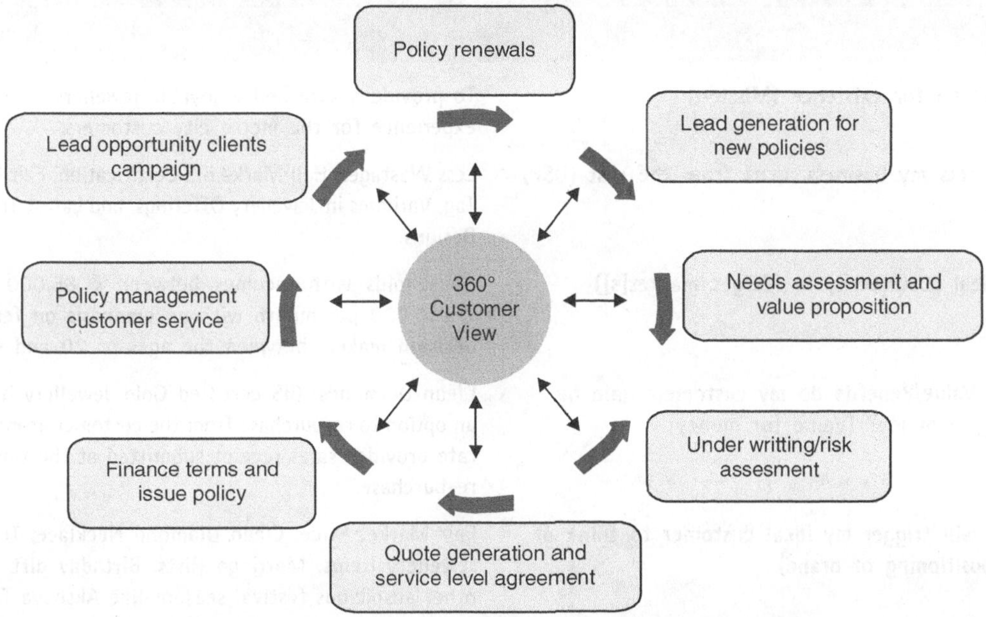

Source: http://www.esavvy.com.au/esavvydnn/Portals/0/eSavvy%20site%20images/insurance360.PNG

India still being an underinsured nation and considering the demographic dividend, it is imperative to spread the message of long-term investments and securing the future as widely as possible by using this opportunity to continue interacting with customers, educate them on benefits of insurance products, focus on need-based selling using CRM module and draw in more customers into this industry.While it is huge challenge for the insurance industry players, these opportunities must be put to sensible use to attain a sustainable growth for the industry.

Discussion Questions

1. Discuss on the Customer Life Cycle in Insurance Industry.
2. Discuss the various modes of distribution channels adopted by the insurance companies to distribute their insurance plans in India.
3. Discuss how as a marketer of a leading insurance company would you generate lead on prospects.

LE-2: One Page Marketing Plan

Based on the sample one page marketing plan given below, prepare a marketing plan of your own for a product of your choice:

Gold and Diamond Necklace Retailing Business	
Category	**Strategy**
My reason for existence (Mission)	To provide a safe and enjoyable jewellery shopping experience for the metro city customers.
What sets my business apart from the rest (USP)	Less Wastages, Hall Mark–BIS Certification, Fair Price Tag, Varieties in Jewellery Offerings, and Latest Trendy Designs.
My ideal customer(s) or (Target market[s])	Households with incomes between ₹ 65,000 and ₹ 150,000 per month with an emphasis on female decision makers between the ages of 20 and 45.
What Value/Benefits do my customers gain by buying from me? (Value for money)	Clean Diamonds, BIS certified Gold Jewellery items, an option to re-purchase from the customer at market rate provided sales receipt submitted at the time of re-purchase.
What will trigger my ideal customer to think of me (positioning of brand)	Fair Market Price, Clean Diamond Necklace, Trendy Jewellery Items, Marriage Gifts, Birthday gifts and other auspicious festival seasons like Akshaya Tritya
Offering to customers (Product/Service/Both)	one lower-priced design and two higher priced designs
Brand Name, Logo, and Tagline (Positioning Statement)	The Emerald – "Pure & Clear - Always"
Price Strategy	***Lower Price Design:*** Price 5% lesser than our closest competitor. ***Higher Price Designs:*** Price 5% higher than our closest competitor.
Distribution Strategy	Distribution and sales through Internet by using retailer's online stores and other leading online gift stores. Available through Exclusive Showrooms opened in all Metro cities.
Promotion Strategy	Develop a new campaign that focuses on the positioning, emphasize fair price and trendy-designer look.
Sales Strategy	Expand sales revenue by 10% for each product line.
What I want to accomplish this year	Lease a building for showroom, Establish online retail store, Recruit employees and train them for showroom sales, and Enter into an agreement to sell through channel partners

The top 3 things that are going to get me there	Direct mail to target customers, Promotional campaign in print, audio-visual and electronic media, and Efficiency in wastage management while jewellery making.
How much will each program contribute to my revenue/profitability:	Retailer's E-Store: 30%, Channel Partners: 30%, Exclusive Showroom: 40%Total Expected Profitability for Jan'13 to Mar'13 = ₹ 50 Lakhs.
How much money will I need to get it done?	₹ 5 Crores

One Page Marketing Plan

Company Name: Year:

COMPANY OR BUSINESS TITLE	
Category	**Strategy**
My reason for existence (Mission)	
What sets my business apart from the rest (USP)	
My ideal customer(s) or (Target market[s])	
What Value/Benefits do my customers gain by buying from me? (Value for money)	
What will trigger my ideal customer to think of me (Positioning of brand)	
Offering to customers (Product / Service / Both):	
Brand Name, Logo, and Tagline (Positioning Statement)	
Price Strategy	
Distribution Strategy	
Promotion Strategy	
Sales Strategy	
What I want to accomplish this year	
The top 3 things that are going to get me there	
How much will each program contribute to my revenue/profitability	
How much money will I need to get it done?	

❑❑❑

Chapter 6

EMERGING TRENDS IN MARKETING

Chapter Objectives

After studying this chapter, you should be able to update yourself with the latest trends and development in the field of marketing:

- **6.1.** Rural Marketing
- **6.2.** Social Marketing
- **6.3.** Green Marketing
- **6.4.** Viral or Buzz Marketing
- **6.5.** Direct Marketing/E-Marketing/Online Marketing
- **6.6.** Permission Marketing

UNIT 6.1: RURAL MARKETING

(a) Why Companies Target Rural Markets

The Indian rural market with its vast size and demand base, offers a huge opportunity that companies cannot afford to ignore. To expand their market share, more and more companies are foraying (entering) into India's rural markets.

(b) What is Rural Marketing

Rural marketing can be defined as identifying the specific needs and wants of rural people, customising the product and service offerings in accordance to the rural people's needs and lifestyle, distributing of offerings using Self Help Groups and Non-Governmental Organisations along with traditional distribution system and pricing it affordable to the target market and satisfying the specific needs and wants of the rural people. Let us understand the rural marketing using Godrej's Mini-Refrigerators 'Chotu Kool'.

EXHIBIT 6.1.1 **Godrej's Low Cost Refrigerator 'Chotukool' for Rural India**

EXHIBIT 6.1.2 **Godrej-Indian Post Office Tie-Up for Distribution of 'Chotu Kool', a Mini-Refrigerator for Rural India**

Product: Product is a customized mini-refrigerator which can operate even during power-cuts. Branded as 'Chotu Kool', is a thermoelectric cooler to preserve vegetables, milk, and water. It is suitable for residential and small commercial outlets.

Place or Distribution Channel: It is distributed through India Post offices which has got a very strong network penetration in India. These would include head post offices, sub-post offices and branch offices. The post offices will accept orders from the public, collect the amount by cash, and deliver the product through Express Parcel Post facility.

Price: The product is priced at ₹ 3,790 a piece which reflects low-cost orientation strategy that addresses the affordability requirement of the rural customers.

Promotion: A sample cooler will be on display at the post offices[1].

(c) How Companies Market their Offerings to Rural India

Companies use the same 4Ps to market their offerings in rural India. But marketing to rural India is not as same as marketing offerings in urban India. To be more specific, companies are facing **four challenges** in rural marketing. They are

1. Availability
2. Acceptability
3. Affordability
4. Awareness

Now let's see how these 4As or challenges are met by some leading companies by using the Marketing Mix – 4Ps Product, Place, Price and Promotion.

1. Availability (Managing Distribution Challenges in Rural India using the Marketing Mix 'Place')

The first challenge is to ensure availability of products and services through appropriate distribution channels. India's 6,27,000 villages are spread over 3.2 million sq km. It is estimated that around 700 million Indians may live in rural areas. Reaching them is not going to be easy. Given the poor state of roads, it's even a greater challenge to make the products regularly available to the rural India. Any marketer would try to reach at least 13,113 villages with a population of more than 5000. Reaching these remote villages is sure to increase the distribution or transportation costs. But Hindustan Unilever has succeeded in having a strong rural distribution network. It helped its brands to reach the interior parts of rural India. The company supplies the goods twice a week to the large distributors who in-turn appoint sub-stockiest and act as hubs. To service the remotes villages, the large distributors use auto rickshaws, bullock carts and even boats in backwaters in Kerala. These stockiest appoint smaller distributors and supply them the goods on a weekly basis. Apart from the traditional distribution network, HUL's capitalised on self-help groups in rural India with its project entitled *Project Shakti*, launched in 2001 covers over 80,000 villages in more than 12 states. It targets small villages whose population is less than or equal to 2000. The objective is to empower rural women by providing income-generating opportunities by creating an organized self-help group.

---

[1] http://www.thehindu.com/business/companies/post-offices-to-market-coolers/article2461929.ece

2. Affordability (Managing Affordability Challenge in Rural India using the Marketing Mix 'Price')

The second important challenge is to ensure affordability of products and services. The rural market is characterized with low disposable income as most of them are daily wage earners. Moreover, their spending is largely influenced by good monsoon and harvesting. Therefore the product offerings need to be affordable for the rural consumers. HUL took it as an opportunity and launched Lifebuoy soap at ₹ 2 for a 50 gm pack. Coca-Cola offered 200 ml of coke for ₹ 5 and also launched SUNFILL, an instant ready-to-mix powdered soft drink at ₹ 2 for 25 gm sachet. Cavincare launched Chick shampoo for just 50 paise per sachet. Today companies offer shampoo sachets priced at ₹ 1 or 2 and toothpastes at ₹ 10, which has become the order of the day to reach the hinter land of India. Godrej's mini refrigerators priced just ₹ 3,790 a piece.

3. Acceptability (Managing Product Acceptability in Rural India using the Marketing Mix 'Product')

The 3rd challenge is to gain acceptability for the product and service offerings. The product offerings should suit the needs of the rural market. The companies should indigenously develop product offerings to cater to the demands of rural India. Recently, Godrej's launched refrigerators tailored made for rural India. The low cost 'refrigerator' Godrej's 'Chotukool' are sold through Post Offices, in India. Similarly, Coca-Cola provides low cost icebox for the outlets in rural India to address the electricity problems, as refrigerators tend to become useless without electricity. LG Electronics in 1998 introduced a customized TV for rural market called *Sampoorna* in North India. It sold 100,000 units in the very first year. An advanced technology is used for plastic coating in VIM bar soap to prevent it from wearing out quickly.

4. Awareness (Managing Awareness Challenge in Rural India using the Marketing Mix 'Promotion')

The next challenge is to build awareness about the company's product offerings. Only 41% of rural households have access to television. Outing for rural Indians is confined to local fairs and festivals. TV viewing is also confined to the state owned Doordarshan to a large extent. Godrej Consumer Products uses radio to reach local people in their own regional language to push its brands. LG Electronics and Philips Electronics use vans and road shows to drive growth in the rural areas.

Apart from these traditional medias, companies resort to innovative methods of advertising like trade fairs, exhibitions and festivals to reach their potential customer base. One such incident is gathering of many companies at the Ganges River for the Kumbh Mela festival where about 30 million people, mostly from rural areas visited. The companies provided 'Touch and Feel' demonstrations and distributed free samples. This proved to be an extremely effective way of promotion where companies use sponsorship as a tool to reach rural markets.

(d) Conclusion

Even today, more than 50% of India's population is in rural India. Keeping this in mind, companies resort to rural marketing as it shows the way for sustainable growth and better earnings.

UNIT 6.2: SOCIAL MARKETING

(a) Social Marketing—Meaning

Social marketing is also called as societal marketing. Peter F. Drucker used to say that Society's problems must be considered as an opportunity for organization. Commitment to social welfare activities will help out to acquire positive corporate image, brand awareness, loyalty and improved sales. This is called as social marketing. Social Marketing is aptly defined by the Management Guru Prof. Philip Kotler, "Management orientation aimed at generating consumer satisfaction and long-run consumer and public welfare as a key to satisfying organizational goals and objectives". Marketers today have recognized that the cause related marketing or societal or social marketing is a way for sustainable growth.

(b) How Companies Engage in Social Marketing?

Corporate India and (MNCs) Multi-National Companies operating in India identify the key social challenges and relate themselves either to create awareness about it or promote their brand as a solution for such social issues. Following examples would help the future managers to know how companies engage in social-marketing:

Company	Brand	Social Marketing Initiative
1. Hindustan Unilever	Pepsodent Toothpaste	Dental Insurance Cover
2. Eureka Forbes	Eureka Forbes Water Purifier	Sponsored 'Pollution Watch' in Star-news
3. Tamil Nadu New Print Limited	TNPL Notebooks	Papers made from Bagasse (sugarcane wastes) and not from chopping of trees
4. ITC, India	Class Mate Notebooks	Papers made from Bagasse (sugar can wastes) and not from chopping of trees
5. Tata	Tata Steel	Built hospitals and schools for its employees' children in Jamshedpur, the steel city
6. Microsoft	Microsoft OS	Offered US$100 Million to India to combat AIDS
7. Mahindra & Mahindra	Mahindra Reva	Electric Cars – Zero Pollution to environment
8. HUL	Fair & Lovely – Fairness Cream	Fair & Lovely Foundation providing career guidance and scholarships for women in India
9. Bisleri, Pepsi and Coca-Cola	Packaged Drinking Water	Providing Clean Drinking Water in India
10. Parle	Parle-G Biscuits and Confectioneries	'Parle Unndathirkana' – A scholarship scheme for "all round performance", in for School Students in Tamilnadu

11. HUL	Clinic Plus-Shampoo	Awarded Scholarships amounting ₹ 10,000 each for three best girls for their academic achievements. 67 girls received ₹ 1000 each
12. State Bank of India	Banking service	Installing water purifiers in rural and semi-urban schools
13. Steel Authority of India Limited (SAIL)	Steel	*Education*: 139 Company-run schools, with over 90% students retention *Health*: Running 18 Hospitals and Speciality Hospitals and 53 Primary Healthcare Programmes across India. Efforts have lowered infant mortality rate and maternal mortality rate compared to national average

(c) Benefits of Social Marketing

Following are the benefits of social marketing:

(1) It helps the company to establish a two-way communication between the organisation and the general public who may or may not be the consumers today.

(2) Promote company's offerings indirectly using PR campaigns, Sponsoring well regarded events and providing scholarships.

(3) Promoting social responsibility like reduction in pollution, wastes re-cycle management, water harvesting and management, electricity for rural using Photovoltaic Solar Cell Panels and so on.

(4) Promoting and building the corporate image of the company through (CSR) Corporate Social Responsibility initiatives.

(5) Increase in earnings.

(6) Attain sustainable growth.

Conclusion

Today companies like 'Grameen bank' in Bangaldesh enhanced the well-being of rural poor by financing the Self-Help Groups through 'Micro Finance' which empowered rural women. Here, social service is integrated with business. This the best way forward for being socially committed and that is what is all about social marketing.

UNIT 6.3: GREEN MARKETING

(a) What is Green Marketing?

Green marketing is a way of doing business by creating value to the consumers by reducing carbon footprints and green house gas emission. It is a strategy where, branding and positioning will be based on being 'Green' or 'Environment Friendly'. Simply put, the entire business process and the product and service offerings would be eco-friendly. This will be highlighted in the promotional campaigns of the company to create a positive brand (both corporate and product brands) image to see sustainable growth in the market.

(b) Why do Companies Go Green?

It helps the green business in the following ways:

(1) To create new market opportunities.

(2) To drive-up the sales revenue.

(3) To build brand equity or value.

(4) To reduce environmental degradation by reducing the green house gas emission.

(5) To increase efficiency and low costs through optimum usage or utilisation of resources.

(6) To gain an edge over the rival brands using its 'Green' image as a Competitive Advantage.

(c) How do Companies Go Green?

In this section, the readers will learn what the corporate India and the MNCs operating in India are currently doing to become more eco-friendly:

Electrical and Electronic Appliances Business

Bajaj Electricals and Philips' CFL bulbs. The Compact Fluorescent Light Bulbs are now used extensively in India replacing the old version incandescent bulbs. On an average CFL bulbs use just 25% of energy to power an incandescent bulb. They also have a better longevity versus traditional bulbs.

Electronic and Electrical Appliance and Energy Stars

All Leading Electronic and Electrical Appliance brands today offer their products with 'Energy-Stars' that indicates how much energy efficient the appliances are. The Energy Stars are available on Water Heaters, Iron Box, Microwave Ovens, Washing Machine etc.

Telecom

Bharti Airtel: Bharti's Airtel 'Green Towers P7' initiative reduced its diesel usage and air conditioners usage in its towers which have been replaced with solar panels and free cooling units. As a result the company was able to save ₹ 47 Million in Diesel Cost and also lead to reduction in carbon footprints.

Real Estate

Indian Government was planning in 2010 for developing four smart cities in Manesar, Shendra. Changodar and Dahej in association with Japanese firm Hitachi, Mitsubishi and Toshiba. These smart cities are to be build based on the principles of '3-Rs', viz. Recycle, Reuse and Reduce. These smart cities would have energy efficient facilities with extensive networking capabilities along with eco-friendly public transportation system.

Footwear

Woodland, the footwear and apparel major launched an online store woodlandworldwide.com in March 2012. The company intends to make 'Eco-friendliness' as their brand recall. For that they are using the materials and chemicals that do not harm the nature, make the manufacturing process less harmful to the environment. Thus intends to promote its brand as 'Eco-Friendly' brand.

Automobile

Mahindra Reva, the only Indian brand, in the electric car market segment reached the total sales of 5000 units in 2011, is now a well established global brand which is exported to 24 nations. Other MNC players who ventured India with hybrid technologies were Honda Civic and Toyota Prius.

Stationery Items

ITC and TNPL offers eco-friendly notebooks made of sugarcane wastes rather than from chopped trees.

(d) Conclusion

In 1990s, quality was the key differentiator for the corporate players to differentiate from their rivals. But today, 21st century business is going green and the green marketing is seen by the corporate houses as the competitive advantage to outsmart their rivals in a sustainable way. Sooner or later, all players in the market will be compelled to join the green bandwagon.

UNIT 6.4: VIRAL MARKETING

The Viral Marketing or Buzz Marketing concept emerged in 1999. It refers to the spread of information about the company or brand at a rapid pace through word-of-mouth. As the company constantly maintains a buzz (make people continually talk about the company and the brand) in the market, it is also called as Buzz Marketing. Today, in the era of technological advancement, viral marketing takes place in social networking sites like facebook.com, twitter.com, flickr.com, LinkedIn.com, Foursquare.com and other famous blogs.

Quite often, the viral marketing campaigns would be in the form of 'refer-a-friend' email campaigns. It is defined as an addictive and self-propagating advertisement, which is integrated with entertainment.

Following strategies are followed by the companies for developing and executing their viral marketing campaigns:

(i) Offer incentive to forward the messages

(ii) Forward the (viral) message only through known persons

(iii) Provide 'opt-in' and 'opt-out' options to the prospects

(iv) Measure the performance

(v) Viral campaigns are to be continuous

(i) Offer Incentive to Forward the Messages

To make individuals to forward the company's promotional messages to their known people, a financial or a non-financial incentive has to be provided by the company. To make the first individual to accept receiving the promotional messages, permission marketing may be adopted. A word of caution, every financial and non-financial incentive has to be capped so that there is a control over the promotional costs.

(ii) Forward the (Viral) Message Only Through Known Persons

Today companies are restricted from sending bulk sms or email messages by TRAI. Usually, they are viewed as SPAMS or unsolicited email letters, where the prospects simply ignore them. In order to overcome this issue, the company must send promotional emails only through the known people like friends, relatives etc. where the response would be far higher than sending them directly by the companies to their prospects.

(iii) Provide 'Opt-In' and 'Opt-Out' Options to the Prospects

All the prospects have the right to protect their privacy and freedom to decide whether to 'Opt-in' or not. An option of 'Opt-in' shall be provided to join official blogs, receive promotional emails with special offers, enroll as a fan in the official page of the facebook.com. At the same time, an option to 'Opt-out' must also be provided, which indeed protects the freedom of choice of the prospects.

(iv) Measure the Performance

The company engaging its customers through viral marketing must track its performance based on conversion rate, 'Opt-out' rate this would help the company to know the exact effect of viral or buzz marketing on the target market.

(v) Viral Campaigns are to be Continuous

Marketers must try to forward appropriate brand messages to its target market quite frequently in the form of emails, blogs, networking sites like facebook.com and so on, and it has to be a continuous process instead of one-time business activity.

UNIT 6.5: DIRECT MARKETING/E-MARKETING/ONLINE MARKETING/SOCIAL MEDIA MARKETING/VIRTUAL WORLD MARKETING

(a) Online Marketing or E-Marketing

If a company promotes and sells the product and service offerings through internet, it is called as internet marketing or online marketing or e-marketing. According Chaffey, Internet Marketing is "achieving marketing objectives through applying digital technologies". A few famous online marketers are ebay.com, paypal.com, jabong.com, snapdeal.com, yahooshopping.com and makemytrip.com, bharatmatrimony.com.

(b) Emerging Trends and Techniques in Online Marketing Programmes

Today corporate players are using various online marketing techniques for acquiring and engaging with the customers in the internet. Following are the emerging trends and techniques for acquiring and engaging with the customers on the web:

(i) Social Networking Sites
(ii) Blogs
(iii) Pay Per Click
(iv) Instant Messaging
(v) E-Mail Marketing Campaigns
(vi) Search Engine Optimisation
(vii) Placing Mobile Ads on Third Party Applications
(viii) Virtual Marketing

(i) Social Networking Sites

Companies today promote their brands through social networking sites like facebook.com, twitter.com, flickr.com, LinkedIn.com, foursquare.com, google+, myspace.com, orkut.com and so on to have a direct contact with the customers.

Any positive and negative experiences of the users of the product would get shared and spread among the registered user-group through word-of-mouth (of course in the form of text) in lightning speed. In a way it can also be called as viral marketing due to its nature. Let us understand how facebook.com used by the leading corporate to address the customers' concern immediately and maintain its positive image. When a customer lodges a complaint or his bad experience in the open forum, the company sees this as an opportunity rather than a problem as if it can resolve the problem at once; its image would get boosted up. When the company acknowledges the customer's problem and resolves it in a reasonable time, immediately, everybody following this message or page would click 'Like' symbol which in turn will create a positive image towards the brand. This would eventually end up in increased sales as customers know that the company or the service provider care for them. 44% of people in India (compared to 22% worldwide and 39% in BRIC nations), have said that they had bought a brand because their friends follows or 'likes', a brand on a social network.[1]

(ii) Blogs

Blogs are online discussion forums where people with similar thoughts and values would share their views on any topic. Marketers use this to understand attitude, tastes and preferences and mindset of the consumers towards their brands. Say for instance, Direct-To-Home Entertainment Television Service Providers like Reliance DTH, Airtel DTH and Dish TV. would engage themselves in reputed blogs related to Television Entertainment to understand the tastes and preferences of their prospects.

(iii) Pay Per Click

It is internet based advertising where the advertisers pay only when an user or the visitor of the website actually clicks on an ad link to visit the advertising page or website. Such links are called as 'Sponsored Link' or 'Sponsored Ads'. Social networking site Facebook.com puts video ads,

---

[1] *The Hindu Business Line,* "My Friend Likes a Brand. Hmmm.....", dt. 03-07-2013, pg-5.

promotions and sponsored stories in the user's News Feed which facilitates high level brand visibility which in turn generate high 'click through' rate[1].

(iv) Instant Messaging

It refers to the ads appearing on the sides of instant messaging platform to promote brands. Example: twitter.com

(v) E-Mail Marketing Campaigns

Companies send email to stimulate the prospects to buy its products and services.

(vi) Search Engine Optimisation

Search engines like google.com, yahoo.com, bing.com offers search engine optimisation service where the company's or advertiser's website URL link appears at the top of the search result. It is a paid service.

(vii) Placing Mobile Ads on Third Party Applications

Youtube.com offers wide range of videos which can be accessed anywhere and at any time. All famous videos will carry a paid advertisement before the chosen video starts streaming with an option for the views to skip the same, if they are not interested. Facebook.com use this promotions very well where it allows a few websites and apps to use facebook.com's information to target their users with better ads through their social networking site, where ads would promote a website or provide a link to download an app and the brand presence will be in the apps.

(viii) Virtual Marketing

Creating a buzz online on any brand using video clips using youtube.com, skype.com, interactive flash games, e-books, e-magazines using flash, and usage of virtual 3D communities like Second Life, Small worlds, Active worlds is a part of virtual marketing. Pothys, a famous brand of Fashion and Ethnic (Cultural) Wear Retailer uses virtual marketing extensively for promoting its Silk Sarees (see Exhibit-6.5.1). It uses facebook.com, twitter, skype.com for networking with the customers and uses 'Paypal' for safe online transactions. When customers share good news or information online about a brands they use, and when marketers use these data for promotion and marketing of their brands, it is called as virtual marketing. Today companies like WIPRO, IBM- India have their offices operating in the Virtual World 'Second Life'. WIPRO was the first Indian Organisation to make its presence successfully in Second Life, a Virtual World. Business organisations across the world, especially, Fortune 500 companies are using Second Life for product launches, promotional activities etc.

Say for instance, an US apparel major encouraged the people (called 'avatars' in Second Life) to buy its apparels in virtual world using its internal currency Linden Dollar (L$) and get 15% discount on their real world apparel stores[2]. Godrej, India's leading consumer goods marketing

---

[1] *The Hindu Business Line*, "This is how Facebook 'cashes in on you'!", dt. 25-12-12, pg-3.

[2] Indian Management "Vitues and Veracity of Second Life", by Nityesh Bhatt and Sapna Choradia, dt. November 2011, pg-91.

company has launched its own version of Virtual World like second life, at its gojiyo.com with a caption "Create your own Avatar".

EXHIBIT 6.5.1 **Indian Players Making Use of Virtual Marketing Effectively**

Source: Pothys: www.pothys.com and Godrej Virtual World: http://www.gojiyo.com/

(c) Opportunities and challenges in online marketing

Every coin has two sides. Similarly, every technology will have both opportunities and challenges. This section discusses on the opportunities and challenges in e-marketing.

Exhibit 6.5.2 **Opportunities and Challenges in E-Marketing**

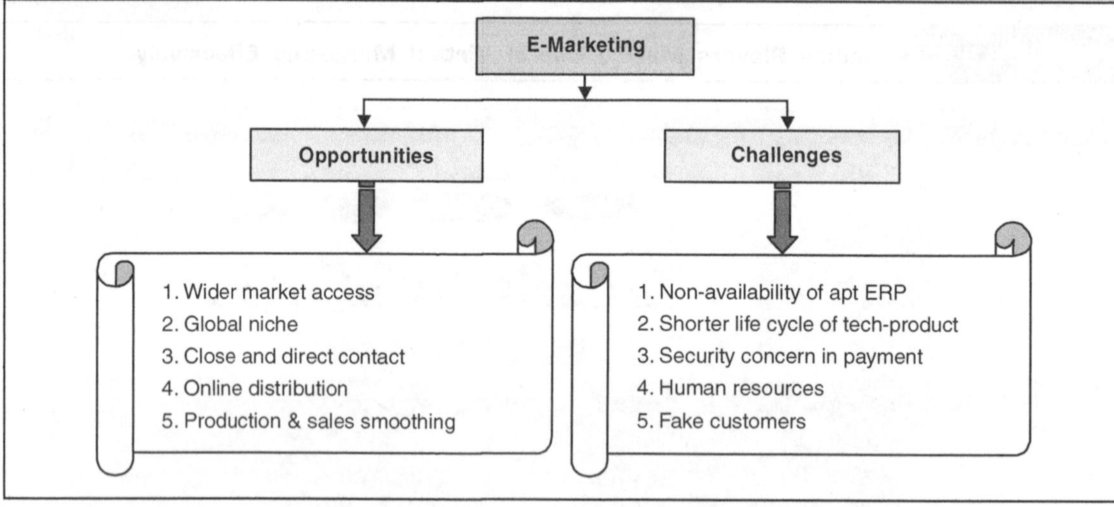

Opportunities in E-Marketing

Following are the opportunities in e-marketing:

(1) *Wider Market Access:* It helps even a small company to expand its business globally.

(2) *Global Niche*: A web based company can standardize its user interface and offerings targeting the global niche.

(3) *Close and Direct Contact:* Internet marketing enables a close and direct contact between a company and its customers that help it to customize its offerings as per the taste and preference of the customers.

(4) *Online Distribution:* Internet facilitates online companies to distribute their offerings cheap and efficiently. Say for instance, Apple sells music to its iphone customers for 99 cents a song, online. Reliance Bigflix distributes rental videos and movies online in India.

(5) *Production and Sales Smoothing:* Internet marketing helps real time inventory management and operational scheduling. It helps to find the trade leads quickly and clear the excess inventory in very short period of time.

Challenges in E-Marketing

Following are the challenges in e-marketing:

(1) *Non-Availability of Apt ERP:* There is no single software solution that takes care of all the operations of the company that come under any industry. Hence it takes time to develop customized software as (ERP) Enterprise-wide Resource Planning package.

(2) *Shorter Life Cycle of Tech-Product:* Online companies have to invest a huge sum of money in hardware and software for e-marketing. Today, new technologies are developed at higher cost compared to its previous version (one may argue that latest cell phone model costs less compared to previous ones but look at anti-virus, operating system, ERP package

prices levels. There is definitely a price rise). When the company switches from its existing technology to a new one, there must not be any disruption in the 24x7 (24 hours and 7 days a week) service. If so, then it will lead to customers switching to rival brands for purchase, which in turn leads to decrease in profitability of the firm.

(3) *Security Concern in Payment:* No technology in this world is 100% fool proof. Hackers around the world steal critical information like credit card PIN and online bank account password from the online companies. Hence customers hesitate to buy online.

(4) *Human Resources:* It is a huge myth that online companies require less employees and the software programmes can do everything. In reality, the software programmes can only assist the business and marketing process where the companies still need efficient people to succeed in the hyper-competitive virtual market. It is also found that the online company needs to spend a huge amount of money and time for training and motivating the employees to make them work in the e-business environment efficiently and effectively over a longer period of time.

(5) *Fake Customers:* Today, online companies have started facing the problem of fake customers who would make a purchase order online and provide an incorrect address to the company. These customers choose 'COD or Cash-On-Delivery' option when it comes to payment mode. When the company delivers the ordered goods to the customers, they come to know about the fake customers, where the time, money and effort spent on this business transaction go wasted, which would eventually end up in loss. Thus the working capital and profit margins of the online companies is affected. It also leads to unrecoverable loss of transportation costs, including the shipping cost.

(d) Merits and Demerits of Online Marketing and Communication (Online Ads)

Following are the merits and demerits of online advertisements:

Merits

(i) It facilitates one-to-one communication for the company with its target market

(ii) It caters to the specific interests of the prospective customers

(iii) It facilitates promotion and sales across borders

(iv) It helps in reaching global customers

(v) It helps the online company to provide different content to the customer by choice

(vi) It is of relatively less cost compared to traditional business model

Demerits

(i) There is always a security concern in online cash transactions

(ii) No use if customers have no access to computers and internet

(iii) High transparency in pricing leads to cut-throat price oriented competition

(iv) It leads to worldwide competition, where small players may not scale its production and operations to match the larger ones

(v) Fraudulent transactions of select group of cyber criminals result in 'Sales Return', which affects the working capital and profit margins of the online companies.

UNIT 6.6: PERMISSION MARKETING

(a) What is Permission Marketing?

'Permission marketing' is a sub-discipline of marketing. It was propounded by Seth Godin, the father of permission marketing. Permission marketing does not approve mass marketing and mass communication as they are obsolete. Today, marketers have adopted this marketing style to succeed in the cluttered and cut-throat competitive market.

EXHIBIT 6.6.1 Permission Marketing of 'The Entrepreneur Magazine'

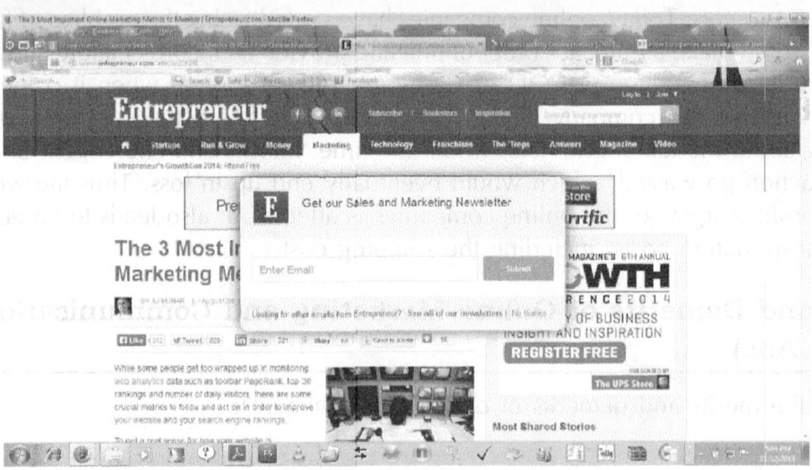

Source: http://www.entrepreneur.com/article/224291

Marketers, first segment and target a specific market. Get their permission so that their sales personnel can officially approach them to promote the company's offerings, where the chances of rejection is minimized as the prospects themselves had already shown some degree of interest in the company's offerings. This process is called as permission marketing. Say for instance, let us see the example of 'The Entrepreneur' Online Magazine. For sending its promotional letters it seeks the permission its web-page visitors by asking their email. One can see the 'No Thanks' option which provides a freedom of choice.

(b) How it Works?

Companies use permission marketing both off-line and online quite successfully in the market. In case of online, let us take the example for email account registration. Most of the online users would have given their preferences or areas of interests like cricket, politics, stocks, science etc. by checking the check-boxes at the time of registration of email account. This is a formal way of getting the prospects permission to send promotional emails with their consent related to their areas of interest. If the email users had not checked any options provided, obviously, the promotional emails sent to the prospects email account would instantaneously gets dumped into 'Spam Box'. This is where mass marketing and communication fails and permission marketing finds its place.

As far as mass marketing in offline is concerned, it can be understood by usinig the example of Club Mahindra, a holiday or timeshare service provider, which has successfully adopted Permission Marketing to succeed in the market. The service provider posts their employees in social spots, viz. petrol stations, high-way toll-booths, premium cinemas etc. Their target market is high income group. Hence, the company has promulgated a set of criterion, which includes owing of cars.

Thus, when people are seen in these social spots with a car, they would get qualified as the prospects of the company. Once they are targeted as the prospective buyers, the company personnel would approach them and ask permission to talk to them.

If permission is granted by the prospects, they are provided with 'Lead Generation Form', in which the prospect would enter their personal details (like name, address) and confirms that they would like to get sales call on Club Mahindra's offerings. As an incentive for showing interest towards the acceptance of 'sales calls', the prospects are offered with a free holiday stay at its facilities or a chance to participate in contests sponsored by Club Mahindra. By this, 'sales calls' do not become 'nuisance calls' to the customers and the chances of converting prospect into a consumer brightens.

This style clearly shows that instead of mass communication, companies resort to mass customization for marketing their offerings in the market. This style is still evolving and will take its own shape according to the changing market dynamics.

LEARNING EXERCISES

1. Prepare a report on rural marketing distribution model of HUL's Project Shakti.
2. Prepare a report on ITC's E-Choupal (check their official website).
3. Check the ITC's role in Incense Sticks or Agarbatti Business India empowering rural SHGs and NGOs. (Refer: Indian Management, "The Journey of Incense Stick"dt. December 2012).
4. Prepare a report on how www.google.com makes money from its sites.
5. Prepare a report on how www.facebook.com makes money from its social networking site.

Field Work: Visit any NGO that is operating in your area, identify their core purpose of existence (mission), find a corporate entity of your choice and get their financial or non-financial assistance to the NOGs for facilitating their work. Your team must take care of all the work until its execution and a report shall be prepared and submitted to the corporate entity and the NGO as a documentary evidence of execution of the project as stipulated by the company and the college faculty-guide.

Note: LE-Learning Exercise.

❑❑❑

GLOSSARY

A

Above the Line

Advertising for which a payment is made and for which commission is paid to the advertising agency. See also 'below the line' and 'push versus pull promotion'

Account Management

The process by which an agency or supplier manages the needs of a client.

Added Value

The increase in worth of a product or service as a result of a particular activity - in the context of marketing, the activity might be packaging or branding.

Advertising

Promotion of a product, service, or message by an identified sponsor using paid-for media.

Advertorial

An advertisement which is designed to have the appearance of an editorial. Advertorials are normally labelled as "Advertising" or "This is an advertisement". Similar in practice to an infomercial.

Advocacy Advertising

Advocacy advertising expresses a viewpoint on a given issue, often on behalf an institution. Examples are to be found in anti-Drink-Driving campaigns.

Adware

Free software which includes pop-up banner advertisements which cannot be dismissed. See 'Banner Averts' and 'Pop-up'.

Affiliate Marketing

A form of marketing or advertising used on the internet. Companies that sell products or services online link to relevant sites. The advertising on the other or 'affiliate' sites is paid for according to results.

Affinity Marketing

Marketing targeted at individuals sharing common interests that predispose them towards a product, *e.g.*, an auto accessories manufacturer targeting motoring magazine readers. Also, a campaign jointly sponsored by a number of disparate organisations that are non-competitive but have a particular interest in common.

After Sales Service

Services received after the original goods or service have been paid for.

AIDA

Attention, Interest, Desire, Action: a model describing the process that advertising or promotion is intended to initiate in the mind of a prospective customer.

AIUAPR

Awareness, Interest, Understanding, Attitudes, Purchase, Repeat purchase: a buying decision model.

Ambient Media

Originally known as 'fringe media', ambient media are communications platforms that surround us in everyday life—from petrol pump advertising to advertising projected onto buildings to advertising on theatre tickets, cricket pitches or even pay slips. See also 'buzz'.

Ambush Marketing

A deliberate attempt by an organisation to associate itself with an event (often a sporting event) in order to gain some of the benefits associated with being an official sponsor without incurring the costs of sponsorship. For example by advertising during broadcasts of the event. See also 'buzz'.

Ansoff Matrix

Model relating marketing strategy to general strategic direction. It maps product-market strategies—*e.g.,* market penetration, product development, market development and diversification - on a matrix showing new versus existing products along one axis and new versus existing markets along the other.

Asset Led Marketing

Asset led marketing uses product strengths such as the name and brand image to market both new and existing products. Marketing decisions are based on the needs of the consumer AND the assets of the product.

Assignments

An assessed work based project report. Assignments are part of the assessment procedure when studying for a qualification.

B

Balanced Scorecard

A technique allowing a company to monitor and manage performance against defined objectives. Measurements might typically cover financial performance, customer value, internal business process, innovation performance and employee performance.

Banner Adverts

Adverts on web pages used to build brand awareness or drive traffic to the advertisers own website.

BCG (Boston Consulting Group) Matrix

Model for product portfolio analysis. Products can be classified as:

Stars—high growth and market share

Cash Cows—high market share and low growth rate

Question marks—low market share in high growth rate markets

Dogs—low market share and low growth rate.

Below the Line

Non-media advertising or promotion when no commission has been paid to the advertising agency. Includes direct mail, point of sale displays, giveaways. See also, 'above the line' and 'push versus pull promotion'.

Black Space

The business opportunities that a company has formally targeted and organised itself to capture. Compare with 'white space'.

Blended E-Learning

An integrated programme with a blend of interactive online tuition, face-to-face classroom workshops, assignments and a Learning Log.

Blogs/Blogging

An internet publishing device allowing an individual or company to express their thoughts and opinions. Businesses can use blogs as a marketing communication channel.

Bluetooth

Open specification for short range communication between wireless devices.

Brand

The set of physical attributes of a product or service, together with the beliefs and expectations surrounding it—a unique combination which the name or logo of the product or service should evoke in the mind of the audience.

Brand Extension

Process by which a company develops new products to be marketed under an existing brand name.

Brand Management

The process by which marketers attempt to optimise the 'Marketing mix' for a specific brand.

Brand Value

The value which a brand would be given if represented on a company balance sheet.

Brown Goods

Electrical goods such as TVs, videos, stereo systems etc, used for home entertainment. So called because they were originally cased in bakelite, a brown plastic.

Business Plan

A strategic document showing cash flow, forecasts and direction of a company.

Business Strategy.

The means by which a business works towards achieving its stated aims.

Business to Business (B2B)

Relating to the sale of a product for any use other than personal consumption. The buyer may be a manufacturer, a reseller, a government body, a non-profit-making institution, or any organisation other than an ultimate consumer.

Business to Consumer (B2C)

Relating to the sale of product for personal consumption. The buyer may be an individual, family or other group, buying to use the product themselves, or for end use by another individual.

Buying Behaviour

The process that buyers go through when deciding whether or not to purchase goods or services. Buying behaviour can be influenced by a variety of external factors and motivations, including marketing activity.

Buzz

Buzz marketing uses 'word-of-mouth' advertising: potential customers pass round information about a product. See also 'viral marketing'

C

Category Management

Products are grouped and managed by strategic business unit categories. These are defined by how consumers views goods rather than by how they look to the seller, *e.g.*, confectionery could be part of either a 'food' or 'gifts' category, and marketed depending on the category into which it's grouped.

Cause Related Marketing

Partnership between a company or brand and a charity or 'cause' by which the charity benefits financially from the sale of specific products.

Channels

The methods used by a company to communicate and interact with its customers.

Chartered Marketer

A marketing professional who has achieved 'individual Chartered Status' awarded by the Chartered Institute of Marketing.

Click-through

The act of a user clicking on an internet advertisement that opens a link to the advertiser's website.

Comparative Advertising

Advertising which compares a company's product with that of competing brands. Must be used with caution to avoid accusations of misrepresentation from competitors.

Competitions

Sales promotions that allow the consumer the possibility of winning a prize.

Competitive Advantage

The product, proposition or benefit that puts a company ahead of its competitors.

Competitors

Companies that sell products or services in the same market place as one another.

Confusion Marketing

Controversial strategy of deliberately confusing the customer. Examples are alleged to be found in the telecommunications market, where pricing plans can be so complicated that it becomes impossible to make direct comparisons between competing offers.

Consumer

Individual who buys and uses a product or service.

Consumer Behaviour

The buying habits and patterns of consumers in the acquisition and usage of goods and services.

Cookie

Small data file downloaded on to an end-user's computer which allows a web site to identify the visitor. Cookies can be used to build profiles of repeat users of a website.

Copyright

The law that protects an author's original material, usually (in the UK) for 70 years after the author's death. Similar law covers logos and brand names.

Copywriting

Creative process by which written content is prepared for advertisements or marketing material.

Corporate Identity

The character a company seeks to establish for itself in the mind of the public, reinforced by consistent use of logos, colours, typefaces and so on. See also 'corporate reputation'.

Corporate Reputation

A complex mix of characteristics, such as ethos, identity and image, that go to make up a company's public personality. Corporate reputation hinges on investor confidence, unlike brand reputation which is contingent on customer confidence and reflected in sales. See also 'corporate identity'.

Corporate Strategy

The policies of a company with regard to its choice of businesses and customer groups

Cost Leadership

The strategy of producing goods at a lower cost than one's competitors.

Culture

The philosophy of a company, reflected in aims such as the maximisation of customer satisfaction.

Customer

A person or company who purchases goods or services (not necessarily the end 'consumer').

Customer Lifetime Value (CLV)

The profitability of customers during the lifetime of the relationship, as opposed to profitability on one transaction.

Customer Loyalty

Feelings or attitudes that incline a customer either to return to a company, shop or outlet to purchase there again, or else to re-purchase a particular product, service or brand.

Customer Relationship Management (CRM)

The coherent management of contacts and interactions with customers. (This term is often used as if it related purely to the use of IT, but IT should in fact be regarded as a facilitator of CRM).

Customer Satisfaction

The provision of goods or services which fulfil the customer's expectations in terms of quality and service, in relation to price paid.

Customer Service Programme

Strategy for assuring customers a positive buying experience in order to improve customer loyalty, increase cross-selling and promote advertising by word-of-mouth. See also 'customer satisfaction'.

Cyber-stealth Marketing

Covert attempts using the internet to boost brand image, to make websites appear more popular than they are or to manipulate search engine listings.

D

DAGMAR

Defining Advertising Goals for Measured Advertising Response—a model for planning advertising in such a way that its success can be quantitatively monitored.

Data Processing

The obtaining, recording and holding of information which can then be retrieved, used, disseminated or erased. The term tends to be used in connection with computer systems, and today is often used interchangeably with 'Information Technology'.

Database Marketing

Whereby customer information, stored in an electronic database, is utilised for targeting marketing activities. Information can be a mixture of what is gleaned from previous interactions with the customer and what is available from outside sources. See also 'CRM—Customer Relationship Management'.

Decision Making Unit (DMU)

The team of people in an organisation who make the final buying decision.

Demand and Supply

Demand is the desire for a product at the market price: supply is the quantity available at that price.

Demographic Data

Information describing and segmenting a population in terms of age, sex, income and so on, which can be used to target marketing campaigns.

Differentiation

Ensuring that products and services have a unique element to allow them to stand out from the rest.

DINKY

Double Income No Kids Yet—a demographic grouping.

Direct Mail

Delivery of an advertising or promotional message to customers or potential customers by mail.

Direct Marketing

All activities which make it possible to offer goods or services or to transmit other messages to a segment of the population by post, telephone, e-mail or other direct means.

Direct Response Advertising (DRA)

Advertising incorporating a contact method such as a phone number, address and enquiry form, web site identifier or e-mail address, with the intention of encouraging the recipient to respond directly to the advertiser by requesting more information, placing an order and so on.

Distribution

The process of getting the goods from the manufacturer or supplier to the user.

Diversification

An increase in the variety of goods and services produced by an individual enterprise or conglomerate. It may be encouraged, either by business owners or by governments, in order to reduce the risk of relying on a narrow range of products.

E

E-commerce or E-marketing

Marketing conducted electronically, usually over the Internet.

Efficient Consumer Response (ECR)

Having the right product in the right place at the right price with the right promotions. See also 'category management', with its emphasis on how products look to the customer - is seen as an integral part of achieving ECR.

Electronic Point of Sale (EPOS) System

A system whereby electronic tills are used to process customer transactions in a retail outlet. Local EPOS systems are usually connected to a central computer system, so that financial and inventory-related data can be exchanged between the store and head office, allowing automatic accounting and replenishment.

Emotional Selling Preposition (ESP)

The unique associations established by consumers with particular products. For example, the emotional response to certain car marques ensures their continual success, even though other makers may offer superior performance at the same price.

Endorsement

Affirmation, usually from a celebrity, that a product is good.

Entrepreneur

Someone who sees an opportunity and risks their own money to set up a business organisation in order to respond to it.

Ethical Marketing

Marketing that takes account of the moral aspects of decisions.

Experience Curve

The plotted relationship between the amount of products produced and the cost per unit over time from launch. As more units are produced, the cost per unit usually declines, an effect that is partially attributable to the accumulation of experience.

Export Marketing

The marketing of goods or services to overseas customers.

External Analysis

Study of the external marketing environment, including factors such as customers, competition, and social change.

F

FAST Marketing

Focused Advertising Sampling Technique: an approach concentrating promotions into a short space of time to saturate the market.

Field Marketing

The practice of sending representatives or agents to retail outlets with a view to building brand and supporting sales. They may for example conduct in-store promotions, set up point of sale displays, and ensure that products are displayed to best advantage.

FMCG

Fast Moving Consumer Goods—such as packaged food, beverages, toiletries, and tobacco.

Focus Groups

A tool for market research where small groups of customers are invited to participate in guided discussions on the topic being researched.

Forecasting

Calculation of future events and performance.

Four M's

Money, Material, Machine and Manpower—traditional framework for viewing the resources available to a business, which can be useful when designing a marketing plan.

Four P's

See 'marketing mix'.

Franchising

The selling of a licence by the owner (franchisor) to a third party (franchisee) permitting the sale of a product or service for a specified period. In business format franchising the agreement will involve a common brand and marketing format.

G

Geodemographics

A method of analysis combining geographic and demographic variables.

GLAM

Greying, Leisured, Affluent, Middle-aged—a demographic grouping.

Grey Market

Sometimes called 'silver market'. Term used to define population over a certain age—usually 65.

Grey Marketing (also called Parallel Importing)

The illicit sale of imported products contrary to the interests of a holder of a trademark, patent or copyright in the country of sale.

Guarantees and Warranties

Legal documents committing a company to deal with faulty goods or services by a variety of methods including repair, replacement or compensation.

Guerrilla Marketing

The strategy of targeting small and specialised customer groups in such a way that bigger companies will not find it worthwhile to retaliate.

GUPPIE

Green YUPPIE—a demographic grouping. See also 'YUPPIE'.

H

House to House Distribution

Delivery of goods or literature to the consumer's front door or mailbox.

I

Inducements

Incentives offered to overcome resistance to purchase, for example 'special offers' or money-back guarantees.

Industrial Marketing

The marketing of industrial products.

Infiltration Marketing

Marketers joining chat rooms posing as ordinary users in order to spread marketing messages, usually as personal endorsements.

Infomercial

Paid-for television programme purporting to be a genuine station programme. Its use is restricted to certain countries including the USA, but not the UK. Similar in practice to an advertorial.

Innovation

Development of new products, services or ways of working.

Institutional Market

A market for goods or services consisting of universities, schools, charities clubs and the like.

Internal Analysis

The study of a company's internal marketing resources in order to assess opportunities, strengths or weaknesses

Internal Customers

Employees within an organisation viewed as consumers of a product or service provided by another part of the organisation—products or services which the employees need to do their own work. For example, the marketing department could be internal customers of the IT department.

Internal Marketing

The process of eliciting support for a company and its activities among its own employees, in order to encourage them to promote its goals. This process can happen at a number of levels, from increasing awareness of individual products or marketing campaigns, to explaining overall business strategy.

International Marketing

The conduct and co-ordination of marketing activities in more than one country.

IPTV

Internet Protocol Television. Technology allowing television and video signals to be received via an internet connection.

J

Joint Venture

A business entity or partnership formed by two or more parties for a specific purpose; for example, 50 : 50 joint venture

JUPPIE

Japanese YUPPIE—a demographic grouping. See also 'YUPPIE'.

K

Key Account Management

Account management as applied to a company's most important customers. See also 'account management'.

Keyword Buying

Advertisers paying for links to their websites to appear on internet search engines along side search results, sometimes as "sponsored links", based on keywords entered into the search engine. See 'Search Marketing'.

Kidults

Adults who buy products that are predominantly aimed at children.

Knowledge Management

The collection, organisation and distribution of information in a form that lends itself to practical application. Knowledge management often relies on information technology to facilitate the storage and retrieval of information.

L

Logo

A graphic, usually consisting of a symbol and/or group of letters, that identifies a company or brand.

M

Macro Environment

The external factors which affect a company's planning and performance, and are beyond its control: for example, socio-economic, legal and technological change. Compare 'micro environment'.

Mailing Preference Service (MPS)

A database of individual home addresses where the occupiers have elected not to receive unsolicited direct (marketing) mail.

Market Challenger

A firm attempting to gain market leadership through marketing efforts - see also 'market follower' and 'market leader'.

Market Development

The process of growing sales by offering existing products (or new versions of them) to new customer groups (as opposed to simply attempting to increase the company's share of current markets).

Market Entry

The launch of a new product into a new or existing market. A different strategy is required depending on whether the product is an early or late entrant to the market; the first entrant usually has an automatic advantage, while later entrants need to demonstrate that their products are better, cheaper and so on.

Market Follower

A firm that is happy to follow the leaders in a market place without challenging them, perhaps taking advantages of opportunities created by leaders without the need for much marketing investment of its own - see also 'market challenger' and 'market leader'.

Market Leader

Seller of the product or service with the largest market share in its field - see also 'market challenger' and 'market follower'.

Market Penetration

The attempt to grow one's business by obtaining a larger market share in an existing market —see 'market share' and 'market development'.

Market Research (or Marketing Research)

The gathering and analysis of data relating to market places or customers; any research which leads to more market knowledge and better-informed decision-making.

Market Segmentation

The division of the market place into distinct subgroups or segments, each characterised by particular tastes and requiring a specific marketing mix. See also 'marketing mix'.

Market Share

A company's sales of a given product or set of products to a given set of customers, expressed as a percentage of total sales of all such products to such customers.

Marketing

Marketing is the management process responsible for identifying, anticipating and satisfying customer requirements profitably.

Marketing Acronyms

Usually, abbreviations such as P3G (Page3Generation), Babyboomers, YUPPIE, BUPPIE, and GLAM. See individual acronyms for a description.

Marketing Audit

Scrutiny of an organisation's existing marketing system to ascertain its strengths and weaknesses.

Marketing Communications

All methods used by a firm to communicate with its customers and prospective customers.

Marketing Information

Any information used or required to support marketing decisions—often drawn from a computerised 'Marketing Information System'.

Marketing Metrics

Measurements that help with the quantification of marketing performance, such as market share, advertising spend, and response rates elicited by advertising and direct marketing.

Marketing Mix

The combination of marketing inputs that affect customer motivation and behaviour. These inputs traditionally encompass four controllable variables 'the 4 Ps': product, price, promotion and place. The list has subsequently been extended to 7 Ps, the additions being people, process and 'physical evidence'.

Marketing Myopia

Lack of vision on the part of companies, particularly in failing to spot customers' desires through excessive product focus. Term derives from the title of a seminal article by Theodore Levitt published in Harvard Business Review in 1960.

Marketing Orientation

A business strategy whereby customers' needs and wants, as identified by the marketing function, determine corporate direction.

Marketing Plan

A written plan, usually in-depth, describing all activities involved in achieving a particular marketing objective, and their relationship to one another in both time and importance.

Marketing Planning

The selection and scheduling of activities to support the company's chosen marketing strategy or goals. See also 'marketing strategy'.

Marketing Strategy

The set of objectives which an organisation allocates to its marketing function in order to support the overall corporate strategy, together with the broad methods chosen to achieve these objectives.

Media Neutral Planning

A customer focussed review of media options during communications planning based on research, analysis and insight, not habit and preference.

Merger/Acquisition

Merger: The formation of one company from two existing companies.

Acquisition: One company acquiring control of another by purchase of a majority.

Micro Environment

The immediate context of a company's operations, including such elements as suppliers, customers and competitors—compare 'macro environment'.

Mission Statement

A company's summary of its business philosophy and direction.

MMS

Multimedia Message Service. Text, audio, graphic and video messages sent by mobile phones, or other compatible devices, over a wireless network.

Models (or Marketing Models)

Graphical representations of a process designed to aid in understanding and/or forecasting. Computerised models allow the simulation of scenarios based on different assumptions about changes to the macro environment and micro environment. See also 'macro environment' and 'micro environment'.

Mood Board

A visual illustration tool used either to represent the atmosphere or feel of an intended advertisement, or to research a consumer's experience of a brand or product.

N

Neuromarketing

Technique to quantify how consumers will respond to brands and advertising. The brain is mapped, using functional Magnetic Resonance Imaging (fMRI), to record conscious and subconscious responses to advertising, products or brands.

New Product Development (NPD)

The creation of new products, from evaluation of proposals through to launch.

Niche Marketing

The marketing of a product to a small and well-defined segment of the market place.

NILKIE

No Income, Lots of Kids - a demographic grouping.

O

Objectives

A company's defined and measurable aims for a given period.

Offensive Marketing

A competitive marketing strategy, the purpose of which is to win market share away from other players in the market.

OINK

One income, no kids—a demographic grouping.

OPAL

Older People with Active Lifestyles—a demographic grouping.

Organic Growth/Development

A company's expansion by the growth of its activities and ploughing back of profits, rather than by mergers/acquisitions. See 'mergers/acquisitions'.

P

Packaging

Material used to protect goods; also an opportunity to present the brand and logo.

PANSES

Politically Active and Not Seeking Employment—a demographic grouping.

Payment By Results (PBR)

Remuneration of an employee or service provider according to productivity or other measure of performance.

Peer to Peer (P2P) Marketing

Technique of encouraging customers to promote your product to one another, particularly on the Internet. An example might be a web site that offers users a discount on products in return for recruiting new customers for the site. See also 'word of mouth'; 'viral marketing'.

PEEST

Political, Economic, Environmental, Socio-cultural and Technological—a framework for viewing the macro environment. See 'macro-environment'.

Personal Data

Data related to a living individual who can be identified from the information; includes any expression of opinion about the individual.

Personal Selling

One-to-one communication between seller and prospective purchaser.

PEST

Political, Economic, Socio-cultural and Technological—a framework for viewing the macro environment. See also 'macro-environment'.

Pester Power

The influence children have over purchases by adults: an influence which, controversially, advertisers may seek to stimulate.

PESTLE

Political, Economic, Socio-cultural, Technological, Legal and Environmental—a framework for viewing the macro environment. See 'macro-environment'.

Physical Evidence

The elements of 'marketing mix' which customers can actually see or experience when they use a service, and which contribute to the perceived quality of the service, *e.g.*, the physical evidence of a retail bank could include the state of the branch premises, as well as the delivery of the banking service itself.

PIMS

Profit Impact of Marketing Strategies: a US database supplying data such as environment, strategy, competition and internal data with respect to 3000 business. This data can be used for benchmarking purposes.

Podcast/Podcasting

Term used to define the broadcasting of multimedia files to iPods or other similar devices. Subscribers are able to view or listen to podcasts online.

Point of Sale (POS) (also called Point of Purchase)

The location, usually within a retail outlet, where the customer decides whether to make a purchase. See also 'EPOS - Electronic Point of Sale'.

Pop-under

Automatically launched internet advertisement that appears in a small window behind another webpage.

Pop-up

Automatically launched internet advertisement that appears in a small window in front of another webpage.

Porter's Five Forces

An analytic model developed by Michael E. Porter. The five forces in terms of which the model analyses businesses and industries are: Buyers, Suppliers, Substitutes, New Portfolio (and Portfolio Analysis).

The set of products or services which a company decides to develop and market. Portfolio analysis is the process of comparing the contents of the portfolio to see which products or services are the most promising and deserving of further investment, and which should be discontinued.

Positioning

The creation of an image for a product or service in the minds of customers, both specifically to that item and in relation to competitive offerings.

Product Life Cycle

A model describing the progress of a product from the inception of the idea, via the main period of sales, to its eventual decline.

Product Placement

The use of a product or service within a television or radio programme, or a film: an example would be the appearance of a leading coffee brand on a table in "Eastenders". There are strict guidelines as to the payments that can be given for such appearances.

Promotional Mix

The components of an individual promotional campaign, which are likely to include advertising, personal selling, public relations, direct marketing, packaging, and sales promotion.

Promotional Plan

Detailed plan describing promotional objectives and activities involved in achieving the role of promotions as laid down in the marketing plan.

Public Relations

The function or activity that aims to establish and protect the reputation of a company or brand, and to create mutual understanding between the organisation and the segments of the public with whom it needs to communicate.

Pull Promotion

Pull promotion, in contrast to Push promotion, addresses the customer directly with a view to getting them to demand the product, and hence "pull" it down through the distribution chain. It focuses on advertising and above the line activities.

Push Promotion

Push promotion relies on the next link in the distribution chain—*e.g.,* a wholesaler or retailer—to "push" out products to the customer. It revolves around sales promotions—such as price reductions and point of sale displays—and other below the line activities. See also 'Sales Promotion'.

Q

Qualitative Research

Market research that does not use numerical data but relies on interviews, 'focus groups', 'repertory grid', and the like, usually resulting in findings which are more detailed but also more subjective than those of 'quantitative research'.

Quantitative Research

Market research that concentrates on statistics and other numerical data, gathered through opinion polls, customer satisfaction surveys and so on. Compare 'qualitative research'.

R

R & D

Research and development.

RAPPIES

Retired Affluent Professionals—a demographic grouping.

Reference Group

A group with which the customer identifies in some way, and whose opinions and experiences influence the customer's behaviour. For example, a sports fan might buy a brand of equipment used by a favourite team.

Relationship Marketing

The strategy of establishing a relationship with the customer which continues well beyond the first purchase.

Return on Investment (ROI)/Return on Capital Employed (ROCE)

The value that an organisation derives from investing in a project.

Return on Marketing Investment (ROMI)

The value that an organisation derives from investing in marketing.

Return on Sales Enablement (ROSE)

The value an organisation derives from investing in activities that drive sales.

S

Sales Promotion

A range of techniques used to engage the purchaser. These may include discounting, coupons, guarantees, free gifts, competitions, vouchers, demonstrations, bonus commission and sponsorship.

Sampling

The use of a statistically representative subset as a proxy for an entire population, for example in order to facilitate quantitative market research.

Scamp

Preliminary design or layout of an advertisement or other promotional material.

Screening

The evaluation or testing of a new product, and sometimes its 'marketing mix', at various stages in the 'NPD' cycle.

Search Marketing

Promoting a company's website using internet search engines. Either getting a company website listed in search results (unpaid) or as a listing on the same webpage as the search results (paid).

Shareholder Value

The worth of a company from the point of view of its shareholders. Maximising shareholder value is a common objective for business management.

SINBAD

Single Income, No Boyfriend and Absolutely Desperate—a demographic grouping.

SINDI

Single Independent and Divorced—a demographic grouping.

SITCOM

Single Income, Two Kids Outrageous Mortgage—a demographic grouping.

Skimming

Setting the original price high in the early stages of the product life cycle in an attempt to get as much profit as possible before prices are driven down by increasing competition.

SLAP

Skills Levels Analysis Process, an online tool to assess skills of marketing professionals and to measure them against business aims and objectives.

SLEPT

Socio-cultural, Legal, Economic, Political and Technological—a framework for viewing the 'macro environment'.

SME

Small to Medium Enterprise.

SMS

Short Message Service. Text only messages sent by mobile phones, or other compatible devices, over a wireless network.

SOSTT

Situation, Objective, Strategy, Tactics and Targets.

SPAM

Unsolicited e-mail, often advertisements sent to a very large number of recipients.

Spin

The attempt to manipulate the depiction of news or events in the media through artful public relations.

Sponsorship

Specialised form of sales promotion where a company will help fund an event or support a business venture in return for publicity.

SUPPIES

Senior Urban Professionals—a demographic grouping.

Supplier Relationship Management (SRM)

Managing relationships with suppliers often through the use of IT systems - compare 'customer relationship management'.

Supply Chain

The network of suppliers, manufacturers and distributors involved in the production and delivery of a product.

SWOT Analysis

A method of analysis which examines a company's Strengths, Weaknesses, Opportunities and Threats. Often used as part of the development process for a marketing plan, or to feed the results of a marketing audit back into a revised plan.

T

Targeting

The use of 'market segmentation' to select and address a key group of potential purchasers.

Telemarketing

The marketing of a product or service over the telephone.

Test Marketing

Making samples of a new product available to see what representative consumers think of it and its proposed 'marketing mix'.

TINKIE

Two Incomes, Nanny and Kids—a demographic grouping.

Trade Marketing

Marketing to the retail and distributive trades.

Tweenagers

8 to 12 year olds or 7 to 11 year olds.

U

Unique Selling Preposition (USP)

The benefit that a product or service can deliver to customers that is not offered by any competitor: one of the fundamentals of effective marketing and business.

Unmentionables

Groups of products that are considered 'too delicate' to mention or to advertise. These may include sanitary towels, condoms or incontinence pads.

V

VALS

Values and Lifestyles: the categorisation of people according to their way of living, using groupings such as Belongers, Achievers, Emulators, I-am-me, Experiential, Socially conscious, Survivors, Sustainers and Integrators.

Value Preposition

The set of qualities of a good or service that allows it to fulfil the customer's needs and desires, as opposed to simply benefiting the seller.

Viral Marketing

Spreading a brand message using word of mouth (or electronically—'word of mouse') from a few points of dissemination. Typical techniques include using email messages, jokes, web addresses, film clips and games that get forwarded on electronically by recipients.

Vision

The long-term aims and aspirations of the company for itself.

VoIP

Voice over Internet Protocol. Technology allowing voice communication to be delivered using internet protocol, an alternative to delivering voice communication over a public switched telephone network.

W

WAP

Wireless Application Protocol. Specification allowing wireless devices to interact with information sources. A common application is the use of microbrowsers for wireless internet access.

Weblogs

An internet publishing device allowing an individual or company to express their thoughts and opinions. Businesses can use weblogs as a marketing communication channel.

White Goods

Large electrical devices for domestic use, such as fridges, freezers and dishwashers. Used to be cased in white enamel, hence the name.

White Space

Areas of any company where strategy and authority are vague, and where useful entrepreneurial activity can flourish. Compare 'black space'.

Wi-Fi

Wireless network connection standards allowing computers LAN (Local Area Network) access via a wireless link.

WiMAX

Worldwide Interoperability for Microwave Access. Technology to deliver wireless broadband access over distances of up to 6 miles, an alternative to broadband access via a fixed line local loop.

WOOF

Well Off Older Folk—a demographic grouping.

WOOPIES

Well-Off Older People—a demographic grouping.

Word of Mouth

The spreading of information through human interaction alone. Some campaigns have used this as key element, for example, the British Gas privatisation's 'ask Sid' promotion. See also 'viral marketing'.

Workshops

Interactive training sessions involving role play and syndicate group work exercises.

Y

YAPPIES

Young Affluent Parents—a demographic grouping.

Youth Market

Young customers viewed as a marketing opportunity. Typically the term denotes those aged 16 to 24, but various age ranges are in use, from '12 to 24' to 'under 35'.

YUPPIE

Young Urban Professional—a demographic grouping.

❑❑❑

BIBLIOGRAPHY

Books

1. Philip Kotler, "Marketing Management", X Edition, Prentice Hall of India Pvt. Limited, 2007.
2. Michael R. Czinkota, David Mercer, "Marketing Management", II Edition, Blackwell Publishers Ltd,1997
3. Douglas J. Dalrymple, Leonard J. Parsons "Marketing Management", VII Edition, 2002.

Journals

1. Indian Management, "The Buzz of Viral Marketing", by Prof.Pradip Kumar Deb, Eastern Institute for Integrated Learning in Management, Kolkata, June'12, pg 91.
2. Indian Management, June 2012, 'is going just a fad' by Sudipta Das, Advisory partner and Climate Change and Sustainability Leader Ernst & Young (India), pg 18.
3. Indian Management, June 2012, 'Is India ready for a green drive' by Arushi Thakur & Suheil Murgai, Senior Consultant & Senior Manager at IPSOS Business Consulting, pg 22.
4. Indian Management, June 2012, 'Living La Vida Verde (Living the Green Life [Spanish translated]): Green Buildings, Lighting, Natural Foods and Life Style.', pg 43.
5. Indian Management, June 2012, "Reaching out, the eco-friendly way", by Richa Prakash, pg 41.
6. Indian Management, June 2012, 'Doing Business the Green Way", by Mr. Arvind Sharma, Director-KPMG, pg 30.
7. Indian Management, "Virtues and Veracity of Second Life", by Nityesh Bhatt and Sapna Choradia, dt. November 2011, pg 91.
8. PwC-COAI-White-Paper-Indian-Mobile-Services-Sector, "Indian Mobile Services Sector - Struggling to maintain sustainable growth" August 2011, "Decrease in ARPU", pg 16.
9. The McKinsey Quarterly News Letter, "New ideas for customer segmentation", "Getting more from prepaid mobile services", February 2008.
10. Business Today, "For a Few Eyeballs More", dt. 25-02-2007, pg 20.

Newspapers

2013:

1. The Hindu Business Line, dt. 4-12-2013, pg 19.
2. The Hindu Business Line, "30% sourcing from SMEs not possible, Walmart tells Govt". by Bindu D.Menon, dt. 24-07-2013, pg 2.
3. The Hindu Business Line, "My Friend Likes a Brand. Hmmm.....", dt. 03-07-2013, pg 5.

2012:

4. The Hindu Business Line, "This is how Facebook 'cashes in on you'!", dt. 25-12-12, pg 3.
5. The Hindu Business Line, "Biometric QR Codes", dt. 7-8-2012, pg 18.
6. The Hindu Business Line, "Competition Panel slaps Rs.6300 cr fine on 11 cement makers", dt. 22-6-12, pg 1.
7. The Hindu Business Line, "Cement Companies disappointed with Competition Commission order", Dt. 22-6-12, pg 3.
8. The Hindu Business Line, "Why fear FDI in Pharma?" by Mr. P. Bhaskara Narayana, Dt. 6-6-12, pg 9.
9. The Hindu Business Line, "Eyewear retailer makes the pen special for women", by Purvita Chatterjee, dt. 12-5-12, pg 1.

2010:

10. The Economic Times, dt. 30-07-2010, pg 4.

2009:

11. The Hindu Business Line, "How many telecom companies should India have?", DT. 29-09-2009.
12. The Hindu Business Line, "Truly Rural", by Sudhanshu Ranade, dt. 6-3-2009, pg 5.

2008:

13. The Hindu Business Line, "What's Surrogate about advertising" by Ramesh Narayan, Thursday, Mar 28, 2008.

2007:

14. The Hindu Business Line, "Corporation Bank ties up with dabbawallas", dt.5-5-2007.

2003:

15. The Hindu Business Line dt. 19-03-2003.
16. The Hindu Business Line, "Fairness Cream ads acquire darker hue", dt. 04-03-2003

2002:

17. The Hindu Business Line- Catalyst, "when size begets size", dt. 8th August 2002.

Websites

1. http://www.retrobrick.com/moto8000.html.
2. http://www.itexaminer.com/pagers-are-almost-history.aspx.
3. http://upload.wikimedia.org/wikipedia/commons/thumb/e/e5/ASUS_Eee_White_Alt.jpg/220px-ASUS_Eee_White_Alt.jpg.

4. http://www.thehindubusinessline.com/companies/itc-q1-net-up-at-rs-189133-cr-noncigarettes-fmcg-segment-back-in-red/article4952195.ece?ref=wl_economy.
5. cks.in,readbetweenps.blogspot.com,agencyfaqs.
6. "Branded soups packing it hot" by Ratna Bhushan, http://www.thehindubusinessline.in/2002/12/09/stories/2002120901830100.htm.
7. "New standard packaging norms for FMCG cos from Nov: Govt", dt. August 21, 2012, http://www.thehindubusinessline.com/marketing/new-standard-packaging-norms-for-fmcg-cos-from-nov-govt/article3803431.ece.
8. http://www.bpni.org/cgi/update7.pdf.
9. http://www.interpack.com/cipp/md_interpack/custom/pub/content,lang,2/oid,7773/ticket,g_u_e_s_t/~/Product_packaging_plays_an_important_role_in_the_marketing_mix.html.
10. 'Milk, snacks, poultry to drive packaged food industry growth to 9% a year in 15 years'- Thrust on branding could further push growth to 30%: CII-McKinsey report, BY Vishwanath kulkarni, DT. April 12, 2013; http://www.thehindubusinessline.com/industry-and-economy/agri-biz/milk-snacks-poultry-to-drive-packaged-food-industry-growth-to-9-a-year-in-15-years/article4610841.ece.
11. "'Flawed' sales model stops Reebok run", by Roudra Bhattacharya Priyanka Pani, The Hindu Business Line http://www.thehindubusinessline.com/industry-and-economy/marketing/article3401274.ece.
12. "Adidas Route 2015 plan ", the Hindu Business Line, http://www.thehindubusinessline.com/companies/article3381077.ece.
13. http://1.bp.blogspot.com/-kSNq2cDyLqg/UHGaRGz1n9I/AAAAAAAAAIA/tISdEjWgEXc/s1600/coca-cola-billboard-india.jpg.
14. www.6pins Forums.htm.
15. http://ezinearticles.com/?Guerilla-Marketing:-4-Ways-To-Generate-More-Traffic-Next-Week&id=43480.
16. http://www.gmarketing.com/.
17. CNBC TV 18, Scam ads: Here's why Ford, JWT India are in a mess, dt. Mar 28, 2013, www.moneycontrol.com.
18. http://www.thehindubusinessline.com/todays-paper/tp-brandline/whos-the-whitest-of-them-all/article1010817.ece.
19. http://3.bp.blogspot.com.
20. http://www.moneycontrol.com/news/market-edge/who-really-gainedpetrol-deregulation_985689.html.
21. The Indian Telecom Services Performance Indicators, July - September 2011, TRAI, www.trai.gov.in, DT. 9th January 2012.
22. The Indian Telecom Services Performance Indicators, July - September 2011, TRAI, www.trai.gov.in, DT. 9th January 2012, 'Table 1.12: Group-wise Market Share (in terms of subscription) within GSM Service' page 19.
23. "Why Nokia Money was axed?" By THOMAS K THOMAS, the hiindu-businessline http://www.thehindubusinessline.com/features/eworld/article3007049.ece.

24. http://timesofindia.indiatimes.com/city/jaipur/Rajasthans-traders-cheer-hike-in-import-duty-on-jewellery/articleshow/22904691.cms.
25. http://www.thehindu.com/business/companies/post-offices-to-market-coolers/article2461929.ece.
26. www.valuebasedmanagement.net.
27. http://www.siliconindia.com.
28. http://www.zigwheels.com/news-features/news/quadricycles-like-bajaj-re60-finally-get-govt-nod/16439/.
29. http://economictimes.indiatimes.com/opinion/guest-writer/customer-centricity-for-insurance/articleshow/7199398.cms.
30. http://www.esavvy.com.au.
31. http://www.livemint.com/2010/11/01203044/Customer-centricity-should-be.html.
32. http://www.thehindu.com/business/companies/post-offices-to-market-coolers/article2461929.ece.
33. http://www.knowthis.com/general/terms.htm.
34. http://www.cim.co.uk/cim/ser/html/infQuiGlo.cfm?letter=H.
35. www.pothys.com.
36. http://www.gojiyo.com/.
37. http://www.thehindubusinessline.in/2004/01/08/stories/2004010800690600.htm.
38. http://www.thehindubusinessline.in/2004/01/08/stories/2004010800690600.htm.
39. "How the dabbawallas do it?", Pradip Thakker; dt. 25-7-06, www.moneycontrol.com.
40. http://www.blonnet.com/2009/11/09/stories/2009110951610100.htm.
41. http://articles.economictimes.indiatimes.com/2011-05-20/news/29565146_1_indian-consumer-godrej-refrigerator.
42. http://www.bestmediainfo.com/wp-content/uploads/2011/07/goair-kingfisher.jpg.
43. http://articles.economictimes.indiatimes.com/2012-02-25/news/31099752_1_hul-s-rin-detergent-brand-laundry-brand.
44. http://www.travopia.com/2012/12/market-share-of-indian-domestic-airlines-nov12-indigo-still-leads-other-interesting-pointers.html.
45. http://www.travopia.com/2012/12/market-share-of-indian-domestic-airlines-nov12-indigo-still-leads-other-interesting-pointers.html.
46. http://www.engadget.com/2013/04/29/virgin-galactic-spaceshiptwo-commercial-space-plane-first-test-flight/.
47. http://articles.timesofindia.indiatimes.com/2013-07-02/ahmedabad/40328719_1_liquor-permit-fees-health.

❑❑❑

INDEX

T

U

V

W

❑❑❑